12 Steps for Recovery

& Recovery Companion Workbook

A guide to overcoming addiction using the spiritual
and moral principles of any 12 Step program anywhere

LINDA LYONS

Copyright © 2011 Linda Lyons
Published by VisionPoint Publications

ISBN: 057807494X
ISBN-13: 9780578074948

The Twelve Steps of Alcoholics Anonymous are in public domain. The use of the 12 Steps of A.A. does not mean that A.A. has reviewed or approved the contents of this publication, nor that A.A. agrees with the views expressed herein. A.A. is a program of recovery from alcoholism. Use of the Twelve Steps in connection with programs that are patterned after A.A. but that address other problems does not imply otherwise.

This book is dedicated to all those who have contributed to my purpose, my pain, and my recovery, either by holding my hand, or teaching me lessons that I could not have learned without knowing them. This book is dedicated to those who understood that spirituality was the key to recovery – the pioneers of Alcoholics Anonymous - and to all who follow in their footsteps lighting the way for others. This book is also dedicated to my son, Adam, who gave me a very good reason to get in recovery and then stay there, and to my husband, Richard, who has loved me through all my steps and missteps.

TABLE OF CONTENTS

RECOVERY COMPANION WORKBOOK

Introduction

Recovery Phenomenon

The 12 Steps of Alcoholics Anonymous serve as the foundation of a <u>recovery phenomenon</u>* that has healed countless people. I have personally experienced a miraculous transformation and, as of this writing, have over 22 years of continuous sobriety. With the Steps, meetings, therapy, my personal Higher Power, my husband's love, and AA support, I moved through a cleansing, cathartic process to find my true self. One layer at a time, the wounds of abandonment and shame diminished with each discharging episode of tears and grief. As the scales of denial fell from my eyes, the clear blue horizons of all my future tomorrows were shining brightly in the distance. I was getting to know me, the real me, for the first time in my life.

I believe the 12 Steps can be used as guiding principles for those seeking contentment, serenity, peace of mind, better relationships, self-love and forgiveness. Recovery may be the goal but so much more will be added to your life, until one day you realize that you are living in a state of grace. A state where the sins of the past have been forgiven and much of the time you actually feel good about yourself. You will be astonished to discover that you have developed new tools for living and behaving, replacing the broken and rusty strategies you once used to merely survive.

It is well-known within the recovery community that emotional and physical sobriety depends upon changing thoughts, feelings and behavior while developing and sustaining a new way of life. This takes commitment, resolve, determination and practice. Our recovery depends upon the ability to take emotional risks; courage and humility will be required to step out of our comfort zones. These may be in short supply right now. That's okay. 22 years ago, I could barely drag myself to my first meeting. Each of us arrives at the doorstep of recovery in varying degrees of co-dependence, acting out neuroses or addictions in our own distinct fashion. But as we share our experiences, we find there is a similar thread running through all our lives. We feel

---

*   **All underlined words or phrases can be found in the Glossary of Twelve Step Recovery Sayings.**

alone, dissatisfied, restless, angry, afraid, bored and adrift. We feel no one has any answers. We are hopeless, embittered, disempowered, and, some of us, disenfranchised.

This book is for those who desperately seek a program of recovery, for those who are curious about the 12 Steps, for those who have been in rehabs, for those who are terrified, for those who think they don't need to change, for those who are severely co-dependent and have picked up this book for someone else, and for those who feel the need for spiritual guidance and are looking for a higher purpose in life.

12 Step Groups and Meetings

Currently, there are over 140 different kinds of 12 Step groups. The ideas that propelled the pioneers of Alcoholics Anonymous, and gave the gift of hope to so many alcoholics, have expanded to include every conceivable dysfunction and addiction.

Millions of people are in a 12 Step meeting right now. Thousands are having a strong cup of hot coffee and participating by telling their stories of how they are addicted, dysfunctional and neurotic. After the meeting, people of every color, creed, nationality and ethnicity will hold hands and say a prayer – sometimes the Lord's Prayer or the Serenity Prayer. Many will hug and share their experience, strength, and hope, feeling good that they can give something back to another lost soul. Some will go out for more coffee at the all night diner.

Parts of the <u>Big Book</u> are read at each meeting, enumerating the 12 Steps and characterizing the problems that face alcoholics, but there is little discussion on how they are actually approached or practiced on a daily basis. There are Step Study meetings where passages are read from another book called the "Twelve Steps and Twelve Traditions," but again no specific instructions are given for working each and every Step. Step Four through Step Eleven are contained in 24 pages of the Big Book. So, much of the information is picked up informally.

At first, many won't even understand the Steps and might feel intimidated by their wording. Taking a ***fearless and moral inventory*** sounds daunting and beyond the ability of newcomers. Some people may not even listen to those parts that sound too complicated. That's normal. But since our lives hang in the balance, there is no reason why the Steps should be a mystery beyond the initial month or so of sobriety. Getting an interpretation of the Steps and information about how they will eventually be incorporated into your life is crucial. In order to alleviate anxiety about the process of recovery through 12 Step programs, the 12 Steps need to be explained.

The problem is that sponsorship is limited, and a person could go for months without finding a knowledgeable person to support their journey through the Steps. Many of us tried to rectify this situation by going to a lot of meetings, but hearing the Steps in each meeting and working the Steps after each meeting are two very different activities.

The distinction between 12 Step meetings and the 12 Steps is critical. Meetings are the fellowship of the program. Meetings are important and necessary for support through the early days of disorientation, confusion, detoxification, fuzzy thinking, distorted beliefs and ideas and anger. Valuable social skills are learned by conversing with others on a daily basis. Becoming intimate with ourselves and then others begins with the sharing process, allowing ourselves to be vulnerable, receiving and giving unconditional love, listening to others with compassion, and gaining a sense of usefulness by taking another newcomer to coffee.

Finding Our Way – Sponsorship

The wisdom of the 12 Steps and the particular meaning and execution of each Step is usually transmitted by a sponsor. A sponsor is a person with a significant length of sobriety, who has worked all of the Steps and can take a new person through the program by spending time, energy, and patience for a sustained period. Even members with many years of sobriety still have a sponsor that provides confidential guidance and advice through difficult times in recovery.

With the large number of people who require effective sponsorship, realistically it's just not possible that every newcomer will find that perfect sponsor right away. There are far more newcomers than there are people who have attained consistent long-term sobriety, have worked the program, and can honestly say they have the experience to be a capable sponsor.

Additionally, there are those who suffered from sexual or physical abuse that may find it difficult to trust strangers or open up about their experiences. Statistically, research indicates that a higher percentage of sexual and physical abuse is present among women who are addicted to drugs and alcohol, and other mind or mood-altering behaviors, than in the general population. These special circumstances warrant therapies and incest survivor groups that target the specific problems of these members. Sponsorship must be available for women and men by those who understand the needs of these survivors. I, too, suffered humiliation and inappropriate sexual touching from my stepfather when I was about 8 years old, a memory repressed for over 27 years. I remembered what had happened when I was six months sober. Was I staying drunk so I wouldn't remember? It was a horrible price to pay. I feel relieved that I remembered what happened so I could get angry and comprehend the phenomenon of repression, and how certain traumatic events infected my whole life and contributed to my sickness.

In the beginning, I was completely ignorant about 12 Steps, what I was supposed to do, what a sponsor does, or what good sponsorship was. I was reluctant to ask for help but many AAers extended their friendship and advice and made me feel very welcome. Soon, I found several mentors and relied upon the wisdom of these remarkable people. Everyone has something to teach, even those who go out and drink again and return to relate their failure to control their destructive behavior. I read the Big Book of Alcoholics Anonymous and went for coffee every night with our motley crew from the midnight candlelight meeting. They saved my life. The generosity of those in AA is legendary and very real. Because other programs use AA as their model of recovery, including the format of meetings, steps, and sponsorship, the comforting similarity of these warm and welcoming practices are available in every kind of 12 Step group.

Even if sponsors are in short supply, you can find a way around this if you truly want sobriety and freedom from your addictions, dysfunctions and neuroses. Reading this book will help you to understand the Steps on your own and assist you in having sufficient knowledge to choose a sponsor wisely.

The Steps are multi-layered and recovery, multi-faceted, gaining momentum and acquiring more depth with each stage of your spiritual growth. Cognitive and behavioral changes co-exist with increased insight and spiritual awareness. I share my experience with the Steps and with recovery to **energize the resolve** of those who undertake the challenge of hacking through the Amazon jungle of their psyche. As we cut our way through this dense undergrowth, we will find support and encouragement from our 12 Step group, and a Higher Power that we may, or may not, believe in yet.

To further clarify and underscore the spiritual and moral rationale of each step, I include exercise sections to accompany **"12 Steps For Recovery"** called the **"Recovery Companion Workbook."** It is vital to write down our observations through each Step as part of a course of action. Each aspect of your particular addictive style, beliefs and personality must be scrutinized and understood for reconstructive change to become internalized and operable. There is much that needs to be explored and my goal is to give you a starting point. No one book can completely cover all aspects and stages of recovery. I want to keep it simple yet comprehensive so that you can achieve physical and emotional sobriety.

The Spiritual Foundation of the 12 Steps

The 12 Steps of Alcoholics Anonymous, and all other 12 Step Groups that originate from the original AA model, utilize spiritual and metaphysical principles that are present in many various types of spiritual teachings. Members of 12 Step are encouraged to create and develop a relationship based upon their own individual concept of a Higher Power-God-Goddess-Divine Spirit, as well as any other mainstream or non-mainstream beliefs found in religious texts. The 12 Steps allow for any and all religious and spiritual beliefs that help you to achieve recovery.

Some books written on the 12 Steps use the Bible as a basis for the interpretation of the recovery process. This excludes many who want to nurture their spirituality but don't want to join any particular religion. This kind of thinking is what turns many people off and has them accusing people in AA of being a *cult*. This is not true. Most people in AA do not use the Bible to work the Steps. The Steps are based on concepts of humility, unselfishness, and brotherly (sisterly) love. 12 Step groups have no religious or political affiliation and are not allowed to have any outside affiliations.

Tested and Proven

At this time, the 12 Steps, including meetings and sponsorship, have proven to be the best treatment available. Although there is no cure for addiction-dysfunction-neuroses, there has been complete remission of the actual addiction/dysfunction itself, a return to better than ever functioning, and freedom from addiction and/or dysfunction by using the 12 Steps of recovery. The success rate using this methodology is significantly higher than the rehabilitation community alone can produce. While many people go into rehabilitation facilities, exposure to 12 Step concepts and the guidelines to work them, is minimal. My book is designed to introduce and take a deeper, intuitive journey into the Steps, while using the Recovery Companion Workbook for further hands-on exercises with the Steps.

My Particular Program of Redemption

You will not *get* the program all at once. Every day was an adventure because I didn't know anything about recovery or rehabs or what people were doing to get sober. I was scared straight at first. Terrified that I would be *struck drunk* while on automatic pilot. Fear was a great motivator because I did not want my old life back. Slowly, I realized that each moment holds the option of whether or not I will resume my addictive or dysfunctional behavior. I met instrumental people who directed me to books or meetings that had great significance in my journey. I went through several sponsors, finally finding a truly remarkable mentor. If you remain open and willing you will be led to what heals you. I was flying blind much of the time in my earlier sobriety and, sometimes, I reached the rarified airspace of the bliss of innocence, of feeling that everything was exactly as it was supposed to be in that moment. I stayed in the program, no matter what, and I stayed sober. Along the way I was taught how to be happy, joyous and free (well, most of the time, anyway).

This was my program of recovery:

- I went to meetings almost daily for over two years and spent most of my time with other alcoholics, who by implication and definition are dysfunctional and extremely neurotic. Most of us were very sick but being loved for being sick was a healing tonic.
- I read the Big Books of Alcoholics Anonymous.
- I read three books that became, and still are, important touchstones of my recovery, "Healing the Shame That Binds You" by John Bradshaw, "You Can Heal Your Life" by Louise Hay and "The Road Less Traveled" by M. Scott Peck. These books offer insight into our mental, emotional, spiritual, and psychological problems. Through inner child re-parenting, positive affirmations, and cohesive observations into the meaning of *moral and spiritual psychology*, each writer provides necessary tools for further development.
- I started going to ACoA (Adult Children of Alcoholics and Other Dysfunctional Families) and CODA (Co-Dependents Anonymous) meetings. If you are an incest survivor, you may need specialized groups and therapy. Some recovering people may experienced flooding when attending ACoA meetings because the memories were emotionally overwhelming. Reach out immediately if that happens.
- I began working with my inner child and learned to re-parent myself with a loving Higher Power and a loving inner parent.
- I began doing affirmations and changing deeply instilled, self-destructive beliefs about myself and the world.
- I grieved the loss of my parents who abandoned me at 10 months old, the lack of parental love and guidance, and the loss of many relatives that I didn't know very well because of the absence of family get-togethers.
- I worked the 12 Steps of Alcoholics Anonymous with the help of an understanding and knowledgeable sponsor.

All of this would have been useless without a compelling motivation for staying sober despite my feelings of pain, abandonment, rage and loneliness. I wanted to stay sober more than I wanted to be drunk and dysfunctional.

Eventually, I stopped engaging in destructive relationships and two and half years into my sobriety, met a wonderful man who is perfect for me. That time I let my Higher Power do the picking. Richard keeps a picture of me when I was three years old on his nightstand. We have a lot of fun when our inner children come out to play with each other.

I have since read many books about recovery from co-dependence, the effects of being an adult child in a dysfunctional family system, and other aspects of addiction and dysfunction, as well as various treatment approaches and therapeutic interventions. I also received a certification in Addiction Counseling from Los Angeles Mission College and, more recently, a Bachelor's Degree in Psychology from California State University.

On that first horrible, humid, hot day that I walked on shaky legs up to a disheveled store-front and went inside for my first AA meeting, I could never have foreseen the path my life would take. I am forever grateful to all those who have been with me on the journey. You have taught me so much about myself and, in turn, taught me about the resiliency of the human heart, and our ability to heal the wounds of our shattered childhoods with unconditional love and acceptance.

Chapter One

12 Steps for Life

A Recovery Model for All

The 12 Steps, created from the hearts and minds of the early pioneers of Alcoholics Anonymous, have been adopted as a recovery model for other addictions, dysfunctions and neuroses. For seemingly hopeless cases, the 12 Steps have produced astonishing recoveries. Through attraction and word of mouth, those counted out by society have regained their dignity and survived the incomprehensible demoralization of their illnesses; mental, emotional, spiritual and physical. For many, the 12 Steps are nothing short of a miracle.

This successful program has expanded to include anyone suffering from spiritual deprivation. The fundamental idea is that those who lack a conscious contact with a Higher Power are disconnected from a Universal Force that has sufficient energy and love to guide and direct their lives. Participation does not require adherence to any religion, cult, fanaticism or guru, as the program is founded upon spiritual principles that are present in many religions and metaphysical philosophies and can be adapted to whatever you choose to call your Higher Power.

What is Addiction?

Addictions, chemical and non-chemical, are part of a neurotic defense system designed to protect you from yourself. Neurosis is defined in the Dictionary of Psychology as "a benign mental disorder characterized by (a) incomplete insight into the nature of the difficulty (denial); (b) conflicts; (c) anxiety reactions; (d) partial impairment of personality; (e) often, but not necessarily, the presence of phobias, digestive disturbances, and obsessive-compulsive behavior." Neurotic defense systems are derived from unconscious and unresolved conflicts that are acted out in some kind of symptomatic behavior (addiction).

> *__Addiction__ is a pathological (diseased or disordered) relationship with any mood or mind altering substance or behavior that comes between you and feelings you don't want to feel that ultimately creates crisis in your life.*

Pathological behavior also includes criticism, anger, sarcasm, rage, withdrawal, playing computer games, working too much, being sexually promiscuous, or any other behavior causing problems in your life that you cannot control. If the activity keeps you emotionally numb and shuts you off from others, while creating havoc and unnecessary chaos in your life, then most likely, your behavior is pathological.

Some of Our Problems

Recovery is possible for anyone who can get honest with themselves and apply a spiritual and moral solution to their addictions, dysfunctions and neuroses. What are some of these problems?

Your drinking and/or drug abuse is out of control.
Your work hours are crazy and everyone is complaining.
You eat and make yourself vomit.
An addict or alcoholic is wreaking havoc in your life.
You have a child that's out of control.
You have been sexually molested and you feel crazy.
You are cutting yourself to feel alive.
You feel *less than* most of the time.
You are angry most of the time.
You have a tendency to blame others for the problems in your life.
You do more than you have time to do.
You give too much.
You take too much.
You have a physical ailment.
You are living a half-life without much joy or happiness.
You feel empty and alone.
You feel sad.
You are obsessive/compulsive.
You have unreasonable expectations and are always letdown or disappointed.
You feel like a victim.
You have no boundaries.
You have unprotected sex with strangers.
You have gambled money that you can't pay back.
You feel fat even though you weigh 98 pounds.
You allow yourself to be abused.
You continue patterns of self-defeating behaviors.
You are trying to control everything and everyone.
You feel shame and hopelessness.

This list could go on and on and on.

One obstacle to recovery is that many people don't believe their life has gotten that bad *yet*. The *yet* is the rationalization of the mind not wanting to be disturbed and the ego not wanting to be displaced. Reasons are not rational when they keep you in the maelstrom of defensiveness and conflict with life and others. Here are some of the irrational reasons people use to prevent inner peace and enlightenment that can be found from working the 12 Steps.

- It's too hard.
- I don't understand it.
- I'm not that bad.
- Life is okay.
- I'm not out of control.
- I don't know why I don't want to do it, I just don't.

Whatever the reason, it will certainly sound good, but if trauma, distress and crisis are marching relentlessly through your life you might want to *reconsider your resistance*.

The Corrective Dynamic - Crisis

Acting out in addiction, dysfunction and neurosis are the ways we use to cope with extreme stress, duress, violence, abuse and other forms of inner psychological terror. Our coping mechanisms keep us occupied and distracted from exploring deeper issues. But sooner or later, crisis forces us to recognize we have problems that must be acknowledged.

Crisis is the warning that something has gone drastically wrong. It may be a catastrophic event, such as losing your job or a significant relationship, getting caught doing something illegal, continuous self-hatred, abusing a child or someone else in your life, financial ruin, extreme feelings or reactions, homelessness or victimization, or serving jail time for your drug use or other associated addiction issues. Most likely, negative events in your life are occurring with more frequency and severity and you are left reeling from the consequences of your addictive and dysfunctional behaviors.

Physical consequences can provoke a crisis. One afternoon, a business neighbor came into my office where I worked as legal assistant and asked me a question about Xerox supplies. I remembered I had once told her I was a recovering alcoholic so I sensed that something was up. Next, she blurted out that she had lesions in the back of her throat. I was taken aback for a moment and then I asked how this could have happened. She started to cry, and as I held her in my arms, she confessed she had been bulimic for years. This lovely woman was a successful business owner, attractive, smart, capable and independent. But she was killing herself.

Experiencing a physical crisis forced her to evaluate the price she was willing to pay to continue her addiction.

A CRISIS THAT ULTIMATELY GETS YOU TO RECOVERY IS ACTUALLY

A GOOD CRISIS AND CAN ACT AS THE CATALYST FOR CHANGE.

Awareness of our condition increases as we experience escalating crisis that compels us to look at unproductive aspects of our personality and behavior that just don't work anymore. Instead of being afraid and anxious, we can take a deep breath and understand that something needs changing.

CHANGE IS THE ANTIDOTE TO CRISIS.

Stages of Change

There stages of change are recognized by many in the recovery field. In order to determine where you might fall in this spectrum, the stages are as follows:

Stage 1 – Pre-contemplation: At this juncture, a person is vaguely aware that something is wrong. There may be slight to moderate discomfort when practicing addictions/dysfunctions or neuroses, but the fall-out is perceived as manageable and there is no intention to change.

Stage 2 – Contemplation: At this point, consequences are starting to accumulate and one realizes that addiction/dysfunction is causing great anxiety and harm to oneself or others. A crisis might be a tipping point that forces recognition of one's dire circumstances. A person might seek more information, start reading books about their problem or asking others what to do. There might be physical consequences that frighten the addict. If law enforcement and the legal system are involved, a person might have the choice between going to jail or a diversion program. Sustained pressure from the repercussions of addictive or dysfunctional behavior has the person seriously considering changing their life.

Stage 3 – Preparation: Changing one's behavior is uppermost in the person's mind. Now, one is determined to do things differently and makes a plan with themselves and others how they will handle future problems of addiction and dysfunction.

Stage 4 – Action: A plan is implemented that includes specific acts, such as counseling and therapy, 12 Step meetings, reading, getting a sponsor, and writing on the Steps.

Stage 5 - <u>Maintenance</u>: One day at a time, we improve and work the program, while maintaining our sobriety from our addictions, dysfunctions and neuroses.

Naturally, each individual is different and the circumstances of their lives and family systems, as contributory factors, will modify each one of these stages of change. Some people may fall right in and get better, others may resist, struggle and relapse into old behaviors. The corrective experience by its very nature is not linear. Old ideas will continue to battle against new ways of thinking and behaving. We must arm ourselves with information, sponsorship, 12 Steps, surrender and a spiritual connection.

The Dynamics of Addiction and Dysfunction

In most cases of addiction and dysfunctional behavior, negative and damaging experiences in birth, infancy, and childhood created a foundation of self-loathing, becoming the catalyst for the destructive behaviors we now exhibit. We feel crazy, defective and abnormal and, for many of us, from birth to now, we live in constant fear that something is not quite right. As we work on changing behavior through our recovery program we must also look into the past for answers.

It is imperative to acknowledge what happened in order to understand the events of our lives and get beyond the torment and unresolved issues that haunt us. We must grapple with our innermost selves, even as we take responsibility for the present and a future that is possible once we acquire the necessary tools.

Some childhood experiences were so overwhelming that we repressed the events. We forget what actually happened but still live with the effects of those events. Some people may claim that they had a good childhood experience and this could certainly be true. However, addiction and dysfunction were not created in a vacuum. No one wakes up one morning and decides to have a pathological relationship with a person, substance or behavior that destroys the quality of his/her life. If you do suffer from addiction or dysfunction, keep an open mind about what occurred in your childhood. This is not an indictment of our caregivers.

Factors that affect the addictive and dysfunctional process are:

Genetics:

Genetic pre-disposition determines our personality and temperament and has been proven in twin studies to be a risk factor for alcoholics and drugs addicts. Many alcoholics and addicts come from alcoholic and drug affected homes. Some alcoholics have no tolerance for alcohol and can go into a blackout after a few drinks. This escalating type of alcoholism occurs primarily between alcoholic fathers and sons, indicating a genetic factor in the disease.

Environment:

Children at risk for developing later addictions, live in homes where there is active alcoholism, drug addiction, co-dependence, or other forms of addiction and dysfunction. Disordered environments are created by unhealthy individuals and maladjusted family systems.

In the normal course of childhood development, feelings of safety and security are introduced by the bonding that takes place at birth or soon thereafter. Bonding with a primary caretaker and receiving nurturing has a great deal to do with the healthy development of a child, laying a foundation for self-esteem, positive self-image, competence, and the ability to reason and view reality correctly. Reflective positive mirroring, support, and unconditional love and acceptance are essential for future self-acceptance and self-love. Conversely, when a home environment is hostile, over-repressive, tense, anxious or fearful, a child may view the world as a negative and untrustworthy place. Constant criticism, rage, alcoholism, physical abuse, and passive aggression from parents and primary caregivers makes a child feel crazy and doubtful of their feelings and inner life. Rejection, abandonment, ambivalence, enmeshment, neglect, over-control, or any other factors of dysfunctional parenting, can result in a child feeling sad, depressed or anxious, and these feelings carry over into adulthood. Children also model behavior they observe from adults in their immediate environment. Children learn to accept themselves by internalizing the acceptance which emanates from their parents. The cumulative effect of a hostile environment, together with specific incidents of abuse, can result in trauma-induced symptoms.

Trauma:

Significant trauma and violence intensifies an already negative environment and depletes the inner reserves of the developing ego. If a child is sexually molested or physically abused by a family member or a person outside the family, boundaries are shattered and safety destroyed. Trauma is also witnessing other members of the family subjected to physical violence, emotional battering or molestation. Many victims of trauma suffer from post-traumatic stress disorder and need programs specifically designed to manage trauma symptoms, in addition to working the 12 Steps. If trauma co-exists with chemical dependencies, then the two treatments must be integrated for any meaningful recovery from either condition.

Toxic Shame:

Toxic shame is feeling we are irrevocably defective, intrinsically flawed and powerless to change this condition. As children, we rely upon our caregivers to nurture and support our growth and applaud our efforts. When this mirroring is absent, we begin to misinterpret and distort incoming messages from our caregivers in more negative ways. This culminates into a pervasive message that communicates, "we're not good enough." Alcoholics and addicts internalize this shame-producing message as a mandate to kill themselves in a slow and painful manner. One drink or drug at a time. Other ways to express toxic shame is by having relationships with inappropriate individuals, such as addicts or abusers and engaging in a continual struggle to *fix* them. This refocuses and projects the toxic shame outward. However, shame reaches into deep, secret places and operates on a subconscious level, shaping our reality with negative and erroneous input. Toxic shame produces a distorted defense system, sometimes complicated and elaborate, that becomes our only means of keeping our psychic integrity or public face intact.

Dysfunctional Family System

Psychologists began assessing certain characteristics of maladaptive family systems by comparing them with adaptive ones. Healthy systems are open, flexible and the flow of information goes in and out of family boundaries without tension or anxiety. Each part of the system is validated, supported and respected by other parts (members) of the system. This does not happen in a dysfunctional family system.

My description of certain traits of the dysfunctional family is for the purpose of assisting you in making a preliminary identification of possible family problems that contributed to your addiction/dysfunction/neuroses. Our examination of family dynamics allows you to process feelings and analyze behaviors that are detrimental to further emotional growth. Our past has the power to kill us if we give it permission to interfere with our recovery. However, it is unproductive to excuse our present behaviors because we didn't have good parenting. One problem for recovering people is that certain developmental phases were incomplete or missed entirely. One of the goals of maturity is to finish these developmental tasks and engage fully in reclaiming ourselves, which includes healing our childhood wounds. We can't heal what we don't know exists.

Some characteristics of a dysfunctional family are:

1) *Neglect and Abandonment*:

Neglectful parenting is a failure to nurture a child consistently and transmit unconditional love and acceptance. Neglect is what the parent *didn't* do rather than what they did. Neglect can be as extreme as leaving a child alone in the house without food or proper clothing.

Abandonment can be physical or emotional through addiction, mental illness or other traumatic family situation. Emotional absence telegraphs the message to a child that s/he is unloved, defective and unworthy of attention or love. These behaviors invalidate a child and make it very difficult to develop self-esteem, self-respect and trust in one's thoughts or feelings later on in life. Children need an encouraging, reflective mirror to internalize positive feelings about themselves.

2) *Over-Permissiveness or Over-Control:*

When a child is allowed to do whatever s/he wants without sufficient consequences, a parent communicates they are not willing to take the extra time and effort to commit to their child's emotional, mental and moral growth. Lack of parental discipline and guidance produce a sense of entitlement within a child that is unrealistic. Later, difficulties arise in adolescence or adulthood caused by lack of social skills and inconsideration for others. The person finds it difficult to conform to the rules and laws that govern all of us. The child/adult feels unable to take responsibility for their actions.

At the other extreme, excessive control makes a child feel inadequate and dependent upon the parent for everything. The parent wishes to put their stamp on a child by molding him/her into what the parent wants or needs for their own purposes. Autonomy and separation is not encouraged. Affection and attention may be withheld dependent upon the *performance* of certain acts on the part of the child.

3) *Enmeshment:*

The parent communicates their helplessness and inadequacy, relying upon the child to provide emotional support beyond the maturity level of the child. Self-serving and destructive dependence causes the parent to use a child to fulfill their unexpressed desires, needs, and ambitions, either emotionally or in cases of sexual abuse, sexually. The child is not allowed to differentiate herself/himself from the parent. Separation is frowned upon and the child feels anxious and guilty over any perceived violation of this unspoken directive of the parent. Divorce provides fertile ground for this kind of improper behavior on the part of one or both parents. In a dysfunctional situation, a parent will try to get the child to choose sides in a divorce or custody battle. The child feels confused and angry but cannot express this without risking emotional abandonment. I call this taking a hostage.

4) *Boundary Violations:*

A boundary is either a physical or invisible line that defines your emotional, mental, psychological, physical or spiritual space. In enmeshed family systems, boundaries are not respected. Many times, no one even understands they have a right to their boundaries so trespasses are considered normal. Violations can be subtle or overt, such as excessive tickling, snide or sarcastic comments about outfits or budding sexuality, teasing about bodily parts or functions that are gender-specific, using sexually provocative language or telling off-color jokes. A parent may intrude upon the privacy of a teenager, or use manipulation to make a child feel guilty for wanting his or her own thoughts or feelings. As in enmeshment, parents do not allow the separation and differentiation necessary for development of certain stages of childhood. In more extreme cases, children will be sexually or physically abused causing serious emotional damage and trauma.

Boundaries are shattered when normal developmental phases are sacrificed to the parental needs and the dysfunctional family system.

5) *Sick Family Member:*

A family burdened by addiction, mental or emotional disorders, absentee parents, or divorce may become abnormally concerned or obsessed with those members engaged in maladaptive behavior. Focus is directed to the **problem** person and children are expected to accommodate the insanity of the behavioral abnormalities. This becomes a training ground for dishonesty, denial and other defensive survival mechanisms that allow the child to live in such distorted circumstances. The child may be forced to switch roles with the parent(s) or primary caregiver, burdened with information and activities far beyond his or her level of emotional maturity and comprehensive ability. This is called **parentifying** a child. Carrying the responsibility of adult-hood and the family legacy eventually steals their childhood.

Other children in the family system may do just the opposite, rebelling against their assigned role, acting out in addiction, truancy, juvenile delinquency or other destructive behavior.

6) *Rigid Rules and Roles, the Practice of Denial, Silence and Isolation:*

In some families, rigid rules and rigid roles are engaged to provide an illusion of stability. Family members are assigned roles that are inflexible and confining, preventing the flow of real communication or acceptance. In a dysfunctional or unhappy family, complying with the family blueprint for behavior, as demanded, imitates what the family believes normal life to be. Denial is necessary to block out the reality of the extreme threats of abuse or violence going on in the home and to maintain the façade of normalcy. However, this robs family members of the freedom to experience their feelings and maintain healthy boundaries. The roles given us are sometimes negative and self-destructive because roles are confining. Children experiment with many different roles and attitudes as part of the normal process of developing an identity. Denying these opportunities for role exploration stifles the natural creativity and spontaneity of our childhood.

For example, my role was the **abandoned child**. The subtle messages conveyed were I was not complete and I was to be pitied by other family members because of my abandonment. I internalized this message by believing I was somehow responsible for my own abandonment because of some terrible defect inside of myself over which I had no control. I dutifully played this role, grateful and over-friendly for any attention, acting out in inadequacy and clumsiness which was not my real self. I am intelligent, graceful, and extremely competent but my family did not encourage or support that role. Was I allowed to express my feelings about my family system? No.

Silence and isolation are used to keep the troubled family safe from the prying eyes of the outside world which is very often seen as threatening to the dysfunctional family system.

Losing Ourselves

Losing ourselves is our misguided attempt to save our dysfunctional family. We continue to uphold the banners of inadequacy and self-destruction that were instilled in us as children, maintaining the status quo just as we've been taught. We shoulder the burden, as it gets heavier and heavier, demanding more of us with each passing year. We don't allow ourselves to question the love we receive from our families because it's the only love we've ever known and it will have to suffice. It's imperative that we deny our true feelings.

We may construct a hard, outer shell that alternates between indifference and anger designed to push others away, or we placate others out of fear of further abandonment. Sometimes, we develop a compulsion to find *fixer-uppers* who resonate with our deeply held belief that someone normal and kind is too good for us. It feels familiar and strangely comforting to choose relationships with people whose problems resemble those of our family of origin. Usually there is an instant, unconscious recognition that propels us headlong into one relationship disaster after another. Even for those who've stayed in the same relationships for years, rituals and tribulations are reenacted in painfully familiar interactions and events that resemble our dysfunctional family.

Violence perpetrated upon children and other members of the family system, or children witnessing violence leads to addiction and other pathological behaviors in adulthood. Terry Kellogg has defined violence as "anything that keeps us from being who we are." Many of us were denied our inherent right to express our true feelings of anger, hurt, fear, and sadness, or denied the right to be spontaneous and joyful, which resulted in violence against our spirits. As adults, we then swim the treacherous and muddied waters of our past, feeling sucked down in the undertow of our childhoods. Until we examine closely what lies beneath the surface of our existence, we will never truly know freedom.

Who's To Blame?

Much of our thinking may center on wanting to find someone to blame for our life circumstances. Perhaps we became aware that our parents or significant caretakers treated us badly or violated our rights, and we feel they are responsible for the mess we now find ourselves in. Although, it may be true that they contributed to our current addictive and dysfunctional behaviors, accusation necessitates going back generation after generation. Our parents were influenced by their parents in an ongoing learning process. In turn, they modeled behaviors that we ourselves learned, and perhaps have modeled to our children. Even if we are aware of this vicious cycle and try to send different messages, without changing our underlying subconscious beliefs, we will unwittingly pass on the dysfunction. Assigning blame may bring momentary relief but it is not the same as processing the pain of our dysfunctional circumstances. Remaining angry and resentful keeps us in the prison of our past.

Addiction Process

The addiction process will demoralize us over time. As we succumb to our disordered thinking and addictive, obsessive behavior, our lives become full of chaos, crisis, neediness and desperation. We grab the *fast fix* to fill the emptiness, the bottomless well of our despair. This cycle repeats itself over and over.

First, we feel pressure, stress, and need; then, we demand to feel better fast. So we engage in our behaviors and addictions, feel slightly better, engage in more of our destructive behaviors and addictions and feel the pressure easing momentarily. However, shorter and shorter intervals between episodes leave us feeling drained, humiliated, shameful and empty. We feel as if we've let ourselves down once again. We discover that our addictions and behaviors don't fix our pain but only provide temporary relief. The consequences of our adverse behaviors are now worse than the pain we are trying to avoid.

Where is the Bottom?

Hitting bottom is a common phrase heard in the rooms of 12 Step programs.

A low bottom is a person who has lost everything – home, children, and job, has suffered physical and mental problems related to their drug and alcohol usage, and may be on the verge of alcohol-induced dementia, or drug induced psychosis, and requires hospitalization. Low-bottom addicts could also be relatively healthy physically but find themselves in and out of jail because of their drug usage, or other drug-related issues, such as selling drugs or prostituting to buy drugs.

In the early days of AA, it was believed that only low bottom alcoholics had sufficient motivation to actually get sober and stay sober. It was only being put through life's wringer and wrung out dry that got a drunk's attention. Is this always the case?

No. Many late stage alcoholics do not get sober. Strangely, although a person on the outside looking in might call this hitting bottom, the person at this *supposed* bottom continues their downward spiral until death. Drug addicts and alcoholics die every day as a result of their addiction.

Sometimes death is a bottom.

Alternatively, there are many people who are ready to stop their self-destructive behaviors because they suspect there might be something better for them only they don't know what it is or how to access it. These individuals have not lost everything to drugs, alcohol, or addictive behaviors, but lost enough of themselves to hate what they see in the mirror. I was not a low bottom drunk, or on skid row, or prostituting my body on the street to get drugs or alcohol. But I did other things to myself that were just as degrading in other ways. I allowed men to abuse me, physically and emotionally. I had no self-esteem or any idea how to live positively with self-respect and love for myself. Though not a low bottom alcoholic, I got sober.

My brother, Matthew, who lived with my violent and battering father, did not. He died of AIDS in 1998. He was a heroin user and injected a dirty needle into his vein. His wife was severely co-dependent, believed that my brother just needed love and took on the job of *fixing* him. He gave her HIV; she may or may not be alive today. They had a child, Matthew Jr., who was born with HIV. This is a family tragedy that spans three generations.

Hitting bottom is the devastating realization that your life is spinning out of control. You are hurting everyone around you and yourself most of all. Hitting bottom is acknowledging emotional, physical, mental and spiritual distress. It is being destroyed by soul-crushing humiliation, shame, guilt, sadness and anger over your inability to get this thing called life to work. It is feeling that you are broken, bleeding, defective and lost. Hitting bottom can run the gamut from being a skid row drunk, dying of AIDS from an infected needle, to divorcing your 4th wife and working 18 hours a day to forget it. As your stress and anxiety increase you may finally become ready to admit that you need help.

Hitting bottom can also be as simple as being sick and tired of being sick and tired of whatever behavior or behaviors are self-defeating and self-destructive. Where's your bottom? You decide.

Feel the Feelings

Feelings can be friend or foe in your recovery. Feelings can get us out of recovery and into our disease very quickly. Some feelings may have been considered inappropriate in your family system or gender based, such as anger or sadness. While anger was appropriate, sadness and crying was not. Or, anger was not appropriate but contempt was okay. When we have emotions that are uncomfortable, we may substitute them with another feeling or try to stop feeling altogether. We accomplish this by drinking, using drugs, eating, gambling, sexualizing, or other addictive and dysfunctional behavior. We may also get angry, defensive, withdraw, become busy, intellectualize our feelings, and various other methods that we have used over the years that seem to alleviate our distress.

In recovery, we are attempting to experience our emotions and it is counterproductive to judge what we are feeling as good or bad. Emotions are guideposts that support our intuitive process. Grieving our childhood losses, re-parenting our inner child and uncovering our past trauma will bring up painful feelings. As we move through and discharge these emotions with a sponsor or therapist, or even a compassionate friend, we are in healing mode.

One thing helped me get through the rough times. I promised myself to feel my feelings, no matter how painful, and do so without drinking. Addictions and dysfunctions ultimately numb us. Give up the addiction and feelings come back with a vengeance, angry that they've been ignored and screaming for attention. However, the pain of the consequences of my drinking ultimately became more painful than just feeling the original pain I was avoiding.

I finally reached out. I realized recovery was about getting to know myself, the real Linda, in all my pain and shame. Learning to let others love me taught me how to love myself. I remodeled positive behavior as I nurtured new emotional states that guided me out of the wasteland that had been my childhood. I attended meetings every day for more than two years, got sponsors, got my heart broken a couple of times (that was another bottom), worked through my issues, raged, cried, grieved and ultimately healed. 12 Step is a simple program for complex people.

Feelings are not facts, but as we gain more trust in ourselves we discover they are messages from our gut in response to the world around us. ***Our feelings navigate the past and inform the present***. If your gut is letting you know that something has gone terribly wrong in your life, then it's time to take yourself seriously and give yourself the gift of restoring your whole self. Somewhere you've misplaced vital and beautiful parts of yourself. Learning to love and honor yourself by restructuring your inner life takes a serious commitment. If you have reached a bottom then you are ready to take certain steps. Of course, you won't be alone even if you think you are. You have already begun.

Chapter Two

12 Step Groups

My First 12 Step Meeting

I knew nothing about Alcoholics Anonymous when I wobbled into my first meeting. It had taken years of degradation and demoralization to finally get me to acknowledge that I was powerless and my life was unmanageable. My last few days were the final indignity.

One drunken night, I looked into the bathroom mirror and saw a woman with red-rimmed, swollen eyes in a bloated face and I didn't know that person. Was this the beautiful woman who once had so much promise? The woman who sang and danced in many theatrical productions? The woman who had co-owned an acting school? The woman who had survived an abusive marriage, only to be right back where I had been 4 years earlier? About to be evicted and homeless once again? Debasing myself to another man because I needed rescuing? I hated that woman. It didn't matter what I had accomplished. There was something drastically wrong with my mind, my soul and my spirit. I had survived so much, only now to be broken beyond recognition. I asked God to put me where It would have me be. I ended up remembering something vaguely about Alcoholics Anonymous. I looked in the telephone book and got the number of Central Office, called, and got a meeting time and place. I didn't have a group of well-meaning friends and family to **persuade** me to go to a 30-day rehabilitation facility. There was no intervention. I knew I was on my own. No one was coming to rescue me except perhaps, another man who was going to mistreat me. And if that was going to be my life, I didn't want it.

My first meeting of Alcoholics Anonymous found me in front of a disheveled-looking store-front building in a rather seedy part of North Hollywood on a hot, sweltering day in late summer. It was September 3, 1988. The meeting hall was nothing like the glamorous private clubs and mirrored bars I had frequented in Beverly Hills and Studio City. Some of the people looked a little ragged around the edges. However, I had surrendered and I didn't care how they looked or dressed. They weren't rich, they weren't hip, but they loved me as soon as I walked into the room because I was one of them. I felt the warmth and curiosity as I sat down and found a pair of large brown eyes looking at me with compassion. The Hispanic man's name was Ernie and he asked if

I wanted a cup of coffee. I was shaking but managed to say, "yes, thank you." He felt my pain; it was in his eyes, too.

At the meeting, several people shared their experience, strength and hope but I didn't understand a thing anyone said. I only heard these words, "the mind lies." What the hell did that mean, I thought?

Several years of active alcoholism had dug its claws into me before I got to that storefront. I had journeyed far into my own personal hell. I had lost my job two weeks earlier because I was still drunk at 9:00 a.m. and too ashamed to call in sick for fear they would hear me slurring my words. A temporary agency was finding work for me but I couldn't get sober to get to those jobs. I called and left messages that I couldn't go, all the while feeling myself drowning in the quagmire of something dark, slimy, frightening and increasingly painful.

So, it didn't matter who those people were in the dingy storefront meeting; I was holding on to them because there was nothing left holding onto me. From that meeting, I went to another meeting, and then another, until around midnight I knew I wasn't going to drink. I had gotten enough of the message to hold me until the morning. Then it started all over again: meetings, tears, hugs, self-pity, coffee, pain and a sense that I was home.

As time and experience with my AA group and my Higher Power grew, each new step brought me closer to the real Linda, the one who had been afraid to reveal herself for fear that she couldn't be loved. I grew stronger. I got sober in a roomful of drunks for which I am eternally grateful.

12 Step Groups

It is very important that you find a 12 Step group because of our tendency to isolate. Part of recovery is building relationships with other people. It will be easier to start with those who already know you best, those who are as sick as you. There are many 12 Step Groups represented in any typical American community and also, worldwide, that can accommodate your specific problems.

Some of these 12 Step Group programs are:

AA	Alcoholics Anonymous
ACoA	Adult Children of Alcoholics and Other Dysfunctional Families
CODA	Co-Dependents Anonymous
NA	Narcotics Anonymous

GA	Gamblers Anonymous
DA	Debtors Anonymous
SIA	Survivors of Incest Anonymous (they define incest broadly)
SRA	Sexual Recovery Anonymous
SLA	Sex and Love Addicts Anonymous
OA	Overeaters Anonymous
Al-Anon	Friends and family of problem drinkers
Ala-teen	Youth groups for those involved in alcoholic families
Ala-tot	For the very young, who are affected by addiction in their families

We have denied much of our reality and it can be quite frightening when memories emerge, once buried and repressed, evoking feelings we have kept at bay. The consequence of our unrealistic and distorted thinking is that as we acknowledge each new truth, we could become devastated with the implications for ourselves and others in our lives. Let's face it, we've been living on the edge of emotional, physical, mental, and spiritual disaster for so long, even something good happening could cause feelings we don't yet know how to deal with.

Addicts, and those who lived in dysfunctional families have a high baseline tolerance for hurt, cruelty, and abuse, which diminishes over time as we work the Steps. The 12 Steps, although a journey to forgiveness, do not require that we tolerate inappropriate behavior or violation of our boundaries. Without drugs, alcohol, and other substances and addictive behaviors to numb our pain, we will need help to work through our feelings. It could be greatly beneficial to find a therapist who is familiar with 12 Step programs who can also help you process the feelings that will inevitably come up as you work the program. I suggest that you utilize the 12 Step Groups, a sponsor, and a 12 Step therapist. According to AA statistics, 62% of its members work with a therapist.

12 Step Meetings

12 Step meetings are spiritual gatherings of people recovering from the tumultuous world of dishonesty, dysfunction and addiction. Each affected person learns from the next how to cultivate acceptance and serenity.

We have a lot of fun in meetings because we feel as though we've been rescued from impending doom. There is emotional release in our laughter. Even though it is frightening to reveal certain darker aspects of ourselves, it is also liberating. As we learn to love others and ourselves unconditionally, our lives keep changing for the better. 12 Step meetings are non-judgmental, safe places to share our feelings, our experiences in recovery, our strength to the newcomer and our hope for the future. 12 Steppers will love you until you can love yourself.

Long-Term Recovery

It has been proven that short-term rehab will not lead to long-term recovery. That makes sense, doesn't it? There are no quick fixes in recovery. Intense work with a sponsor, therapist and a 12 Step Group should continue for at least 2 years. It took many years to create the distortions, denials, and defenses so that your disease could take over your life and it will require persistence, tenacity, and determination to join the disconnected pieces of this puzzle you call "me."

Your commitment to feeling your feelings, everyday meeting participation, getting a sponsor and working the steps, is a great start to long-term sobriety. Receiving love from others like ourselves fulfills a very basic need inside of each of us. In the philosophy of Maslow's Hierarchy of Needs, there are five tiers of needs, each tier building on the last; survival needs, safety needs, love and belonging needs, self-esteem needs and self-actualization. Your 12 Step group will provide many of these needs, some of which have been denied us by our family of origin. Don't deny yourself these fundamental rights and connections by isolating into your own world. It could be dangerous for you, your loved ones, and your future.

Chapter Three

STEP ONE

We admitted we were powerless over alcohol (people, places or things)
and our lives were unmanageable

Powerlessness

Here we are. At the first step.

Does anyone really want to admit they are powerless and their lives are unmanageable? Hell, no! It runs counter to everything we are taught in this power-driven, ambition-fueled world that we inhabit. Although we may not want to admit we have no power, it is quite evident we have none. We cannot force another to change for us or demand their love. There are some who might comply but usually for only a short time. Then we're back to fighting for power and wrangling for love. But power cannot be willed nor love commanded. We can't change anything or anyone to our satisfaction. This lack of power and love are the primary difficulties we encounter on all sides.

When we experience both lack of power and love in our lives, we exert tremendous effort to regain our footing, even as we slip and slide on the rocky terrain of our egos. We hide bottles, drugs and other paraphernalia of our addiction and dysfunction, and lie to ourselves and others about the severity of our dependence. We live in a hidden, shame-based purgatory that is created from our refusal to ***accept our condition or ask for help***.

Unmanageability

How each person experiences the unmanageability of their lives varies but very often we find that the fracture point in our lives happened far sooner than we were willing to admit. It seems we must turn fracture into break, and break into crippling inability, to admit that we are on the verge of collapse.

You may be a practicing addict/alcoholic who's lost your children, your home, your job, your friends and are now living out of a cardboard box. You may be an executive determined to control everything around you only to find that the world fights back adamantly, refusing to succumb to your will. You may be living on the quiet edge of desperation as your gambling debts mount up and you face bankruptcy. You may find yourself feeling incomprehensible demoralization as your behavior towards yourself becomes more and more destructive.

A state of unmanageability assumes that we have no power to control the person, place or thing that has come under our scrutiny. We have fallen into the quicksand of our ego-driven denials, and the harder we fight against the reality of unmanageability, the faster we sink. We will only get angrier, more stressed out, depressed, anxious or suicidal.

Development of the Unhealthy Ego

First, it is helpful to define the ego and how it operates in our lives. The ego is the construct of inner and outer determinants such as temperament, personality, talents, weaknesses, intelligence, beliefs, behaviors, environments (home and school), and parental influences. The ego is conscious (as opposed to our subconscious) and develops by the process of judgment. As we respond to internal and external environmental stimuli, mental and emotional, we judge the responses of others to us and our responses to others. Therefore, the ego's main purpose is to assist the psyche in maintaining its integrity by crafting the tools we think we need to strategize for our mental, physical and emotional survival.

From birth to adulthood, we have received thousands of messages about ourselves from our parents, caregivers, peers and the outside world which were highly influential in the construction of our personality, identity and self-image (ego). If the messages were perceived as negative, critical, sarcastic, angry and unloving, then we were polluted with toxic shame, guilt, fear, anxiety, sadness or other disagreeable emotions. Our ego quickly took charge to mitigate the damage and protect its sense of integrity. Unfortunately, the ego cannot differentiate between helpful and detrimental protection. It uses whatever it has at its disposal.

The ego poses as our ally, shielding us from the worst of the blows but we pay a tremendous price for this protection. With denial as a sidekick, the ego continues to distort the truth of the deteriorating condition of our lives. Our addictive or neurotic behaviors become a momentary haven from a world that, too often, exposes the ugly realities we didn't and don't want to face. If we hurt, we are going to find something to stop the pain even if that something is destroying us. The tools the ego uses are alcohol, drugs, gambling, relationships, sex, chaos, work, food or whatever is available to soothe and comfort our insecurities.

Our addictions and dysfunctions are insatiable because, at first, they are fixing the problem. We feel better, smarter, wiser, prettier, or more handsome, stronger and sexier. I know I did.

As the ego continues its job of buffering our psyches against information we don't want to acknowledge, it separates us from our authentic self.

That's why our damaged egos cannot help us navigate our way through life anymore and so we must put it down, set it aside, and stop listening to it.

The Illusion of Control

One of the despicable tricks of the ego is how it dupes us into believing that we have control over the conditions and circumstances of our lives. The ego borrows from the magician and misdirects us constantly, shifting focus away from our escalating use of drugs, alcohol and other substances, to people, places and things, the chaos and insanity of our lives. But behind the curtain, our lives are unraveling with alarming speed despite reassurances from the wizard who insists that everything's okay.

It is this illusion of control that is spoken of in the Big Book. The alcoholic believes that s/he has control over the consumption of alcohol and that they can stop whenever they want.

Control is a major issue for most people who are addicted, dysfunctional, or neurotic.

The more you try to control the sicker you become.

When challenged, the ego's handiest reactions are to deny what's happening or defend its position. The more fearful and fragile the ego, the more defended it has to become in order to survive. These survival mechanisms, as they are built around the illusion that we are in control of something, fail miserably time and time again.

The only thing we can control is our response to our feelings, our moods, our compulsive urges, our past, the legacy of dysfunction or addiction, and other negative or positive circumstances of our lives. If our response is to engage in addictive and dysfunctional behavior over which we have lost control, then we have no control over anything.

Willpower

Another form of control that the damaged ego enlists is willpower. Many people, including ourselves, may think that those who are addicted or cannot solve their ongoing problems are just weak and have no willpower. Naturally, when we fail time and again we consider ourselves more defective and inadequate, reinforcing the cycle of toxic shame.

Willpower is a very poor method of trying to change anything in this world. You can't change another person using willpower. You can't change yourself using willpower, although you may have tried. Willpower is only as good as the underlying ability to change beliefs which then changes behavior.

Changing behavior takes much more than willpower. The subconscious messages, which form our beliefs, fuel our dysfunctional behavior. These messages have been powerfully re-inforced over years and years of repetition. We are now masters at executing the family and parental directive of maintaining the status quo. Changing upsets the system and that's not allowed. That's why willpower is ineffective in breaking the cycle of self-abuse.

Willpower didn't get me to stop drinking. One moment of clarity when I saw a pathetic, disgusting drunk in the mirror revealed the true nature of my condition. I was appalled and then immediately terrified that I was doomed to live as a stuporous shell of my former self. Admitting to myself I needed help, I reached out by going to an AA meeting. That's the day I started to be abstinent from my mind and mood altering substances.

Commitment to my emotional and spiritual growth continued to keep me sober. I had been an unwitting victim of my family's shame and inability to love and be responsible for my well-being. Saving me meant giving myself permission to stop letting their treatment of me define who I am. Their treatment of me defines who they are. It is doubtful that I could have remained sober without these important discoveries.

Willpower doesn't provide sufficient motivation or strength to support long-term serenity. It's just too hard. Willpower is what we're trying to eliminate in our lives. We are becoming Higher-Powered to effectuate spiritual change in ourselves and in our environment.

Resistance

At first, you may resist the concepts associated with recovery. In fact, you may fight against them with all you've got. That's all part and parcel of **_getting it_**. Resistance is the amount of force or pressure you apply to stop any incoming information and requires a great amount of energy to sustain. We are stuck in patterns of a lifetime and, though we chafe against them until we're bloody and raw, it's a sure thing. There's no guesswork – we know what's going to happen and that is comfortable.

Change, on the other hand, is uncomfortable. We have to reposition our mental state, open our ears, learn some new things, apply solutions and have faith in an outcome that might not be positive. Then we have to start all over again, listening and learning new things.

It's a lot of work for a questionable result. There are no guarantees that anything beneficial will happen.

There is one good thing about change. It will take us where we haven't been before, and considering where we are right now, that's probably for the best. You have taken in one important lesson. Something has gone wrong with your life. This certainty will assist you in keeping an open mind on those days when change seems to be an enormous burden.

Forms of Resistance:

You are probably facing the deadly Ds of denial, defiance, distortions, delusions, and defenses, which are just some forms of resistance the ego throws up as roadblocks on our journey to recovery.

- ### *Denial:*

This one is a particular favorite of those who believe in the ostrich theory; if you stick your head in the sand and someone is shooting at you, you won't get shot. Sticking your head in the sand or in the clouds is not going to absolve you from the consequences of your behaviors, if they are a result of your addictions or neuroses. Unfortunately, as we go deeper into our disease denial gets stronger because it's part of the disease. The devil of denial sits on our shoulders and whispers in our ear "it's not that bad yet." Oh, how we love to hear that! It's not that bad yet. How bad does it have to get?

- ### *Defiance:*

You're tough and you can take it. When people confront you about your unacceptable behaviors – screw them! You're gonna do what you want, when you want, and damn what anyone thinks. Don't mess with you! Defiance comes in all types: quiet, passive-aggressive, smiling, angry, and "rebel without a cause." This strategy is a favorite of those who used to throw themselves on the ground, hold their breath, and turn blue until mommy or daddy did what they wanted. The mistaken goal of defiance is to intimidate others, keeping the defiant one from being questioned or facing the wreckage of their life. A lot of hostility is usually required to stoke the fires of defiance. A lot of shouting keeps your conscience from being heard. These methods work if you don't mind being in conflict with someone or something most of the time. However, others will probably give up on you after banging their head up against the walls of your obstinacy time and again making it unlikely that you can sustain long-term relationships other than with your close relatives.

- *Distortion:*

Dysfunctional, unstable, violent or alcoholic families perceive life through the distorted lens of their immediate need to survive emotionally and physically. Children soon internalize, through a caregiver's gestures, comments, punishments and illogical statements that they must agree with the consensual reality of an insane family system. Behaviors they see and feelings they feel are dismissed and replaced by the interpretations of the caregiver. Agreeing with family reality is encouraged and constantly reinforced by our caregivers with smiles, praise, small kindnesses and acceptance into the family. Later in life, we continue to be able to distort the truth into what is acceptable and non-threatening to ourselves or the beliefs of the family system. As we attempt to solve life and relationship problems while enmeshed in the limited vision of our family systems, we find that we are constantly struggling between finding real solutions and being faithful to family vision.

Some <u>cognitive distortions</u> that pervade our thought processes and direct our behavior are exaggeration, extremism, black and white thinking, mislabeling, misunderstanding, catastrophizing or minimizing, jumping to conclusions, and disqualifying the positive. However, there is a small voice inside us whispering the truth, but many times we negate that voice because we are needy and desperate for the approval of others just as we were in our family system. For example, we know instinctively that a man who acts excessively jealous is reacting abnormally. However, we distort our view of him with excuses and reasons why he acts possessively. Our vision is distorted by our need to see him or her as the **one** or the **savior**, our **rescuer from loneliness,** or whatever role we have decided to assign this possible future batterer, abuser or criticizer that traps us in the cycle of doubt. Because we were victims of the distorted viewpoint of our parents, we continue to use this broken survival strategy for our seeming benefit. We become experts at distorting the truth to suit our momentary needs, but since we're not crazy, we still understand that we are not seeing reality and our distortions don't stop the truth from being the truth.

- *Delusion:*

This particular resistance strategy is more severe than distortion. In distortion, we can see some of the truth but we choose to call it something else, twisting it out of shape beyond recognition. Delusion is the means of seeing something that really doesn't exist or not seeing something that is clearly there, no matter how many facts are presented to contradict the delusion. Delusions are sometimes associated with psychotic breaks with reality as described by psychologists. In the delusions I am referring to only one area of reality is affected, such as body image. For example, an anorexic woman was on a popular talk show and she weighed 60 pounds! She was told that she was very sick and could die but she just didn't see it! However, another anorexic woman came on the show, sat next to the first anorexic woman, and each of them saw the other woman clearly and how dangerously thin the other was, but they still did not see it in themselves! No matter what facts are presented to a deluded person, if it runs contrary to their delusions it won't affect their beliefs.

- *Defenses:*

There are many facets to this form of resistance, such as justification, rationalization, playing the victim, being angry, placating and criticizing which will be further elaborated in the Recovery Companion Workbook for this chapter. We have all kinds of excuses why we can't do something. We wield the sharpness of our anger like a sword so that those who oppose us back down. We apply the crystal tears of our self-pity to elicit sympathy in others as we justify our reasoning in the most ridiculous of ways. For example, how can anyone justify gambling when it is a proven fact that the casino always wins? Yet, thousands of people sit down in front of a black jack table or slot machine thinking that they're going to beat the odds. When we run out of defenses we just get pissed off, withdraw and go into defiance mode. These strategies work in the short term but ultimately they destroy any intimacy you would hope to achieve with significant loved ones in your life.

Reliance on our old coping strategies is like dragging around that tattered, stained, worn-out blanket we used as toddlers to give us comfort. Remember the battle to get you off the blanket or the thumb? Like it's frequently said in recovery, "Everything I let go of has claw marks on it."

Our strategies aren't working and our lives are out of control.

Willingness

The first step across the chasm of uncertainty and doubt is willingness to connect with the concepts of the program. How can this be accomplished? There is some argument about whether or not thinking or behavior needs to change first. Since it's almost impossible to change our thinking in the beginning, a change of behavior and scenery are in order.

You start by not going to places where you practiced your addiction or acted out your dysfunctional behavior. This is called footwork. Footwork can be many things. Such as going to a 12 Step meeting every day, finding a job, going to school, taking parenting classes or anything that, in the reasonable course of one's life, makes it better for ourselves and for those around us. We are willing to comply and compromise with others instead of willfully demanding our own way. We are willing to initiate pro-active problem-solving skills.

You may wonder about the difference between willpower and willingness. Willpower is bending or forcing circumstances to our will without considering the greater good for ourselves and others.

*<u>Willingness</u> is a conscious adjustment of our will as
we set aside preconceived beliefs and ideas to
accommodate new information and solutions to our problems.*

<u>Open-mindedness</u>

Letting go of pre-conceived ideas, we let in the sunlight of the Spirit. Accepting the open hand reaching out for yours. The new place you've arrived at. Giving something a chance. Looking around and not judging who or what you see. Shutting out the old voices yammering away that you're no good and nobody likes you.

It is scary to accept ideas that are alien from our own. Why should we do that? **Because our lives are unmanageable.** Our old ideas and actions didn't work like they were supposed to! For me, open-mindedness was accepting that I knew nothing. All my old ideas had stopped working. I was intelligent but my emotions were scrambled by the conflicting messages of my past and present, and my soul was shattered with loneliness and alienation. I chose to be open and give up the idea that I knew anything about how to live life.

Becoming vulnerable and open is a risk that you take if you want to get better. But you won't be alone. People in meetings will share stories of their lives and recovery that you can identify with – try and find the similarities and not the differences. When you find yourself nodding in agreement to what someone has said in a meeting, you are starting to open up your mind to the possibilities of recovery.

<u>Honesty</u>

Honesty compels us to look truthfully at our motives and agendas, as well as past events, our part in them and the part that others played. Honesty is our companion while we develop a new moral compass, discriminating between the positive and negative outcomes of our behavior. If we have the capacity to be honest, we can recover. Honesty frees us from deception and denial about the true nature of our inner selves.

Your truth, your reality and your viewpoint will be re-evaluated under a new set of principles set forth in the recovery program of the 12 Steps. As our lives became riddled with numerous defenses and resistances, we lost the ability to be honest with ourselves. In some cases, we have been overly critical and harsh which is not honesty but self-flagellation. At the other extreme, we have condoned our lapses in honest and fair behavior and justified our questionable reasoning with more lies.

If we say one thing but end up doing another – that's dishonesty. If we say we're going to stop gambling but end up at the poker hall or in front of the slot machine – that's dishonesty. Saying something does not make it so – behavior must confirm our declarations. The truth is that we may *want* to change but don't have the motivation or complete commitment to change. Assessing our thoughts, feelings, motives and intent accurately, to the best of our ability, is honesty, even if we honestly don't want to work hard to get better.

Fear is one of the first obstacles to honesty. When we start examining our innermost selves we're afraid of what we'll find. That we're weak, lazy, petty and unreliable. That we really don't deserve anything good in life. That other people's assessments of us were correct. At first, those close to us may not believe that we've found our footing or that we're sincerely seeking recovery. Trust is earned and, if we are consistently honest with them, our intention will become apparent. In place of fearing what we've become, we might turn the page into the future of who we are yet to be, to discover that we're often kind, generous and helpful. That we love people to the best of our ability. That we want to do better. That we have done worthwhile things in our lives. As humans, we are good and bad, dark and light, weak and strong, right and wrong. That is our nature.

Yes, we've done damage out of desperation and pain. We've hurt others with our defiance and our defended egos, our excuses, our unkept promises to ourselves and to others, but we are entering a new phase of our life and are willing to be open and honest about what is really going on with us.

If you are able to admit that you are powerless over people, places and things, or alcohol and drugs, sex, gambling, work and other mind or mood-altering substances and behaviors, then you have started to get honest with yourself. Because the truth is, if you have lost control and behave compulsively, then you are powerless.

Surrender

One of the first spiritual paradoxes we encounter is surrender. Mislabeling the concept of surrender is very easy to do and plays into our reluctance to admit defeat over our circumstances, no matter how dire they might seem to others.

Surrender doesn't mean quitting. Quitting is giving up in the middle of the game, losing heart and throwing in the towel. Quitting is feeling defeated before you begin. Surrender is not admitting defeat. Surrender is relinquishing control to a Power greater than ourselves once we turn loose of resistance and self-will. You may begin experiencing the paradox of surrender the first time you let go of something even if it's just for an hour. You will feel more powerful and at peace. You forget there was something to let go of in the first place as you experience serenity. Then, of course, you take it back again. That's okay. We all do that.

The paradox is that once we surrender we have gained another kind of power that comes from our Higher Power. Going with the flow of our recovery, rather than resisting, suddenly gains us access to a Power that is shouldering part of our burden. This may be your 12 Step group or anything you choose. We're still doing the footwork but with a sense of wonder and amazement that *Something* is doing for us what we could not do for ourselves. We are letting in the light of love and acceptance.

The miracle begins with surrender.

It is paradoxical that when you release something or someone into the care of our Higher Power, you open the door for something better to come into your life. I once received an email that I'm going to share with you.

"When God takes something from your grasp, it's not to punish you, but merely to open your hands to receive something better."

I let go of things that are out of my control every day. I let go of people who I wish would change. I don't leave them or stop being with them but I let go of my insistence to have them be what I want them to be. Hoping they're going to change will only make me unhappy. When they want to change, they'll do the work just as I have. My serenity and peace of mind is in jeopardy when I hold onto people, places and things that I have no control over.

As you begin to accept these ideas, exchanging them for old, obsolete beliefs, your thinking will change and your feelings can begin to guide you. In turn, people and circumstances around you will begin to change because you have opened your mind to the possibility that change can now occur.

Chapter Four

STEP TWO

*Came to believe that a Power greater than ourselves
could restore us to sanity*

I was Never in Kansas

From my earliest memories, things around my house were strange. First of all, I couldn't figure out who anybody was. Who were my mommy and daddy? My "mother" (actually my grand-mother) told me not to call her "mommy." Then who was she and where was my mommy? I ignored that question for years. Then I called the man who rented our back bedroom "daddy" and my mommy, who wasn't my mommy, said he wasn't my daddy. Then another man come around who said he was my daddy but by this time I just wanted someone to love me. No, I don't believe I ever experienced Kansas. Things were always "Oz."

I remember one particular Christmas. I was 8 and my little brother, Matthew, was 3. My father and stepmother, Corinne, had invited my grandmother and me for Christmas Eve dinner. The turkey was taking a little longer than expected and my grandmother kept complaining that she couldn't eat late in the day. Corinne was getting more anxious as time wore on and my father, the rageaholic, was getting angrier and angrier. The air was thick and heavy with tension as we sat down to eat. Corinne had made a lovely dinner and everything was just about on the table when my father exploded calling Corinne hideous names, taking the bowl of creamed peas, and dumping them on her head. She ran out of the apartment, crying, and my father followed her. My brother, grandmother and me sat at the table in stunned silence. What was there to say? We did not acknowledge what happened, but bravely tried to continue on with the evening when my father and Corinne returned.

My father was a batterer, an abuser and heaped vitriol on Corinne almost every time I was with them for an outing. My father intimidated and terrorized his family. I was exempt from much of the overt abuse because I lived with my grandmother but the underlying threat of violence was always present during those times I was with them. Love and terror for this man co-existed in an uneasy and disturbing alliance creating an association of love with abuse that had residual consequences throughout my life.

Other passengers on this crazy train were my biological mother, stepfather, Aunt Connie, and two half-sisters, Joanna and Amy. When I was 11, I finally met my older sister, Jo, but we were strangers. My childhood was full of such losses, sadness and emotional chaos and confusion. When asked to create a family motto in one of my addiction studies classes, mine was "you're on your own." I was isolated from important family members, witnessed and subjected to neglect and abusive behavior when I did see my parents and abandoned the rest of the time. However, I minimized my violent and abandoning family history just as I became adept at minimizing my drinking and other self-destructive behaviors. The bizarre interactions and configurations of my family forced me to **accommodate the crazy and ignore the insane**. This took a devastating toll on me throughout the years and into my adulthood.

In families such as mine, there is limited space for nurturing, praise, encouragement, or bonding, so that we become even more alienated and confused about what is normal and what is not normal. As babies, we come into this world as empty vessels with an enormous set of needs that are presumably going to be met by emotionally healthy and loving parents. This didn't happen with you or me. The turmoil of family overwhelms the emotional resources of the individuals trapped in the dynamics of unhealthy interactions of criticism, abuse, sarcasm, rage, violence, intimidation, apathy, sexual innuendo, neglect, betrayal and abandonment.

In the *normal* scheme of things, parents provide the mirroring necessary for an infant to develop a positive self-image, and consistent nurturing throughout childhood solidifies the image the child carries with them. This is what is referred to as self-esteem and self-worth. We get this from our parents. Since none of the people in my life had self-esteem or self-worth, they could not transmit this to me. Though many of you will have different circumstances and constellations of family members in your home environment, much of the behaviors will be similar.

If You Think You're Different, You've Come to the Right Place

As my basic needs for bonding, mirroring, and nurturing were denied, I also carried around this horrible secret – that I was *different*. I didn't like being different at first. Then, in order to survive emotionally, I decided that different was unique, talented and special. I was compensating for feelings of inferiority and worthlessness. We may find ways to *sell* ourselves to others by presenting a false persona because we feel insecure and inept as our true selves. Many of us feel like imposters in our lives, afraid that someone will discover who we really are and determine that we are damaged goods. So our lives are spent desperately scrambling to *repackage* ourselves in an attempt to feel a little bit better.

For me, it was performing as a singer and actress. From an early age, I got applause for singing and being funny. I decided that this was my ticket to get an approximation of love, attention and acceptance.

My yearning for love was so much a part of my childhood that it is what I recall most about growing up. My grandmother protected and loved me to the best of her ability but she was uneducated, had old world thinking, spoke broken English (Spanish was her primary language), was uninformed, didn't read much, and was two generations removed. Never once did my grandmother ask me how my day was or engage me in ordinary conversations. It wasn't her fault – she was a victim of her generation's attitudes toward parenting. I like to think I have modeled some of my grandmother's best characteristics, such as independence and self-sufficiency.

Though my grandmother tried, she didn't know how to parent a child. She provided shelter, clothing, food and basic education. She almost never mirrored acceptance of who I was by praise or encouragement. As I write this I can still feel the pain of that emptiness. I compensated for the lack inside myself, the barrenness of my daily life, with reading constantly, television and movie-going. By 7 years of age, I could watch four movies at a time. I became a masterful *escape artist*. I would then act out scenes from the movies in front of my mirror, imagining that some day I would become a great actress like those beautiful women who mesmerized me from the screen. This became how I mirrored myself, only with impossibly high standards and ideals of beauty and achievement. Is it any wonder that I never measured up?

Later in adulthood, my insanity metastasized into rationalizations of the scariest kind, that my drinking was normal and a rite of passage to becoming a great artist. Great artists are crazy, and use alcohol or drugs to commune with the gods of inspiration. Their lives are full of drama and unrequited love. I followed my script perfectly. I drank a whole lot and I was nuts. All of this specialness took a great deal of effort to sustain. I had to express my talented and artistic soul. I had to be with men who abused me, so I could be in pain, in order to continue following the script. I didn't know how to do it any differently. I realized later that I had to be bigger than life, bigger than I really was because I was not enough. I had been judged and found wanting time and time again.

Your family might have looked normal on the outside while hiding moderate to severe dysfunction. Many times, when we are practicing our addictions and dysfunctions, we are not able to decipher the mystery of our family dynamics. The code remains unbroken until we begin to get better. But that takes time and healing.

The Void – Deprivation Syndrome

Our hearts have been broken with relentless efforts to get the love we've longed for and we've endured countless failures to get any love at all. We justify our addictions and indulge our self-directed will until we have lost any sense of serenity or peace of mind. We suffer from excessive neediness and unrealistic expectations, bound and determined to get blood out of a stone and water from an empty well.

As normal as our needs may have been in childhood, we are now adults and face the challenge of providing our own reservoir of love and approval. Without self-esteem and self-worth, mired in past programming, this is an insurmountable task. To distract ourselves from the baggage of toxic shame and unworthiness we carry around, we repeat the torturous cycle of getting our needs met in inappropriate ways with inappropriate people. We then wear out our reserves of energy, leave ourselves depleted and crash back into the pit of abject aloneness.

The emptiness (empti-mess) inside those who are addicted and maladjusted is a void that can't be filled no matter how many relationships we get into, how many drugs we take, how much food we eat, how much alcohol we drink, how many things we buy or how much control we exert over others. We are suffering from a deprivation syndrome and there is no substance on the planet that can satisfy us. As we desperately try to fill the void, it becomes apparent that we have an excessive need for love and attention that no human person can ever give us. In not having our needs for love and acceptance met in childhood, need has grown into a beast that is never satiated, demanding more and more from others who, ironically, are incapable or unwilling to satisfy our desires.

Another repercussion of unmet needs and unresolved conflicts, both conscious and subconscious, is that many of us continue to practice the subconscious directives of our caregivers and abandon ourselves, abuse ourselves, hurt ourselves, ignore our innermost intuitions, destroy ourselves, addict ourselves and neglect ourselves. We may lash out in rage and anger, blaming everyone else, without realizing the original source of our frustration, rage and anger is usually not the person or present situation now confronting us. Again, these are more symptoms of our insanity.

Something must change in ourselves in order to overcome the neediness, and lack of spirituality and moral direction in our lives. But we continue to look elsewhere for answers, too afraid to look into our souls and see the abyss staring back.

Defining Insanity

In Alcoholics Anonymous one of the definitions of insanity is: "Doing the same thing over and over again, expecting different results." It is not possible to perform the same actions and get a different result. In order to get a different result, the preceding action must be different from what was tried before. Normal people acknowledge what they do doesn't work and try something else. Those who are addicted, dysfunctional or neurotic keep trying the same thing over and over again, hoping against hope, crossing our fingers and not stepping on any cracks, that THIS TIME WILL BE DIFFERENT. He will be different, she will change and they will *see the light*. This almost never happens.

It seems we have a compulsion to repeat our childhood history to achieve a different outcome; where we were loved unconditionally, accepted for our strengths and weaknesses and approved of by those we love. But we pick our parents (symbolically) to accomplish these goals which is why many of us choose *relationships* with partners and others who are detached, emotionally unavailable, incapable of intimacy, critical, rageful and/or unloving. This is why we choose *relationships* with drugs, alcohol, gambling, food, sex, work, fixing others and other mind or mood altering substances or behaviors, over and over again, to *fix* ourselves. Either we're trying to control someone or something else, or we're in pain and use substances and behaviors to alleviate our anguish.

Our insanity has taken us to the edge, where we dangle helplessly, breathless above the precipice waiting to fall and smash into a thousand pieces. Something must be destroyed in us before something new can be created. Out of the pain of our past will come the deliverance of a new way of life, new thinking and a feeling we have been reborn. But first we must let go and let ourselves fall.

Old Thinking

Old ideas die slowly as the mind takes devious twists and turns to justify irrational behaviors. Our belief system is a conglomerate of messages, both verbal and non-verbal, that are received from our caregivers, or significant others, from the moment of our birth (some say even before). How our caregivers communicated their love, understanding and protection toward us will determine how well we trust in the world and its resources. As we grow older, we build upon those initial beliefs and look for evidence to validate them.

Although learning new principles could change our lives for the better, we rarely question perceptions that have dominated our lives for the worse. We have taken in erroneous ideas, repeated them over and over again and now have internalized them as truth. Our needs, sometimes even our deepest, most primal needs, will be sacrificed in an almost trancelike obedience to our beliefs. This is why we sabotage ourselves with destructive thoughts and behaviors and continue to stay addicted and dysfunctional. We are severely co-dependent on people, places and things because our belief system tells us we're not good enough to get love, nurturing, attention or permission to get our needs met in healthier ways.

But in reality, beliefs are like a food court in a mall. There are plenty of choices available and we can pick and choose what beliefs feel right to use – what ideas satisfy our palate, instead of chewing on overdone and monotonous dishes every night. Holding our beliefs up to scrutiny, we can determine several things. First, what do we believe? Where did we get this belief? Why do we believe this? Does this belief serve our well-being? By eliminating beliefs which no longer serve our greater good, we can begin to choose other beliefs that support our new and better life.

Trust

We were once innocents who trusted in our parents as the gods of our tiny Universe. We were dependent upon them for our every need, and without them, certain death. Then our needs were thwarted or interfered with our caregiver's needs. We cried – they did not come to comfort us. Later, in childhood, we were told our feelings were wrong – our sight was flawed. What we felt about what we saw was mistaken. Slowly, we were taught how to perceive and interpret events according to our caregiver's vision. We were corrected when we asked for our own sight. Trust became doubt; doubt became bitterness and bitterness became skepticism.

When you are asked to doubt your reality and told, by what was or wasn't said, that you have no worth or value to those who are in charge of your development, then you don't feel safe in your own family. Trust is dangerous because you must remain constantly on guard in the hostile territory defined by *their* moods, *their* feelings, and *their* needs.

The very foundation of my life was built upon abandonment by my mother and father. Trust was shattered from birth. But children are forgiving. I went back to the empty well time after time, hoping and praying for love and was devastated by each rejection or act of abandonment. Deprived of a normal, emotionally available family that others took for granted, I hated God for the life I didn't want. I really didn't see the point. I doubted life itself.

Most of us lack the ability to trust anyone or anything at first. Important people have let us down. Certainly God has been a questionable source of power or relief. There are very few people who begin a 12 Step program by embracing a Higher Power whole-heartedly.

A Lighted Doorway

Yes, trust may be the dark hallway leading to the door of faith but walk we must, if we are ever to see the light.

In the serendipitous way that grace usually unfolds, one month before I got sober my sister gave me a book, "The Game of Life and How to Play It" written by Florence Scovel Shinn. "The Game of Life" is a metaphysical book based on the spiritual principles from Science of Mind philosophy that uses affirmations to manifest desired conditions in one's life. Affirmations are positive statements that we write down on paper or repeat aloud to ourselves affirming some situation or thing we wish to manifest in our lives. We affirm in the present tense, in the

NOW, and declare all others conditions that *appear* real to be false, and the true condition of our life is that which we desire.

So I started reading the book but didn't even know what to want in my life. Everything I thought I wanted I either hadn't gotten or was killing me. All my desires had turned to dust along with my ambitions, dreams and goals. What could I manifest in my pathetic life? I remember saying over and over, "God, put me where you would have me be." That's all I could say. Soon after I began saying this affirmation, I ended up in AA. I guess that's where God wanted me to be.

This began a dramatic shift in my worldview. I didn't realize until later in my recovery that I didn't affirm something I thought I wanted, like a good man or an acting job. Life had thoroughly kicked my ass and I knew I didn't know how to fix it, so instead I asked GOD what It wanted me to do, where It would have me be.

I had made my first surrender (Step One) and then unknowingly worked Step Two, by asking God instead of telling It, and when I turned the matter over to God, I was doing Step Three. That's when I received the miracle. I know today that's how most miracles are received.

Creating a space for a Loving Guide and Divine Intelligence makes our lives so much easier. We rely on this Power as we start to believe that It is truly working in our lives and in the lives of others. Surprisingly, once we establish a relationship with a Higher Power, no matter how tentative, we begin to shift the burden onto It and feel lighter and less afraid. It works if you work it.

Many times in the rooms of AA, I have seen people dragging into their first meeting, broken and beaten and within a couple of months, their eyes start to shine, their faces glow and they're smiling. They've found something. They've found a Higher Power who loves them, people who love and understand them and they begin to love themselves.

We can reinvent ourselves in a positive and beautiful way. We don't have to continue to beat ourselves up and believe we are defective, bad, less than or more than human. Changing our belief system will support our freedom from addiction, dysfunction and neuroses.

Affirmations

We can take charge of our belief system and free ourselves to choose to believe in a powerful Loving Presence that has not been defined by our birth religion, our parents, our schools or society. Once we gain a firmer footing in faith and God's direction and guidance, we can start to affirm new life conditions. We can affirm whatever we desire as long as our Higher Power has put the stamp of approval on it. I guess that's why I'm in a healthy and somewhat normal relationship. I didn't pick Richard, God did.

I highly recommend Louise Hay's book, "You Can Heal Your Life." She gives any beginner to affirmations much needed information. Just saying, "I am enough," helped me feel better about myself. I'm sure you will work on your own affirmations and continue doing them as part of your daily program. I have a section on affirmations in the Recovery Companion Workbook.

"Slow" briety

When we *come to believe* something, the very nature of the wording implies that belief takes time, grows slowly, arrives gradually and is based on some kind of experience with the belief itself which is that a Power greater than myself can restore me to sanity. I didn't really understand this concept in the beginning stages of my recovery. It didn't seem to matter. Just by acknowledging my problem, it seemed a Presence had already entered into my life even as I struggled to define its meaning. But I am not alone.

There are those of us who don't believe there is a "God," a Supreme Being or a Divine Essence. I had trouble with this myself for the first couple years of my sobriety. Because my instincts had been warped, my intuitions compromised by self-obsession and my spirituality damaged by the indoctrination of childhood religious training, I was finding it hard to believe a Higher Power could help me. Quite simply, I was furious with God. Why did God cause me to be abandoned by my parents or give me this terrible disease of alcoholism over which I had no bodily control? What kind of a "loving God" does this? I railed, ranted, and cursed God, I got mad at God and told God off.

If this contradicts my earlier section on my first affirmation asking for God's guidance, please know, as a newly recovering person, my mind flipped on so many switches that I was dizzy. Yes, I had faith and then I'd get angry. Then I'd let go and let God; next, I'd take it back. Throughout all this new kind of insanity, believe me, there had to be a God watching over me or I wouldn't be here now, although it wasn't a force I was very happy with at certain times in early sobriety. I resented God for Its absence in my life when it seemed I had needed It most.

As time went on, I realized that I had always prayed for things or circumstances that I thought would be best for me, never for God's will for me. I wanted conditions to change for my benefit, never for the benefit of all concerned. I was being selfish, self-centered, self-absorbed and afraid. I have learned that this is counter-productive. Which is why I like affirmations. I affirm a condition I want in my life but always for the greatest good of all concerned.

You may already have deep faith in a Higher Power, God, Allah, Buddha, or Jesus, or may attend church regularly. It may seem that it will be easier for you to accept the principles of the 12 Step program. But many have found that religious and moral convictions were not enough to attain or maintain sobriety. The certainties about religion and faith that were instilled into you as a young person are not a result of your own spiritual search. This does not equal spiritual experience. Experience implies that we have transcended to another level based on our actual encounters with spiritual crisis and resolution of those crises within us. Merely believing what our parents believed will not sustain us through the rigorous self-examination necessary to internalize a new way of life based on spiritual ideals.

A spiritual transformation does not occur by going into a building and listening to words spoken by someone who has dedicated themselves to a particular religion. A spiritual odyssey is necessary to effect a conversion of your most rigid ideas. Church attendance, or adherence to a particular religious belief, does not automatically save you. If this were so, you would already be transformed. The Steps require you to do the work to change your thinking, your words, actions and behaviors that lead to a spiritual awakening.

If you are having trouble believing in God, hopefully you can still believe in Something greater than yourself. Even if you cannot believe in the concept of a God, there are many examples in our natural world that are Powers greater than ourselves. Even those who are atheists, who believe that the universe is a random creation and events are not directed by a Higher Plan, can feel awe at the sight of stars, the powerful ocean, the Earth and it's wonders. The sun bursting through the clouds is a Power greater than you. The Earth, its enormity of scope and size, and the occurrence of unexplainable events that are wondrous and magical, are Powers greater than ourselves. Whether a random accident, or carefully planned creation, the Infinite Universe is a Power most definitely greater than any human.

You may also use your 12 Step group. The combined faith of the group can inspire and educate as you work the Steps. At some point, you will find your own faith which becomes a foundation upon which you can build a spiritual life.

When approached by Ebby Thatcher, Bill Wilson rebuked the idea of God, as do most alcoholics and addicts. As Bill found himself slipping further toward death, Ebby suggested that Bill modify the God concept into something he could live with; a Higher Power as something greater than himself, to be interpreted by each individual according to their understanding.

This was a brilliant turn of events because now, according to the precepts of Alcoholics Anonymous, God is not exclusive to any religious denomination but can be established and created by any person, of any gender, race, color, nationality or ethnic group according to what an individual perceives as God or a Higher Power. The 12 Steps only ask us to believe in a Power greater than ourselves and this Higher Power can be defined by us.

By defining our own Higher Power, we can create a God of our limited understanding that expresses unconditional love and concern for our well-being, and forgiveness rather than hellfire and damnation. God becomes an inclusive Presence who encompasses and enfolds everyone in the comforting glow of spiritual growth and enlightenment.

A Conscious Connection

In prayer, meditation and affirmations, or in a meeting, hearing what you needed to at the moment you needed to hear it, through a life lesson, through nature, and maybe a whisper of a voice guiding you through a tough time, you will know that you have connected with Something and feel the Presence of It acting beneficially in your life. You are developing a relationship with your Higher Power and gradually sanity will return.

By applying the necessary honesty and accountability to your thoughts, words and actions, miracles start to appear. Letting go of our preconceptions about the way the world should work, we watch our lives unfold according to a greater purpose that substantiates our newfound trust. We have a reason to believe because we see a Power working in our lives although it's not known entirely how or why it works. Spiritual rather than religious, the Steps produce a gradual awakening within you and, as you become more attuned to this process, you experience healing.

Chapter Five

STEP THREE

Made a decision to turn our will and our lives over to
the care of God as we understand God

Stop the Madness

In flights of fancy and fury, wrapped in materialism, commercialism and waving the banner of individualism, we have sought to empower ourselves through people, places and things. Even though I advocate empowerment through manifestation, it is a given that my manifestations are for the benefit of all and only if such manifestations are the Will of my Higher Power.

Many of us have made decisions to turn our lives over to the care of our husbands, wives, girlfriends, boyfriends, peers, debts, financial matters, worries, anxieties, fears, drugs and other addictive substances and/or behaviors, rather than create our own lives free of unhealthy dependencies. When this strategy fails, we then blame everyone but ourselves, relinquishing responsibility for our choices and decisions.

Before you can honestly take Step Three, **you must stop indulging your addictions, whether they are drugs and/or alcohol, or other mind or mood altering behaviors or substances.** Stopping the behaviors is just the beginning and the day you stop can be marked as your first day of sobriety but you are far from recovered.

In turning your life and will over to the care of your Higher Power, we must assume that your Higher Power does not want you doing drugs, alcohol, or practicing other addictive behaviors. Indulging in these substances and behaviors causes significant discord in your life and this can hardly be God's Will for you.

If you do not stop the addictive behaviors, you can still work the Steps however, it is doubtful that you will have a spiritual awakening. Maybe you've already stopped practicing your addiction or substance abuse, and have stopped other behaviors that alter your mood or your mind. Perhaps you've gone to few meetings, and feel ambivalent about the people, the Steps, and the hard work ahead of you. You're not quite sure that this is for you. Maybe you're going to a 12 Step meeting for someone else. You still can't identify with the other members of your group. Yet you know you need help. A conflict rages inside you. You thought you surrendered, but again the disease rears its ugly head, as it will many times throughout the first few months of recovery and maybe even longer. This is resistance.

The goal of your misguided will is to continue to do it your way. And what is this way?

Your Will vs. Their Will

Look around you. The execution of free will by anyone you know, hear about, or watch on TV, **devoid of spiritual development**, is a train wreck. The confusion in the world, the violence and atrocities acted out in the name of religious, or political agendas, all demonstrate the corruption of **self-will run riot**. Many indulge in the dubious luxury of thinking they know what's best for themselves but soon find they are not in right alignment with their place in the world, or with God's Will. Still, our voices ring with certainty: "Our way or the highway!"

So, we dig ourselves deeply into a rut of our own creation and insist that we will make it work no matter what evidence is presented to the contrary. It usually takes a major catastrophe and massive doses of pain to prompt any action on our part. The reason for this colossal effort on the part of the Universe is to show us the error of our willfulness. Our will leads us astray because it thinks it knows what is best for us. But the truth is that we are usually self-seeking, self-absorbed and in fear that we will not get our needs met, our fair share, what someone else has or some other thing that we desire at any given moment.

Another complication arising from the use of our self-will is that humans are creatures of intention. We are constantly intending something or other, whether it is to do our laundry or become a multi-millionaire. These intentions and goals are wonderful, they keep us going, in the game and interested in life. However, our wills and our agendas continually collide with the wills and agendas of other people. As we wrestle for our voices to be heard above the cacophony of other voices straining to be heard and grapple for more of everything, we become less and less happy. It seems that what we were sure we wanted or needed desperately becomes the very thing that destroys us.

Most of us have monumental control issues and have convinced ourselves that our will is the best course of action for everyone. As we try to direct the show, the players, the script, the set, the sound and special effects, we produce nothing but chaos, anger and bitterness because others are insisting on doing it their way, not ours. So, we get into conflict with these people. We fight for control, we win some, we lose some, and we are in a constant state of turmoil over the outcomes.

Our self-will constantly finds ways to inject itself into our thoughts, beliefs and behaviors to stamp itself on the environment, other people, places and things. We know when it isn't God's will by the hurt feelings and angry outbursts we leave in our wake. Somehow, when we're operating out of self-will, conditions deteriorate, sometimes beyond repair.

Our best thinking is aided and abetted by the self-obsession of the psyche as it plunders, blunders and stumbles through Life causing mayhem and pandemonium as we travel the pot-holed, gravelly roads of self-will run riot.

Limited Vision

My son took a class in Logic, Truth, and Reasoning, a philosophy subject, and his teacher put a pie chart on the board. He blacked in 2% and told the class, "this is what we know," then he blacked in 2% more of the pie chart and stated, "this is what we don't know." The class gaped in confusion at the 96% remaining in the pie chart. They couldn't understand what that signified. The teacher explained, "this represents what we don't know that we don't know." Beyond our limited vision is a vastness that defies description.

Perhaps because of the awesome presence of the sky, moon, sun and stars, since the dawn of humankind, we have felt the signature of a Being upon our Universe. Primitive cultures drew paintings, constructed rituals and offered sacrifices to a Presence that was not seen but felt to reside in the natural world as an energy which had consciousness inside animate and inanimate objects. We felt a symbiosis with this Presence and, for many, it was a power to be feared.

Out of the fear of nature and our desire to appease the elements, we have offered gestures in the form of prayers, sacrifices and rituals to this Being of a Thousand and One Names, to look upon us favorably, bless our children, our crops, our creations, our endeavors and our ambitions. We pray, placate, plead and beg God to help us in our hour of need. This is the footing on which many of us have based a relationship with our Higher Power.

Asking what God can do for us, never what God would have us do.

Some of us treat God as our own personal genie and are angry when He-She-It doesn't deliver. Then there are those who don't believe there is a God. Atheists think there is nothing, no Higher Intelligence because there is no evidence of this Intelligence. Others would have us all wearing hair-shirts and taking a vow of celibacy. From one extreme to another, humans are sure they have the ultimate answer to the question of the existence of a Higher Power.

It seems that there are those who have the dubious luxury of negating God and Its Presence in the Universe. Yet, who can explain infinity? The cosmos, the never-ending space. The stars. Though outer space is dark and cold, light and heat were created to make stars, then planets.

Scientists have learned that the odds of this Universe containing stars is one in 10^{229} which is a number so large we cannot even comprehend it. It doesn't seem likely that these odds would randomly produce the emergence of stars, then planets, and then the environment to produce a place like Earth which can sustain animal and human life. The human intellect seems driven to create a God. Why?

Only you can answer this question, through time and experience, with your own personal search for the God of your understanding.

Don't Quit Five Minutes Before the Miracle

Personal experience with a Higher Power is as valid as scientific data. These are called case studies. In a larger sample size of individuals, many claim to have experienced miracles. The Merriam-Webster dictionary definition of a miracle is:

> 1: an extraordinary event manifesting divine intervention in human affairs 2: an unusual event, thing, or accomplishment.

There are 67 documented miracles from people who made a pilgrimage to Lourdes seeking cures for terminal illnesses. They were cured. Their illnesses went into remission. I'm sure there are many more documented and undocumented miracles that have occurred around the world. I only know one thing. I am a case study of a miracle.

At a year and a half of sobriety, I was doing my 5th Step with my sponsor, Pat. I told Pat about an incident when I was five years old. My father and stepmother, Corinne, were living with my grandmother and me, and Corinne was pregnant with my brother, Matthew. Even though he was a troubled person, I idolized my father. My grandma and he argued quite a bit. Often, she threw dishes as he threw curses and threats many an afternoon, until one day my grandmother said they would have to go. I was sitting on my bed and my dad walked in with a sad face, sat down next to me and asked if I wanted him to leave. My grandmother was standing in the doorway, glowering. Somehow I had been taken emotional hostage and was being forced to choose between the father I loved madly, who had abandoned me, and my grandmother, who had always taken care of me. With my heart in my throat, I did what my grandmother wanted and I looked at him and said, "Yes, I want you to go."

Well, my sponsor said that I probably felt guilty about lying. She completely misinterpreted the meaning of this family interaction and the inappropriateness of asking the 5-year old to make adult decisions. I was placed in the middle of the conflict between my dad and grand-mother as a manipulative ploy by my father to serve the needs of the adults in this scenario. Pat did not understand how pivotal this event was in my childhood. In her defense, she was not a therapist and we know so much more about dysfunctional family dynamics now than we did in 1990. The proper boundaries between child and adult were violated. My father was holding me responsible for adult behaviors over which I had no control. I shared the rest of my Fourth Step with Pat. She told me to read the Big Book and she left.

I remember sitting in my comfy chair, reading, when I became filled with an intense feeling of shame. It was pouring through my body like molten lead, burning in every cell of my body, overwhelming me. Now, I realize I was feeling what I had used my addiction to keep at bay. I got up and started pacing, as two voices shrieked different messages; one screaming that I was no good, that it was my fault, it was 5-year old Linda's fault, that I was damaged goods, **that God didn't want anything good for me!!** The other voice raged that the 5-year old wasn't going to take the blame anymore. I wasn't going to take the guilt anymore!! I wasn't going to allow my parents to have the power to kill me!! I was finally fighting back but my shame was winning.

My ego (survival skills) kicked in. What did I do when I felt shame? I got dressed up to look pretty, went to a bar, got the attention of a man or men for that quick fix of flattery to feel good about myself, drank a whole lot and did crazy stuff. That's what I usually did in the past. But, I didn't. First of all, I was sobbing, my face was puffy, my eyes red. I ended up calling someone on the program and he talked me down off the ledge.

I had experienced flooding, the overwhelming surge of negative emotions that are so painful they must be stopped at any cost. Once the acute crisis passed, several insights came to my consciousness:

- I had placed the fault of my abandonment on myself, letting this define me. I realized and felt, deep in my gut, that this did not define me – it defined those who had abandoned me.
- I had used my excessive drinking to numb the demoralization of toxic shame resulting from continual abandonment and emotional rejection that formed the deeply held belief that I was defective.
- My inner child was revealed in her pain and wisdom, and it was my job (Big Linda) to keep her safe.
- I realized that the God of my childhood had not sufficient power to relieve me of the burden of my addiction as an adult. Therefore, I had to change my concept of a Higher Power.
- I HAD BEEN GOING TO DRINK WHEN SOMETHING INTERVENED.
- I also realized I had to get rid of that sponsor!

Since these epiphanies which I believe emanated from my Higher Power, I have created a Divine Consciousness of my understanding; my own God/Goddess that I don't understand, that wants the very best for me, is always on my side, does not judge my stupidity, and praises me for the good I do and what I accomplish. Infinite Wisdom loves me unconditionally, without judgment or censure, and is constantly guiding me toward my greater good, which are health, abundance, happiness and the ability to help others. Great Spirit is unlimited - there is plenty of It to go around. There is no lack or limitation in my life, only that which I put there through my own limited views and ideas.

The truth is I'm a drunk, an ACoA, an Al-Anon, and co-dependent. Naturally, when the going gets tough emotionally, I drink. Something stopped me. I can't explain it. And the miracles kept coming.

The next day after this emotionally charged episode, I went to a meeting and Frank, one of my mentors, put his arm around and said, "You're a good girl." It was **exactly** what I needed to hear. I don't know how he knew what to say but my whole being resonated with the certainty that I was good, not damaged goods. These are miracles of divine intervention. Intervention for those with incurable illnesses.

Addiction is a terminal illness. Addiction will eventually kill you. Drugs, alcohol, bulimia, anorexia, gambling, sexing, over-eating and co-dependence generate repercussions that are life-threatening. So do AIDS, accidents, domestic abuse resulting in murder, Hepatitis C, violence fueled by alcohol and drugs, and prescription drug-related medical complications. Prescriptions drugs can and do kill people. Witness Anna Nicole Smith, Heath Ledger, Michael Jackson and Brittany Murphy, to name a few who have died. There are thousands more who are not celebrities that die every minute of every day.

If we can't see that we need a miracle, then we are blind.

Humility vs. Grandiosity

What we don't know is as vast as the infinite and the magnitude of our ignorance, staggering. Or it would be to any person who actually thinks about it for any length of time. The thought may be so daunting that many cling to the temporary certainties of our finite world. Unfortunately, we know little and have mismanaged the rest of what we do know. It becomes a useless exercise to continue the charade of shoring up our deficiencies with useless chatter about how we're going to handle our problems. If we could have handled our problems, we would have. We didn't, therefore we can't. Not without help.

The way you have lived life day after day, year after year, with all the unpleasant results, must be replaced with a new plan for living. It is not easy to attain humility, because our beleaguered and belittled psyches use grandiosity to survive. When you internalize the messages that you are unworthy, over time this causes damage to the self-image. It is the paradox of narcissistic disorders that our egos are actually not strong, but weak, when we cannot practice humility. Our self-inflated ego actually preserves our psychic integrity. This is a coping skill, however, it stops working. When we are called upon to be humble, it may feel as if we are losing vital pieces of ourselves. To apologize or admit wrongdoing can feel devastating to our fragile sense of self. We are sometimes just not strong enough emotionally.

I believe the root cause of grandiosity is toxic shame. Grandiosity disguises our lack of ego integrity and strength behind a façade of false bravado, and suits our needs rather well, if you think about it. The outside is hard, brittle and defiant, while on the inside we are quivering with need and the belief we are intrinsically worthless. We live in conflict between these opposing viewpoints, which battle back and forth over less than versus more than but never good enough.

We must become bigger than life, be more than, when upon closer and deeper investigation we actually feel *less than*. We exaggerate our achievements and attributes to look better than the next person. We are obsessed with the quest for greater leverage against what we experience as a hostile world. Humility will be lacking in those of us expressing unhealthy grandiosity. We must cultivate humility if we are to be granted spiritual freedom.

If we can find any small measure of humility within ourselves, it will become apparent that we are not God, a Higher Power, the Sun, Moon or the infinite Universe. We are not in charge here, over ourselves or over others.

Free Will

We have free will and will always have free will. But what is the purpose of free will?

Free will is the facility by which we **choose**. I choose to surrender to the fact I was addicted to alcohol. I choose to believe that a Power greater than myself can restore my sanity. And I choose - make a decision - to turn my life and my **will** over to the care of God. Before that, my free will was choosing to drink until I became an alcoholic. But was this really my free will?

Once I saw reality and not the delusions my twisted ego had been feeding me, I had choices; keep drinking, kill myself or get help. Until that moment, I had no choice; the dementia of my denial had made me unreachable.

Practicing an addiction is the absence of choice.

Neuroses, dysfunction, addiction and codependence are compulsory behaviors programmed from old patterns and beliefs, and negative cognitive mandates which exist only for the perpetuation of our disease and self-destruction.

I really had no free will because I was in bondage to the will of alcohol and other emotional disturbances. I was abdicating my free will to whatever circumstances alcohol and my dysfunctional behavior created. I had lost the power of choice and control by the time I got to AA.

Turning One's Will and Life Over

With my own free will I have made a decision, to be in alignment with God's will. God's will is connected to God's love. If I presume a loving God, then It's will for me cannot be harmful.

As you can see, both Step Two and Step Three are intricately linked together in the concept of reliance upon a Higher Power. If you are still having problems developing a connection with a Higher Power, please use your 12 Step group as your Higher Power. Most 12 Step members have experienced the same doubts. If you continue to inject your will into the circumstances and fabric of your life, you will follow a self-obsessed course of destruction and emotional instability. It is sometimes difficult to differentiate between our will and God's will. I've seen many people call their will, God's, and then blame God when things don't work out.

The underlying principle of Step Three is faith. Faith is belief in something not yet seen or revealed to us. We cannot know God's purpose or plan in advance. We must take a leap of faith and trust that God's will is positive and life-affirming. As we attempt to turn our life and will over to God, a logical question is: Is this God personally interested in me?

I believe that God reaches back when I reach out. This Infinite Loving Essence can be contacted through prayer, meditation, right action, honesty, truth and love, if we want to be connected. God does not intrude upon us if we don't want Its help. God is far beyond man or woman and to label Higher Power as human is to trivialize the magnificence of God, and presume that we understand God. The 3rd Step states "as we understand Him," which I have changed to "as we understand God." Although I have changed the pronoun to a noun, this does not change the meaning of the Step. We choose God as we understand God, not as God really is, which is beyond our understanding.

In the fertile ground of our personal surrender, turning over people, places and things to the discretion of our Higher Power, we are growing a faith that responds to our current problems and dilemmas. We are a work in progress receiving the strength to accomplish amazing things in our lives. This is a fact for me and so many others. We prepare ourselves for miracles when we stop thinking we know what's best for us and everyone else around us. We are short-sighted when we assume that we have all the answers.

God created order out of chaos. Every day that I don't drink, or engage in my dysfunctional thinking or behavior, is a day that my Higher Power has intervened on my behalf. Now I look for that peaceful silence inside of myself. I can stay calm and centered in the midst of pandemonium. This is the gift from my own work on my spiritual development, together with a daily intervention from my Higher Power. After 22 years, I have the evidence that God simply is.

God's Will vs. My Will

In God's infinite wisdom, It has given us a choice - our will versus Its will. Our will has landed us in bad relationships with ourselves and others, taking drugs, using alcohol to blot out the pain, raging, feeling sorry for ourselves, and becoming a blubbering mass of free-floating neuroses, without a clue of how to live our lives. But nonetheless, we're out there directing ourselves, our spouses, our children, our bosses, our homes and institutions, with absolute surety that we know best. And others are doing the same with the result that, most of the time, we see a world filled with greed, war, hunger, crime, uncertainty, mental illness, hate, and prejudice, spanning from politicians, religious leaders and corporate raiders, to your average Aryan brotherhood member. This is what free will looks like when the ears are closed tight against the still, certain voice inside us that is God.

So, what is my definition of God's will for me? God's will for me is to attain spiritual enlightenment and to have my human survival needs met. I define my human survival needs as follows:

Loving and being loved unconditionally;
Having food, water and shelter;
Having a partner with whom to share my life;
Having my emotional needs for nurturing, comfort and security met;
To be a part of a tribe or group with similar values and goals;
Living a life of low stress and being in harmony with others;
Being comfortable in my own skin and loving myself unconditionally;
Living a life of honesty and integrity;
Forgiving myself and others, letting go of resentments;
Taking care of the planet on which I live;
Helping others to the best of my ability;
Being part of the solution rather than part of the problem.

When God's will and my will are in opposition, since I am in my own body, mind and spirit, my will prevails, however, my choices and my decisions will then bring me pain, anguish and discomfort. This is what I have found. My willpower did not work when it came to not drinking. My free will, gone astray of spiritual development, was a disaster. I have free will to consciously give it up for something much better - God's will - and we always have a choice - which we make daily to give up our will for God's and see what God has in store for us. I do it willingly because my way was just too damn hard. I was terrible to myself. I didn't love me unconditionally then.

God's will for me has turned out to be much better than I ever would have picked for myself of my own free will.

God's Grace

God's grace is lying dormant in each and every one of us waiting to be awakened through honesty, footwork, humility, gratitude, a clear mind and heart achieved through sobriety and working the Steps. If God is the Life Force - we are a drop in the ocean of Its Mind. We are already part of God and always have been.

Living by spiritual principles will magnetize God's grace and produce profound results in your life. Cause and effect is karma. We make a good or bad cause and receive an equal and opposite reaction or effect. Grace moves us into a higher domain of spiritual evolution. Grace is that state wherein we are forgiven and released from karmic retribution for our misdeeds. Though we might still suffer from the ramifications of our wreckage we receive redemption from the *pay-back* so often required in the karmic condition.

If you're out there lying, cheating and stealing, God's grace just isn't going to happen. Drinking, drugging, practicing addictions and insanity, blocks this Grace. Dishonesty about what you're really about, your motives, your hidden agendas and ego delusions, will hamper the flow of energy necessary to achieve your Higher Purpose.

Though God put us through the five wringers of purgatory and the six levels of hell, It has finally gotten our attention. And it hasn't been such a Divine Comedy. We have tried to circumvent the one irrevocable truth of our lives – that we are addicts and cannot control our own lives anymore. The ability to control our addictions has been revoked and, most likely, will never go back to pre-addict status.

Right now, you may not have received God's grace because you have decided **not** to surrender your ideas, will and dominance. You are on an intellectual mission to determine if this program is right for you and you're merely reading through this book, not working the Recovery Companion

Workbook, or intending to turn your life and will over to the care of a Higher Power. That is fine. If it is meant to be for your greatest good and you ask God for your greatest good, something will propel you forward. It might be a lucid moment free of denial, it might be another major disaster in your life that leaves you in a horrible place. <u>It takes what it takes</u>. I do wish God's grace for you.

You may have accepted that you are powerless over people, places and things, your life is unmanageable and you have surrendered. You are open to allowing God to restore you to sanity and following through with action: doing something different than you've ever done before. Soon, you're coming out of the fog of delusional thinking, rationalization and recognizing that Something is there for you. You can't possibly be doing this on your own. You tentatively put God in charge as you turn it over. Your willingness to change is noticed by others around you. You're keeping an open mind instead of doing YOUR WILL which was practicing addictions, dependencies, neuroses and other behaviors that were screwing up your life. Strange things will start to happen.

You will listen to others in the program, find a sponsor and begin treating yourself better. You will start helping others around you and look at them differently. You will be in fear about a certain problem and find that the problem has been resolved through some means or the other. God is handling your needs now. You are receiving God's grace.

Third Step Prayer

God, I offer myself to you
To build with me and to do with me as You will.
Relieve me of the bondage of self
That I may better do your Will
Take away my difficulties
That victory over them may bear witness
To those I would help of Your Power,
Your Love, and Your way of life.
May I do Your Will always.

Chapter Six

STEP FOUR

Made a searching and fearless moral inventory of ourselves

No Guts, No Glory

Somebody has got to be kidding, right? Searching? Fearless? Moral? Inventory? What in the hell kind of business have you gotten yourself into now? Everyone who reads this Step wants to throw their hands up in the air and call it quits. This is the Step that separates the wheat from the chaff, the men from the boys, the women from the girls, the serious from the hesitators and those who want to get well from those who merely just like the idea.

This is the jumping off point for most co-dependents, alcoholics, debtors, drug addicts and other dysfunctional and neurotic individuals who claim they want help. This is the step that determines whether you have the necessary resolve to commit wholeheartedly to yourself and your recovery. This Step requires a willingness to look into the dark crevices of your behavior, announce your presence, and turn on the spotlight to illuminate clearly the mental and emotional attitudes that feed your dysfunctional behavior and character defects. Most likely, in order to hide unpleasant truths about ourselves from ourselves, we have used other people, bad relationships, drugs, alcohol, chaos, confusion, sex and every other damn thing.

This Step will assist you toward forgiveness of yourself and others. There is nothing so terrible that you cannot be forgiven. Be brave, there are others out there who are willing to hold your hand through the dark and storm-tossed night in which you examine your fears, your anxieties, your resentments and your past secrets.

Character Building

It has been said that character is destiny. This is because our character, which is commonly referred to as moral excellence, or lack thereof, determines our persistence in the face of opposition, our courage to challenge paralyzing fears and our willingness to move through an intimidating process. A person of character learns to develop an <u>attitude of gratitude</u>, of thanking the Universe as they stumble, one step at a time toward the healing light. The point is to start and stay the course, one day at a time, one minute at a time until you begin to see something new. Because we are doing something DIFFERENT, we will get a DIFFERENT result than we have in the past.

We are hoping to develop character in the process of recovery. Character is also part of our personality, develops sound judgment and determines how fairly we treat ourselves and others, our level of integrity, humility, accountability, work ethic and produces an inner sense of confidence and compassion. It can be formed by our conscious intervention.

We have probably not been much concerned with good character, rules or standards. Many of us have felt a sense of entitlement or that the rules did not apply to us. We have found out differently. Good character does not overreach our humanness, but is inclusive of our flaws, forgiving of our weaknesses and imperfections, embracing all of ourselves, the good, the bad and the human. It is difficult to develop character without the necessary guidance of those who raised us, or the modeling of the qualities that form character. So often we have not had this positive influence in our childhood and have seen only dysfunctional behavior which we considered normal, up until the point that we realize it is not. Using this dysfunctional template is killing our souls and any chance of becoming free, joyous and happy.

The Components of Character

Becoming an honest person is the beginning of our recovery. Honesty will be an integral function of our newfound philosophy of life because, without honesty, there is little chance of recovery. The Big Book is emphatic in stating that those who cannot get honest will not get sober. In this case, sobriety and the cessation of our addictive and neurotic behaviors hang in the balance and are based on our ability to be truthful about our intentions and subsequent behaviors. This is calling pulling our own covers. If you are unsure about your true motives, check in with your sponsor or others on the program that you trust for guidance.

There are degrees of honesty. There are levels upon levels of truth. Each day, as we surrender to the process of becoming honest, more is revealed about our reality, our intentions, our agendas and the condition of our integrity. However, some people can't handle honesty. They are so thoroughly invested in the lies they have chosen to invent and repeat to themselves year after year that, even the freedom gained from getting honest will be beyond their ability to grasp. In the Big Book, these people are referred to as "being born that way." I don't necessarily believe that people are born unable to grasp the truth or be honest.

Other character assets are openness, willingness, accountability, objectivity and attempting to refrain from the emotional reasoning that so often accompanies justification of our actions, thoughts and intentions.

Courage is necessary, however, there is no perfect courage. Perfectionism is not the goal. Perfectionism is the hubris of the ego struggling to **be** someone or to get approval for some intangible that really only comes from loving and accepting ourselves as imperfect. If you can find enough courage to move forward, just a little, into the astonishing territory of your inner psyche and what makes you tick, you will find many positive character assets and attributes. We make progress, one day at a time, one step at a time, applaud ourselves, do a little better, applaud ourselves, love ourselves, forgive ourselves and go on. Our progress may be slow but our Higher Power only asks that we do the best we can with what we know in this moment. God loves you unconditionally, no matter what you have done or the mistakes you have made in the past.

As you embark on one of the most difficult parts of the journey – Step Four – it is time to evaluate our lives under the microscope of truth. Falsehoods resemble an infected tooth or injury that oozes with germs and decay. The dentist or doctor must clean, sometimes cauterize the infected area to drain it of its poisons. This usually hurts like hell. There is tenderness and soreness together with a sense of relief that we are on the way to being healed. In Step Four, we are clearing away the wreckage of our past so that we may see the truth, acknowledge our part in the problems we find there and walk freely with our head held high with real dignity. Not the fabricated grandiosity of the injured psyche. The more truth we can uncover, the more change will occur in our lives. This is character.

Unconditional Love/Manipulation

Now for the "L" word. In our inventory, we will begin with the inordinate demands and expectations we place on others to fulfill us, heal us, love us, fix us, feed us, have sex with us, carry our water for us, indulge us, and save us from ourselves. We continually make people, places and things our Higher Power, and expect our lives to go well. We have unresolved dependency needs and desires based on distortions and delusions that will ultimately destroy us.

A prerequisite for being with another person in love and honesty is the ability to be with ourselves in love and honesty, and experiencing intimacy with ourselves by acknowledging our vulnerabilities and imperfections. But we don't know how to go about acquiring this intimacy. Is it any wonder that on the battlefield of love, armed with a thousand kind of lies, we still have no genuine relationship with another person? We have no honest relationship with ourselves. We may blame, shame and torment others because of our lacks and limitations in this arena, but in order to find serenity we must begin to see our part in the viciousness of the fight for dominance on the love fields. Some of the acts perpetrated by us were manipulations to get our needs met, be they sexual, emotional, physical, mental, for security, for advancement or other material, Earthly reasons. We must recognize that when we say we love someone, this kind of thinking is not about love. Love is not a negotiation or a transaction between people. Nor is it a battle to be won in getting the kind of love we feel we need. Again, going back to Step Three, we are no longer in charge of deciding how our love needs are to be met – that is up to our Higher Power who only wants our greatest good.

Love, in its purest form, is an exchange of unconditional loving energy. It has no motive or hidden agenda. It is not given to be received in kind (although that's really great when it is), or to get something out of someone else, to prove something to someone, to be righteous, to be right, to be kind, or compassionate so that the giver will feel good about him or herself. All other kinds of words spoken, or actions performed, in the name of love are manipulations and emotional blackmail of some form or another and, although they can be given with the best of intentions, for the other person's own good, for their learning, so they can do better in life, etc., they are mired in fear, arrogance and self-seeking. Any word or deed used to declare love for someone else that's really for your own gain, to lessen your fear, to manipulate or to take hostage, is not love, but manipulation, hostage-taking and emotional blackmail. Before we can stop anyone from using, abusing and betraying us, we must recognize this behavior in ourselves. We must identify the ego - the false self, the addictive self - before we can truly start getting honest and taking responsibility for our actions. Then we no longer wish to force love upon others, or allow others to *force* their love on us.

From our earliest memories, for many of us, the root of our dilemma is lack of love. Love not received, unrequited love, love-starvation, crumbs of love, or the inability to know what love is because of our family crisis and dysfunction. These omissions are tragic, and reverberate in our lives for years until we end up lonely, addicted, sad, desperate, needy and hopeless.

Although we might strive to give and receive ideal love, it becomes apparent that all human love is flawed, as we are imperfect beings. Trying to get love from others may or may not work out. Almost always we feel it is not enough love or the right kind of love, and then we get angry and blame others for their insufficiencies in the love department. How can we blame others, when by expecting love from another, we are not loving them unconditionally? That's why we say in AA <u>for fun and for free</u>. If you cannot give love in this manner, don't beat yourself up. Many of us never reach a state where we can give our love unconditionally. However, it is essential in writing your 4th Step that you realize your limitations in this area and that you elaborate on those many times you felt angry, hurt, upset or resentful over not receiving the love you wanted or felt you deserved.

There is only one source of Unconditional Love that you can receive at any moment and that love comes from our Higher Power.

Preparing for Inventory

Until this Step, much of our focus has been on developing a relationship with a Power greater than ourselves to alleviate the torment of our daily lives once we stopped indulging our addictive and dysfunctional behaviors. Without the distractions and problems created by our addictions, we have been more aware of ourselves, our bodies, our emotions and mental states of being. We've enjoyed the support of our sponsors and recovery partners, those in meetings every day that help us through the tough times. We have also learned to reach out to a Higher Power, accepting the concepts of surrender and reliance.

As you continue to practice Steps One, Two and Three, you will recognize these first three Steps as liberating truths. Challenges and problems require you to reconstruct answers based on the fresh perspectives of what you've taken in from the program to this point. Change may seem slow but there is awe in the progress you've made, and you will begin to feel amazed at yourself. You are learning to substitute a self-destructive activity, such as practicing your addiction or neurosis, with a positive action. Going to meetings, going to coffee after meetings, reading your recovery books, writing out your thoughts and feelings, sharing your crazy thoughts and feelings with the group, getting applause for being a nutcase, getting more hugs and more coffee, taking a 12 Step friend with you to the family "dys" function where Uncle Bill gets so drunk he ends up naked in the swimming pool. Going to a meeting the next day and expounding on your gratefulness for being sober and sane rather than joining Uncle Bill in the pool, like you normally would, and ruining your new outfit.

It is necessary to have a strong foundation in the first three Steps before tackling Step Four. This Step is an action Step and requires us to go into ourselves on our own. Many of us have never looked too closely and it's a daunting proposition requiring that we overcome our worst fears and confront the ghosts that haunt us. Going back through time, we may be meeting younger versions of ourselves for the first time. We may find ourselves speechless at the damage that was perpetrated upon us or that we perpetrated upon others.

We have had a lot of help up to now but like the hero/heroine's journey, there are some roads that we must travel alone because only we know the terrain and monsters that hide behind the rocks and crevices of our denial. No other person can get inside our soul and decipher our past, or the meaning and intentions of the players in our game of life. As we dig through the wreckage of our past, excavating through our life events like an anthropologist at an ancient dig site, our toxic shame may scream that *we dare not go there*.

We will, most likely, face our shame in this Step, which is why so many skip through and make only a rudimentary effort. This is an example of half-measures. I have seen too many times where they have availed a person nothing. If you have been working through some of the exercises in the Recovery Companion Workbook, then you will have already exposed yourself to a partial examination of your behaviors and this can considerably soften the impact as we enter this new phase of the program.

Before you take the frightening leap into the uncharted regions of your character, the depth of your commitment, your integrity and your values, I suggest that you pray each time you write on your inventory. Before you put your nicely sharpened pencil to your yellow lined tablet, or that napkin in Denny's while you're having coffee, ask God to guide your mind and your writings. Ask God to help you get honest with yourself.

Instincts Gone Awry

The Twelve and Twelve is a book that accompanies the Big book of AA in which the authors propound the theory that the basic instincts of the disordered/addictive person go awry as a result of wanting far more from life than is reasonable or fair. I believe this *greediness* is a direct result of *neediness*.

We see natural human instincts gone awry every day. For example, obsession for financial security mutates into greed and this deadly has brought down civilizations, political figures and the man next door. The same with sex, eating, gambling, spending/debting, working, drinking or drugging. We want more and more hoping to fill up the void that inhabits our psyches. This insistence on wanting more injures ourselves and others in our lives. Sexual infidelity harms our spouses and disrupts the lives of our children with divorce and contention in our relationships. Just as abusive drinking or addiction of any kind has harmed our family and friends. Our insistence upon our rights, or our way, has terminated many a promising opportunity or relationship. We must be willing to honestly admit where our natural instincts have gone to the extreme and become harmful. Anything done to extremes will interfere with the proper balance of one's life.

To the point that no human can satisfy our need for unconditional love, **no human power** can save us. Dependency upon others, either through trying to dominate and control them, or allowing them to dominate and control us is another form of wanting emotional security in our lives, and not about loving someone else unconditionally.

Selfish, Self-Seeking, Dishonest and Afraid

As we begin to think about our inventory, it will become apparent that our lives have been controlled by our fears, insecurities, dishonesty, and our selfish and self-seeking ways. It can really be no other way at this time. Fear-based actions are doomed to bring unhappiness. Decisions made out of desperation and based on one's self-will and dishonest rationalizations are bound to be the wrong decision.

Each time we enter that forum and grab for what we can get from someone, from our families, from our jobs, from the world or from anyone unlucky enough to cross our paths, then we will continually do battle with everything and everyone. For others also have their fear-driven desires and seek to use us to fulfill themselves. Relationships based on these rocky foundations of fear and desperation, ambition and exploitation, have little hope of success. Fear and self-seeking makes liars out of all of us. We say we love someone because we fear they will leave us and we'll be lonely. We say we like something when we really don't out of a perverse need to placate and be *one of the guys* or *girls*. If we were to step out of the crowd and live our lives without manipulations or dishonesty, fear or self-seeking, we cannot see how our needs will be met.

Self-obsession and self-seeking are at the root of fear, dishonesty, greed, lust, pride, envy, anger, sloth, gluttony and all the other deadly sins or human frailties of the world. Not getting ours. We must find and root out these attitudes and behaviors before we do more harm to ourselves and those around us.

Inventories

There are actually four inventories that are referred to in the Big Book on this step: the fear inventory, the sexual behavior inventory, the resentment inventory and taking stock of our good qualities and characteristics. I guess the original pioneers and writers of the Big Book thought the first three were our most slippery places. They are the spiritual banana peels. If we don't look closely and carefully and dissect our unspoken motivations, then we are likely to slip and go back to practicing our addictions and neurosis.

Fear

There are many ways that fear mutates into prejudice, anxiety, judgment, greed, self-obsession and anger. Fear of the other, *stranger fear*, causes us to attribute negative motives and intent to the other person. We are constantly judging others by our standards. We may form opinions based on erroneous information and assassinate the characters of those on our jobs, our neighborhoods, or in our communities. These transgressions against others are a product of fear. Self-centered fear. Fear there is not enough to go around. Fear of lack and limitation. These fears are further outlined in the Recovery Companion Workbook.

With very few exceptions, most fears are self-centered. The Big Book tells us that self-centeredness is the root of our problem. Fear is the number one catalyst that sets self-centeredness into motion. You may have some fears based out of real concern for another human being. However, these instances are probably rare. When we are in the grip of addiction and dysfunction, we are too needy to concern ourselves much with others. So many of our negative feelings are concern for ourselves. We are constantly - 24 hours a day – consumed with what's going to happen to little, old me. We become obsessed with ourselves. We become drama Kings or Queens, using our fears and insecurities to evoke sympathy or attract attention from others. Then we become so transfixed on ourselves, our *big show*, we really can't listen or hear what others are saying.

Faith is the antidote to fear.

As we continue to have faith and <u>turn it over</u> to God, much of our daily burden has been alleviated. What happens next is now in God's hands and we can stop worrying or being anxious about the Broadway production of our lives. Let us note the word *care* in the 3rd Step. This means that God, Divine Intelligence and Love is now caring for our needs. This is how we can finally let go. God will and has taken care of every need that I have at this time. Yes, I have needs and God has met these needs. All of them.

Look deeply into yourself and find what you are afraid of. Be honest. How many of the fears listed are about you, your finances, your relationships, your children, your material possessions, how you look to others or your health? How many are about how you feel emotionally? Such as a fear of meeting new people? How many are about things that will probably never happen?

We can never entirely rid ourselves of fear but we can practice turning our lives over to God's care each and every day.

Resentments

Now we can begin listing our resentments. Resentments are the Achilles heel of every addicted person. We are angry and someone has got to pay. We demand revenge for our victimization. We blame something, someone or somewhere for our problems and our minds are churning with how *they're* going to suffer. As we obsess on the egregious nature of the wrongs that have been committed against us, it seems as if we're the only ones fulminating in the stew of our outrage. The other person has long since forgotten the incident and has probably moved on. So we are the ones doing the churning and burning. So much so that we may even begin to resent ourselves.

The dictionary definition of the word resent is: "To feel displeased and indignant about, to feel insulted by (something said or done)."

I don't know about you, but I could go on for a few days about what I'm displeased with and indignant about. Starting with my cell phone company. And I often do - for about ten minutes.

Then I stop myself and realize I'm giving my peace and serenity to nameless people sitting at computer terminals who don't even know me. And I get into action. I actually got rid of my cell phone.

Resentment is re-feeling over and over again, the insult, the hurt, the indignation and displeasure. Even though the event happened long ago. We are angry, hurt and upset and we never let it go!!

In a completely different category are those resentments that we harbor from our childhood against our parents, stepparents or others who abused, molested and abandoned us. For these people or institutions, we only write out the resentments. Some of us may have been in the foster care system and have resentments about that entity. We list each and every resentment as described in the Recovery Companion Workbook. *And that is all.* You are not to blame for anything that happened to you as a child even if you feel guilty for something you can't quite define. ***This is very important.*** If you have ever been sexually molested, you need to work this out in an incest survivor's group. This is the most heinous of boundary violations and could trigger relapse without additional help. Children, adolescents, and teenagers are helpless. We did not ask to be abused, molested, or abandoned and it is definitely not our fault. There was an adult in charge.

For the purpose of this step, we are looking where we were at fault in our adulthood. Around 17 years old would probably be a good start. At this age, we have been exposed to reason, ethics, moral judgment and the elements of good character. Although we may have chosen not to act according to this knowledge, or the examples shown us, we are responsible for our own moral code regardless. We were accountable and the rules of social interaction and personal integrity applied to us.

What part did we play in the drama of our lives that put us in a position to be hurt, used, abused or betrayed? Where were we selfish, self-seeking, dishonest or afraid? Abuse, abandonment, molestation, physical violence and other violence perpetrated against us, or that we were a witness to, may have set into motion many of the destructive patterns of our lives. However, we have left the initial traumatic environment and had ample opportunity to modify our dysfunctional behavior. It is now time to distinguish between making excuses for our behavior because of our family of origin and a sincere effort to attain spiritual growth. This will be possible with a realistic assessment of our participation in the behavior that continues to cause us pain long after we've left home. What causes this continued pain?

Remember: *selfish, self-seeking, dishonest and afraid*. Nine times out of ten, when we got hurt, as an adult and in our pre-addictive and addictive state, we most assuredly did something to bring it upon ourselves. Our ego, the false and defensive self, dictated that we had a need and that this person, place or thing could fulfill it and when s/he or it didn't, we got steamed. But 99.9% of the time, it was a decision the ego made based on self.

First, we write out our resentment:

My resentment: *"I resent Steven because he used me sexually and did nothing for my career."*

What did this affect? We use these listed below from the Big Book:

- My finances
- My security
- My pride
- My ego
- My self-esteem
- My ambitions
- My personal relationship (self, husband, wife, friend, sister, mother, lover, etc.)

Steven's actions affected my security, pride, ego, self-esteem and ambition. I write that beside the resentment. I also write out any additional insights I may have about my resentment.

I write my next resentment regarding Steven. *"I resent Steven because he chose Susan to play the lead part when he should have chosen me."*

Again, I write out what it affected. It affected my pride, ego, self-esteem, ambitions and personal relationship with Susan.

I might have 20 things I resent about Steven. These are all written out separately. After each written resentment, I relate what it affected and other insights I might have about this resentment.

I then go to the next person and write out all of the things I resent about her or him. And what it affected after each one.

Obviously, there are many people and institutions we resent and we're going to have a very long list of who they are, what they did or didn't do that we resent, and what it affected. You might have several tablets full.

It may be overwhelming to look at this list of people and institutions that have completely dominated your life for so many years that kept you turned on and plugged in, via your anger and resentments. How could anyone have a moment of peace or serenity when we are in the 24/7 business of blaming others?

Now, <u>go back over the list</u> looking at your thoughts, actions and/or feelings in the situation, asking yourself where you were selfish, self-centered, dishonest, or afraid.

Concerning Steven and his not helping my career: Yes, he may have used me sexually but I was *self-seeking* for his help in getting ahead in my career. I was *dishonest* about my true intentions. I did not love Steven nor was I sexually attracted to him though I may have tried to rationalize that - another form of dishonesty. I was afraid to ask him for help without giving into him sexually because I knew he might not help me if I asked him directly. So, it becomes apparent that in this human transaction between Steven and myself, there was fear, dishonesty, and self-centeredness, lack of faith and self-esteem. I did not value myself nor did I believe that I was talented enough to make it in my career without compromising my innermost standards. So I *sold myself out* as my sponsor used to say. How many of us do this every day?

You may now ask yourself if it is ever okay to expect someone to help us in our careers, our jobs, our ambitions or our plans. Yes, it can be. If the plan that you have laid out for yourself seems to be in direct alignment with God's plan for you, then the help, be it through a person, place or thing will usually arrive once you have done the footwork. Social negotiations for mutual benefit occur all the time that produce win-win outcomes. But to **expect** is to be constantly disappointed.

Now I can see that I played a huge part in what happened to me. Ah-ha! **Most of the time when we get hurt, abused or used, we had an agenda and expectations of our own that didn't get fulfilled**. When people fight, it's about two differing sets of expectations that each feels the other person should be meeting and they aren't. Having expectations is very self-centered and selfish.

I have found the only way to peace and serenity and reclaiming my power is by discovering my part in the resentment. Most of the time, it's my ego that's been hurt. My false self-image of who I think I am being stomped on by someone who just doesn't understand how important I really am. And didn't give me what I expected. That will send me from calm to rage in no time flat. I get offended and I blow my top. I used to have thick walls of defenses, and layers upon layers of excuses that were all that came between me and a very hostile world. I was extremely sensitive and I needed those walls and defenses. I've since realized that I'm okay just the way I am, my ego is less defended and I'm not that sensitive anymore. I have people in my life who fulfill my expectations without emotional blackmail. I'm not being hurt constantly because my expectations aren't being met. We want to be loved, liked, sexually fulfilled, respected, admired, and told we're great, beautiful, talented and smart. And this is okay. We deserve to be appreciated and have supportive people around us. But if I'm constantly getting hurt - whose fault is that? It's mine. I'm the one in charge of my feelings. No one can fix my feelings for me!!! Being accountable for my feelings and my subsequent actions is necessary to achieve integrity and maintain self-respect.

Resolution of the Resentment Inventory

Through 4th Step work and taking ownership of our resentments, we understand that people have hurt us very deeply. Another realization is that these people were very sick; emotionally, spiritually, mentally and sometimes, even physically. They did the best they could within their limitations, and maybe their best falls far short of appropriate behavior and kindness, but it's all they can possibly be or do. **To achieve peace of mind sometime in the future, we are going to have to forgive these people and institutions for their ignorance and spiritual short-sightedness.** We and they are only human.

However, we do not rush to forgiveness. That would be entirely dishonest. Forgiving someone who has abandoned, betrayed, forsaken, and rejected you takes time. You may need to live inside your own skin, remaining sober for quite a time before forgiveness for others is achieved. The inventory is a start to see what part we played. We are not bad people getting good, we are sick people getting well.

Addicts are people whose natural instincts have been warped and perverted through childhood trauma, emotional over-sensitivity and the continual practice of their addiction which prevents them from acquiring harmony, peace and balance within the self.

We may be progressing spiritually but we don't hope to achieve perfection anytime soon. This is the nature of the human condition. Everyone is at a different point on the scale of spiritual evolution and we are not here to judge the choices of another person. I consider the worst thing that happened to me, my addiction and the horrible nightmare of my life that followed, to be the very best that could have happened to me in this lifetime. Yet, those that were seeing the drunk Linda were probably judging me left and right. How wrong they were. How wrong I was.

Sexual Inventory

Again, we make a list of those events of sexual misconduct such as infidelity, forcing someone to have sex, rape, molestation, using someone sexually or using sex to gain money or other material gain, such as a promotion.

Sexuality has little to do with love for the most part. Sexual needs are not based on altruistic concerns but are biological imperatives to reproduce the species and are very powerful drives within us. Many murders have been committed because of sexual misconduct of one or more parties. Sex is so powerful that institutions and religions have been created to stifle and contain our sexuality. Rules and regulations about who is to have sex with whom abound, and repressive regimes have risen to power all to sanctify only certain kinds of sex between certain kinds of people. Our inventories are not about the rules and regulations of any religion or institution, but our sexual behavior can be examined using the paradigm of the 12 Steps, and analyzing whether or not our actions were dishonest, self-seeking, self-centered or fearful.

For example, a man has sex with a woman and has no intention of letting their encounter lead to any significant relationship with her. The woman sees having sex with this man as a way to ingratiate herself and uses seductive behavior as a bait to silently coerce him into further intimacy. She uses sex hoping that it will eventually lead to a more lasting commitment from him and an eventual long-term relationship between them.

These two people are being completely dishonest with each other, have numerous inappropriate agendas and will end up causing the other pain and distress because they have unrealistic expectations. The man is arrogant and selfish in thinking that he can use a woman sexually and then just walk away from the encounter unscathed. He offers this woman nothing and seeks only to use her sexually (selfish and self-centered, dishonest). On the other hand, the woman in our scenario is moving way too fast, perhaps out of fear and desperation to find a partner, or for a million other reasons. In trying to manipulate the man to invest more emotional energy than he feels, she is being self-centered and dishonest about her real intentions. His subsequent rejection of her will lead to pain, accusation and acrimony between them.

The honest thing to do in the case above is for the man to express his sexual interest and for the woman to express her interest in having a significant relationship beyond one that is only sexual and fleeting. Both now understand what the other's true desires are and can proceed accordingly. Perhaps the woman is also sexually frustrated and can have sex without any strings, and the man may find himself falling in love with the woman, even though he thinks he only wants sex. After we have been honest with our fellow humans, we leave the results to God.

This applies to all the Steps in the 12 Step program. We apply honesty to ourselves and with others, where indicated, and leave the results to our Higher Power. We fight nothing and no one for supremacy because to do this is to enter the fray of human problems and conflicts and risk losing the protection of our Higher Power. Truly having faith is to leave the results to God – our Higher Power – as we stop the madness of our own free will run amuck which has failed us time and again.

Inventory of our Good Characteristics and Qualities and Actions

It is wise to balance the numerous details of our human foibles and frailties with an accounting of our good character attributes and qualities. This list can be written out with accompanying examples of where you have exhibited these characteristics and good points of behavior in your life. Perhaps you have been a good friend to someone expecting nothing in return from that person. Maybe you have saved the family dog from getting run over by the ice cream truck. Are you considerate, kind, empathetic, a good listener, loyal, open-minded or any other characteristic that is positive, loving, caring and unselfish?

Make your list and look at it every day and feel proud of your accomplishments, recovery and growth in the program.

We Are Only As Sick As Our Secrets

Again, fear rears its ugly head to stop us from exposing the dark underbelly of our psyches. This familiar saying of AA describes those who carry the horrible burden of their secrets throughout their lives. Each of us has a few skeletons in our closets. They're in there with the boogieman. We don't want to tell these secrets because we feel ashamed. This is exactly why we must rid ourselves of the power these secrets hold over us. Secrets are crippling to our future recovery. Holding in all that ugliness, without sharing it with a trusted sponsor or therapist, undermines our faith in ourselves and our Higher Power. We can really have no peace until we let it out and get it over with.

Many of us have lived under the injunctive of **_don't ask – don't tell_**, a family motto that trades in secrets, shame, and innuendo. We have been taught to lie about who we are, and what we have done, out of fear that others will loathe us as much as we have loathed and despised ourselves.

Each addict, alcoholic, neurotic and psychologically disturbed person has those situations in their lives where they did something or allowed something to be done to them that could be sickening, disgusting, frightening, deranged, psychotic or otherwise heinous. These secrets must be unburdened and spoken aloud to be free of their toxic stranglehold on our souls. You write them down and share them in your 5th Step.

The Time Frame

It could take you up to a year to do a proper 4th Step. It could take two weeks. Let it take what it takes as you practice the other Steps in your life. You can still make amends before doing the 5th Step. You can certainly pray and meditate as suggested in the 11th Step. You can carry the message as set forth in the 12th Step.

The 4th Step is a thorough housecleaning but the process never ends. We are constantly *checking our motives*, especially when we run into trouble in our lives. Because we can be sure that when trouble arises we are in the grip of dishonesty, fear, selfishness or self-centeredness. I have found this to be the case in my 22 years of recovery.

When you have finished reading this Chapter, you may begin some of the exercises in the Recovery Companion Workbook. You can also choose to wait until you have read this Chapter several times. It is only necessary that you begin to understand the concepts. As you gain more insight, you can begin the 4th Step process as outlined here and in the Recovery Companion Workbook.

Chapter Seven

STEP FIVE

*Admitted to God, to ourselves, and to another human being
the exact nature of our wrongs*

Walking the Talk

The concept and use of confession as a tool for cleansing our souls to receive spiritual insight and guidance has been around for thousands of years. I myself have sat in a Catholic church confessional during my time in Catholic school, droning through a litany of venial (smaller) sins, while omitting those that were most embarrassing. I received absolution many times and learned nothing about the true nature of <u>stinking thinking,</u> self-pity, shame and the dishonesty that breeds more lies, denials, distortions and delusions.

To counteract any natural tendency to minimize or exaggerate our wrongdoing, it is necessary to share our inventory with another person. Though we may have the best intentions in the world to do better, the act of telling someone else what we've done wrong and to whom, illuminating our resentments and fears and admitting these things in the light of another's scrutiny, makes it real for us.

We may also tend to beat ourselves up unnecessarily rather than doing what is prescribed, which is making amends. Faith without works is a static and dead faith. We are now <u>walking the talk</u>. This means we are putting into action the program of recovery as outlined by the 12 Steps. This is our first major outward act that solidifies our membership in the brotherhood and sisterhood of addicts, alcoholics and dysfunctionals. We are crossing the river of commitment and rowing to the other side.

Step Four has taught us how to investigate our intentions and behavior according to the principles of conscience and right action but Step Five puts them into another's hands for further evaluation. If there are still areas where we might slide and slip past without notice, the 5th Step stops us in our tracks.

Cement the Intent

We are striving for integrity, the principle behind this step. Integrity is defined as "adherence to a code of values," "soundness" and "completeness." The integrity integrated into our daily lives becomes the touchstone of our future program. Our recovery grows more rooted in a moral core of values as we construct our lives around these new principles.

We reduce the need to act out in neurosis and dysfunction while developing a daily discipline of meditation, prayer, therapy, meetings, talking to others, writing and positive affirmations. Incorporating integrity into our lives adds a level of consciousness that allows for humility and gratitude on a daily basis. By putting our intent into action, we cement the foundation for the beginning of the rest of our lives. We haven't yet built the whole house, but without laying the groundwork of our newfound resolve, we cannot withstand the harsh, buffering winds of opposition. We are still a work in progress needing support from others to continue growing.

I was terrified to do this Step. It was the first time I allowed another to see me in all my ugliness. This has a powerful impact on the psyche because we are exposed and truly vulnerable. We are no longer bystanders watching others. We are now trapeze artists flying through the air, having faith that another will catch our wrists and swing us to safety. Our sponsors, counselors and therapists, as our designated *listeners,* will be an empathetic presence. There is no judgment in the 5th Step disclosure. Perhaps our sponsors will share relevant stories of their addictive and dysfunctional past that we can identify with in our own inventory. These disclosures are meant to illustrate we can get sober no matter what we have done, and that we are not alone in wrongdoing. Whatever we have done or how we have transgressed, others have committed the same or worse.

Once we complete our 5th Step, we will emerge stronger and more sure of ourselves and our newfound direction.

Objections to Exposure

In the Recovery Companion Workbook, I have listed many of the objections we may have in sharing our innermost secret selves and the wrongs we have done to others and ourselves. We may stumble over obstacles like pride, fear and dishonesty, even though we've cleared out most of the cobwebs in our dark corners. We do not expect perfection or a complete understanding of our transgressions. The process deepens each moment in recovery as we continue to go to meetings, write, listen to others and share our experience, strength and hope. Now we prepare ourselves to *clean house* and *give away* those items that have outlived their usefulness.

Becoming Vulnerable

In the 5th step, a sense of peace settles over us once we tell another person the nature of our wrongs and become willing to set about making those wrongs right. This is far different than someone waving a magic wand, saying a prayer of absolution and forgiving us without our having to make reparations for our wrongdoing. In revealing ourselves and our transgressions, we are liberated from the prison of our shame and guilt.

The self-disclosure required in this Step deepens our commitment and develops our ability to become intimate with ourselves. We will also experience vulnerability with another, for perhaps the first time in our lives. They hear our deepest fears and secrets. It is normal to be frightened and it is courageous to share our sins with another. You will be protected by your Higher Power, no matter what.

We are not alone in our misdeeds. Everyone has committed wrongdoing, lied, been selfish, angry, or fearful. We are not better or worse than another, only human, divinely inspired, and ultimately capable of rising above our indiscretions. When we stop deluding ourselves, we can truly live a life that transcends the ordinary because each day we are a miracle.

The Exact Nature of Our Wrongs

As outlined in the 4th Step, we make our inventories in the prescribed manner and include our deepest and never before shared secrets. However, as we contemplate the entirety of our inventory, it becomes apparent that we cannot divulge every resentment over the entire course of our lives. It is more productive to share those resentments that had the most impact on your life, that hurt you the deepest or seemed to set into motion your addictions and dysfunctions. The *essence* of our wrongs will likely be that we were selfish, self-seeking, dishonest or afraid. For how can we even have a resentment without an expectation for ourselves, our well-being or our own motives? How can we feel fear that is not about ourselves? Perhaps we sold ourselves out (dishonesty), or a seemingly bad thing was done to us, but was, in fact, set in motion by us because we had a selfish agenda. It is important to internalize the concepts of accountability and responsibility for our actions and those actions of others upon us, as having their roots in our agendas, fears, lies or selfishness. It is this act of honest self-examination and pulling our own covers that leads to freedom and true vision.

We may never understand the exact nature of our wrongs, but we can hit fairly close to the mark. The effort is what matters. We are aware that we have done wrong and can distinguish where we have gone wrong. Comprehension, wisdom, and maturity are slower to emerge in our developing consciousness. Many of us have experienced that human resources often fall very short of the kind of power necessary to uplift our psyches or our spirits. Realistically, human power will inevitably fail, like an electrical outage in a thunderstorm.

The Person With Whom We Share Our 4ᵗʰ Step

At this time, you may have a sponsor in a 12 Step Group, who has given you considerable input into yourself and how the program works. Someone who has become familiar with your life and your problems, and has helped you make incremental progress. You may like to share your 4ᵗʰ Step with this person. However, please be aware that anything shared with a member of a 12 Step group does not have the same confidentiality as that of a licensed counselor, psychologist, therapist, priest, minister or other clergyperson. There is no privilege of confidentiality with a layperson who is simply a member of a 12 Step Group, even though anonymity is a cornerstone of the program. If there is anything in your 4ᵗʰ Step that is a criminal act for which you have evaded criminal arrest or other legal consequence, be advised that your sponsor, if questioned in a court of law, would have to reveal what you told her/him in your 4ᵗʰ Step. The law has been decided in these matters. I do not agree with this because we are members of an anonymous group. The very definition of anonymity means we should not be able to reveal someone's last name because we shouldn't know their last name (even if we really do).

That being stated, a licensed 12 Step counselor or therapist is bound by laws of confidentiality and could be a good person with whom to share your 4ᵗʰ Step. If there are no criminal acts, you can share with anyone else. I'm not saying that a person should be absolved from lawful punishment for crimes committed because of the law of confidentiality. But I believe the person must come to that conclusion as a result of working the steps and submitting themselves for punishment if that is the right thing to do.

Revealing the dark crevices and questionable reasoning of our behaviors and characters opens a portal to our souls and makes us extremely vulnerable during the time we are sharing our 4ᵗʰ step. Many people in 12 Step groups are not equipped to hear 4ᵗʰ Steps because of their own unresolved conflicts. Such was the case with my sponsor. Again, if you have even the tiniest connection with a Higher Power, you are divinely protected. As demonstrated by the events outlined in the Chapter Five, I hope you have faith that this is so.

My sponsor was a periodic drinker, who regularly got sober with no more than 4 years between relapses, and this had been her pattern for over 20 years. Being a newcomer with limited knowledge, I didn't understand that she was not a suitable person with whom to reveal my 4ᵗʰ Step. Although she could spout AA clichés and rhetoric, she had only scratched the surface of the underlying reasons for her habitual relapsing behavior.

Choosing someone who understands the nature of toxic shame issues and who has the ability to listen without further shaming us is very important. We need a responsible, accountable, recovering individual or therapeutic professional who interacts with us, using self-disclosure, clarifying questions, reflection and unconditional positive regard, and with whom we can identify and feel psychologically safe. We can't really know who that might be with certainty but we do the best we can and leave the results to God.

Catharsis

As with many of the epiphanies I have received during my recovery, I have discovered that before the rainbow there has to be one hell of a storm.

My 5th Step was no different. In Chapter 5, I shared the realizations that my recovery uncovered. I fired my sponsor, Pat, and reached a different level of sobriety. Even though the first time I shared my 4th step (which is the 5th Step) went awry, it still had incredible power to lead me further into my journey. In actuality, if Pat hadn't triggered my spiral into shame, I could not have achieved the insights of that night.

This incredible catharsis ripped away the lies of my childhood and I saw the beautiful truth for once. I was no longer confused or needing to be deceived. This is the power of the 5th Step.

We may unleash feelings and perceptions that have been repressed for many years. It is important to know that if we are feeling overwhelmed or experience flooding of emotions, we must contact our therapist, sponsor, or someone else on the program immediately.

Further Growth

After the episode with Pat, I worked with another sponsor with seven years of consistent sobriety, who had worked the Steps and had a deep understanding of the concepts of the program. She guided me through my 4th Step, as I felt I hadn't gotten what I needed from Pat.

Stacy and I had much in common, we both had young boys to raise, ambiguous feelings toward our fathers and abandoning mothers. She helped me understand that all the conditions in my life are based on my spiritual condition. As I went through my list of resentments, she was instrumental in helping me see where I had been selfish, self-serving, dishonest and afraid. Some of those resentments, as justified as they might have been, toward my stepfather, mother, father, grandmother, Jim, Ted and a myriad of others, did not serve my higher purpose of peace, harmony, and serenity. But how was I to overcome my resentments toward these people?

It seemed a very large order indeed. This process is ongoing and specifically addressed in the 8th and 9th Steps.

I know that there is a Higher Power. I have also realized something about myself. When I feel toxically shamed and the integrity of my core personhood is threatened, I want to self-destruct. I don't actually crave a drink, per se, but I want to do something to rip myself apart. This is how toxic shame affects me. But I am aware of it and because of my time on the program I know now what to do. Get my ass to a meeting and talk to someone!! Write about it! Pray to God! Meditate!

I have options and choices today. I don't have to react to life and it's capricious twists and turns, with fear, resentment, anger or dishonesty. I can tell the truth, as I perceive it, accepted or not, because my God, my Higher Power has given me clarity and understanding. Truth is the engine that runs my life today. I don't have to hide who I am from anyone anymore.

Chapter Eight

STEP SIX

Were entirely ready to have God remove all these
defects of character

We're Getting There

Writing out our 4th Step and exposing our vulnerabilities in the 5th Step, is a great challenge requiring mature growth and insight. Then here comes Step Six with its seemingly impossible suggestion that we call upon God to extract every character flaw from our lives. Don't get discouraged. It's important to give yourself credit for the tremendous efforts and accomplishments you have achieved up to this point. You are amazing! You have acquired some beneficial character assets and realized some of the promises of the program. Most likely, if you are reading this Step with an intention to follow its suggestion, then you have already taken Steps 1 through 5, probably worked 11 and 12 and made some amends (8 & 9). If you have stopped using your addictions and dysfunctional behaviors to alleviate your pain, you are well on the road to recovery and probably feel heaven-blessed at times.

With all the honesty at our disposal, we told a trusted mentor, sponsor, therapist or counselor where we went wrong by clinging to resentments and anger, or how we stubbornly refused to admit our part in the chaos of our lives. We dug through our past and brought to the surface many seemingly benign personality traits, along with more grievous moral lapses and character problems. We may have decided to take responsibility for these lapses or revised our standards of right and wrong. However, we are now being asked to become entirely ready to reach a lofty, martyr-like state of sainthood that few are capable of achieving at this point in their recovery, or ever, for that matter.

Understanding the Intent

The difficulty of this Step is in the language. The language is in the extreme, "**entirely** ready," "**all** defects of character." First, defect seems a harsh word to apply in connection with our future recovery because it brings up shame-inducing images that already plague many of us who feel fatally flawed and unworthy. Secondly, some of our character defects have been instrumental in our survival strategy. For example, anger. Many of us have used anger to intimidate others to do things our way. Through time and experience, hopefully, we can replace anger and acquire the skills to be assertive, asking for what we need, rather than extracting it through belligerence and temper tantrums. At some point in our recovery, we will realize that our lives are more effective without resorting to the use of negative strategies.

As worded, Step Six seems to point a judgmental finger in our direction and demand that we *want* to become instantly free of any human foible, flaw or shortcoming. This only creates resistance in many people. Even if we did want to be entirely ready to have each and every fault-line of our characters removed, do we even have the necessary insight to know which defects are holding us back and are the most grievous? Before your Higher Power can remove your shortcomings which were acknowledged in your 4th and 5th steps, you must comprehend the extent of destruction that these character defects impose on yourself and others, accept them as serious enough to require removal and honestly want them removed.

So, how can we reconcile this Step using newfound concepts and apply them in the context that was originally intended?

We don't have to worry. Although each person is at a different stage in their spiritual quest, our Higher Power will reveal what needs to be done or changed in us. As long as you have truly turned your life over to the care of your Creator, you are now co-creating a new existence based on faith and truth. We will need to bring into our consciousness certain areas where we need help. As many have said, "God helps those who help themselves."

Getting Ready - Getting Willing

In preparation for the 7th Step where we ask God to remove our shortcomings, there are certain characteristics of our personality that need to be examined and excised if we are to move forward into healthy psychological functioning. In some areas, we are comfortable with familiar patterns of behavior that are resistant to change. However, it will be necessary to confront and challenge our pre-existing emotional conditions.

The principle of Step Six is WILLINGNESS. The willingness to change what is most destructive about the present patterns in our lives.

Willingness opens the door to transformation. Willingness in action is doing what propels us in a positive direction rather than backsliding into old thinking. We may already be more attuned to problem behaviors and traits that held us back before our recovery. Positive, life-affirming options and choices are now more available to us on a daily basis. We open our spirits to receive and accept guidance from our Higher Power, rather than relying upon our misguided judgment.

When we practice the principles to the best of our ability, <u>more will be revealed</u>. This is one of my favorite AA sayings because it implies that our Higher Power will gently guide us toward a purpose or solution that helps others and ourselves. I can't emphasize enough that this is one of the promises in motion. It is truly remarkable that so many times, when I focus my attention on footwork, with absolute confidence that more will be revealed to help me solve my problems, something more is always revealed that enlightens and puts me back on the right path.

But first, I must be willing.

Self-Defeating Patterns

Even as we use the older definition of the 6th Step to give us an ideal, it is important to understand that:

> *Character defects are persistent self-defeating patterns that*
> *once admitted and accepted can be alleviated by*
> *the work of the recovery process and God's intervention*.

In almost every instance, my *defects* alienated me from myself, my loved ones, my Higher Power, and threw my life into turmoil. In early sobriety, there was so much going on emotionally that the motives for my disturbing self-destructive behaviors were difficult to decipher. As I continued writing about the events of my life, attending meetings and talking to other addicts, slowly the picture of how toxic shame had poisoned every aspect of my life came into focus.

As with most recovering people, my sanity was restored in fits and starts. In good moments, I was able to achieve a semblance of emotional equilibrium. However, I was still needy and lonely. I began to develop a closer relationship with my younger sister, Amy, and together we went to ACoA and CODA meetings. We began processing some of our family dysfunction through grieving the many losses of our childhood and getting appropriately angry over what had happened, or didn't happen, in our family system. John Bradshaw's book, "Healing the Shame That Binds You," was instrumental in my recovery process.

However, I learned about John Bradshaw when I was 6 months sober and became insanely infatuated with another AAer who was 20 years sober.

Colin, an Irish-Catholic turned atheist, was avidly involved with the theories of Bradshaw and working the inner child methods. He started flirting with me at the 6:00 p.m. meeting we both attended, and afterwards we would go for coffee with a group of other AAers. Reading the concepts of toxic shame, my head understood that I had been shamed to my core in my childhood, but my old patterns of choosing men who were emotionally unavailable kicked into high gear, as I became more enthralled with Colin. I just knew he was *the one.* Oh, yeah. He was 20 years sober hanging out with a newcomer (a big no-no called the 13th Step), he was unemployed and living with his brother. He was 10 years older than me and had been married 4 times. Oh, yes, he was relationship material, all right. Did I mention that I was still crazy, but sober?

At first, he came on strong with the warning that he only wanted "half a loaf" of a relationship with me. At least he was being honest. But I didn't really hear this because my self-will was riding shotgun with my delusions of true love. I would *fix* him and we would live happily ever after. He was deep into processing his shame and soon our quasi-relationship became more *quasi* than relationship. His lukewarm attitude toward me allowed me to fully experience the pain of my dysfunctional choices. I lay in bed at night, in such emotional pain, it was almost physical. Yet, I knew this pain would not kill me; only alcohol would. My Higher Power was pretty clever. I kept going back to that 6 o'clock meeting and I kept working my program.

After I finally let Colin go (he found a "newer" newcomer), I got involved with another AA man who was also in Narcotics Anonymous and had 8 years of sobriety. Although he was a former felon and rode a Harley Davidson motorcycle, he had a job (a step up for me), an apartment (be still, my beating heart) and he actually asked me out on a date on Thanksgiving Day 1989, two months after my first sober birthday. Our relationship lasted exactly one year and was a whirlwind of break-ups, falling in love, getting back together, fighting and then breaking up again. During the whole year, I continued with my programs of AA, ACoA and CODA and became very well aware of my relationship patterns. But I couldn't seem to stop myself. On Thanksgiving Day of 1990, after I cooked a delicious turkey dinner, the veil of denial lifted and I actually saw that we had absolutely nothing in common. I no longer felt romantic love for the man. We broke up for the final time.

Once again, I had settled for someone who was incapable of honesty, intimacy or consistent love and convinced myself that somehow it was going to work out. I was very discouraged that even in sobriety, my relationship choices had not changed and it seemed as if these patterns were fated and irrevocable. I felt incapable of choosing a healthy, loving, caring man. Did I mention I also felt a little sorry for myself? This was one of my most serious self-destructive patterns and finally, after that break-up, I hit a relationship bottom and began therapy.

Hitting a Bottom In Sobriety

We may have acknowledged some of our character deficiencies in the course of working on our 4th and 5th Steps, yet it may seem that at times we're still struggling with these same problems. Many issues remain stubbornly resistant to change and keep us from reaping the benefits of our recovery. I have noticed that in some 12 Steps programs, other than Alcoholics Anonymous, recovering members skip over some of the more formidable Steps, falsely believing that working Steps 1, 2 and 3, 11 and 12 is enough. This is not so. Doing an incomplete 4th Step and skipping over the 5th Step will stop your developing recovery. So, I really hope you do these Steps. It is vital to your future program.

If you **have** done both previous Steps within your capability to do them, then a door has opened and those self-deceptions that obstruct your spiritual growth may have been removed. Our reasoning powers have improved and can assist us in surrendering the most glaring of our character defects that are holding us back from serenity, peace, harmony and health.

We will never work these Steps perfectly. We are human – flawed, imperfect and have chosen to have an Earthly experience which automatically implies we are here to learn and transcend certain trials. Many of us will hit a bottom in sobriety because our more serious self-defeating patterns have not been eliminated. Bottoms are painful but necessary for spiritual and emotional improvement.

We cannot be absolutely sure if our Higher Power will remove all our character defects or even any of them. The point is: are we willing to have them removed? If we are, then we welcome the changes we've worked for and strive to rid ourselves of the negative characteristics that are holding us back from living a joyous life.

Revelations

The 12 Step program requires us to surrender again and again and the 6th Step is no different. It asks us to be willing to surrender self-destructive traits that harm us and others in our lives. Most likely, we won't see the benefit in surrender until we hit bottom with a character defect that has serious consequences in our lives.

For me, that was realizing I didn't know how to choose a man with whom to have a partnership. Even though I had stopped using alcohol, my dysfunction found expression in the types of men I tried to have relationships with. The causes and conditions of these aberrant patterns were obviously linked to early and repeated abandonment by my mother and father. As I continued to process many of the feelings, I understood that although my past could not be changed, my future had to be in God's care.

So I cried and let go to let God work a miracle in my life. As I realized I was incapable of choosing a man who wanted intimacy and sharing, I was able to view the problem from a different perspective. I recognized my resistance to choose a person with whom I could become truly intimate. I was afraid to be my authentic self because I felt shamed (toxically). I believed if I got close to someone they would see how unworthy and flawed I really was and reject me. Again, more was revealed and I was willing to see this new truth, a deeper one that I had been unwilling to see before. *I was afraid of intimacy, therefore I chose men who were also as shamed as I and incapable of intimacy.* This also corresponds to the Law of Attraction. Without the knowledge of my true beliefs I was doomed to repeat this pattern endlessly.

The immensity of this revelation shook me to my roots. I decided that I was going to accept that I was incapable of choosing a man for myself, accept responsibility for my past mistakes with men and instead take a risk with becoming intimate with a man. In the same breath, I also accepted that maybe God didn't have a relationship in store for me; that I might have to be alone. And I was willing to accept this. Another surrender. The expectation that I somehow deserved a relationship or entitled to one had to be eliminated. Paradoxically (the recovering condition is loaded with them), I reasoned that my Higher Power always took care of my needs as long as I did the footwork.

About two weeks after this epiphany, I went to my nighttime job at the Holiday Inn where I was singing in a duo act with Levon Saxon, a gifted pianist. Adjacent to the lounge was a larger banquet room with another entrance. After a couple weeks of our engagement, I saw a man walk in with a party of about 8 people from the banquet entrance. He was tall, with an athletic physique, dark hair, wearing a tuxedo. I looked across the room at him but I couldn't see him clearly, so I turned my attention to the cocktail crowd and soon the party got up and left. Little did I know that my Higher Power was working in the unseen realm – creating reality - as has been the case very often in my life.

Three weeks after that, still singing in the Holiday Inn with Levon, a man walked in alone, wearing a suit, tall, good-looking with dark hair. He sat down in the cocktail area, ordered a drink and watched as I sang. Since it was around 11:30 at night, there weren't many people in the cocktail lounge and I begin to sing to him while I wondered about his story. Was he the infamous traveling salesman staying at the hotel, was he married, was he available? There was something about this man. He radiated kindness. He had a gorgeous smile. I knew he was a *nice* guy. And my sick head said, "Oh, I won't be attracted to him." That is our sickness. When something good does come along, we feel unworthy and sabotage ourselves. But I had turned my life over to the care of my Higher Power and God wasn't going to let me screw it up.

This mystery man and I started talking after the gig. He was a musician and he was unassuming, handsome, sweet, sexy, and I felt the world turn on its axis.

No, I didn't sabotage myself. I had grown just enough in my recovery to be able to accept this wonderful gift of love and happiness from my Higher Power. Later, we figured out that he had been the man who came into the banquet room three weeks earlier. We have been together and married for over 19 years.

Sabotage

It seems that many people believe they can find an *easier, softer* way to get the rewards of a recovery program. Engaging in our characters defects may seem easier than playing by the rules of life but in the long run easy gets very hard. Unknowingly, in our fear of taking an emotional risk, we have deprived ourselves of the sweetness of life. As illustrated above, I suffered from a fear of intimacy, unable to choose a suitable partner with whom to share life. It became too painful for me to continue my old ways. Doing it differently may feel very awkward at first. That is natural. It may feel like it isn't even you anymore. I assure you that it's still you, just you in transformation, helping your Higher Power remove barriers that have been holding you back from moving through necessary developmental phases. You are becoming the person you always wanted to be without resorting to the ineffectual, self-destructive behaviors of addiction and dysfunction. If it feels uncomfortable – then you're probably doing something right.

I have made a list of both Character Defects and Character Assets in the Recovery Companion Workbook in Step Four. This list is useful in Step 6 or for work in any of the Steps. As we comprehend these defects as **characteristics of our self-sabotage**, we may become more than willing to have our character defects removed by our Higher Power.

No matter how heinous a crime a person has committed, doesn't he or she also condemn himself or herself in the very act of hurting another? Isn't their freedom at risk? Don't they invite the world to view them negatively? This is certainly not positive or self-affirming behavior. Respecting ourselves by having appropriate boundaries and respecting the rights and boundaries of others are character assets that enhance our recovery. Violating another person's boundaries; sexual, physical, mental and emotional, or allowing others to violate our boundaries is self-sabotage. What good can come of forcing or controlling another? Recovery is working on ourselves, our own problems and keeping our nose out of others' business, unless asked.

Acceptance

Willingness is a key concept in any recovery program. How do we achieve this willingness? Gradually. Your ego might fight for dominance but when the problems mount up and you're at a loss, you reach a turning point. You decide to accept life on life's terms. Accepting the circumstances we find ourselves in and realizing they are of our own making. But we can't relieve ourselves of the burdens of our past without the help of our Higher Power.

As more is revealed, we may not like what we see but we can accept something even if we don't like it much at the moment. There are probably a lot of unpleasant truths about yourself that you don't care to see. However, you can look at your character defects without having to judge yourself for having them. It is not your role to judge yourself or your past. In this Step, the goal is to become willing to further examine your character defects and ready to have your Higher Power decide which ones are to be removed. In the co-creation process, our Higher Power can't remove our self-defeating traits without our involvement. This is a reciprocal process between spirit, God, willingness and acceptance.

One of the components of being entirely ready is that we are willing to go to any length for sobriety and recovery. Building character is a slow process and one that requires that we stay honest as we work to reveal, and have revealed, deeper and more profound truths about ourselves that will benefit our lives and the lives of many others.

Chapter Nine

STEP SEVEN

Humbly asked God to remove our shortcomings

The Cost of Pride

Humility is constantly maligned, considered unnecessary for getting what one wants in this life, and seen as weakness in our greedy, power-seeking world. Humiliations are to be avoided at all costs as are wounded pride and losing face. These negative beliefs about humility are seemingly burned into human DNA preventing us from developing a far-sighted outlook on the nature of our place in the continuum of life on this small planet spinning around in infinity. In the wake of pride and dominion, the human species has done more damage to the planet Earth than all the other species combined, recklessly using resources for our own *progress*. One of the main aberrations we have perpetrated in our selfish use of the Earth's resources is that only a few groups of people are obscenely wealthy, while more than 70% of the human family of the world, suffer in abject poverty, war, strife, religious purging and genocide. In looking at the world and its inhabitants in this light, I think it's safe to say that pride is highly overrated. Atrocities are justified every day with specious logic and psychopathic reasoning.

As we learn to express humility, we realize that God's will is not to use other people ruthlessly for our own agendas. Humility has allowed me to see that I am not special or above the law any more than the next person. I am a person among persons, a sister among sisters, and a friend among friends, no better, no worse, no more and no less. It is a relief to be free of the burden to prove myself constantly by being *someone*. Pride shouts for admiration and recognition. Humility quietly seeks to lend a helping hand. In my quest to be recognized and admired for being special, I almost died.

In my recovery, my accomplishments are intrinsically motivated. Feeling good inside of myself is why I do what I do. Be it washing the dishes or writing this book. I don't need praise from others to sustain my efforts. I like praise just as well as the next guy but that isn't my main motivation for achievement. If I can help others, then I feel I've had a good day. Today I am a part of the human race.

Separate But One

It is our apparent *separateness* that many use to justify exploiting others. Separation can be viewed as the greatest evil since the dawn of humankind. Most horrors and atrocities have been perpetrated on others because they were different, despite that the rational mind informs us that these differences are only external.

We are all composed of the same substances. We each return to ash and dust. Differences are illusionary and destructive. The more we try to separate ourselves from others the sicker we become. Some people may feel they are above others by benefit of education, wealth, status, prominence, intelligence, beauty or by believing they know what's right for others. But differentness is only transitory. Once we die, we give back all Earthly gifts including all the material trappings we have accumulated. We are again one with the Earth, our spirit departing to our Higher Power and joining other spirits in a state of *oneness*.

We can bridge the gap of our isolation by finding similarities in our experience with those around us. A newly sober person listens to others in recovery and identifies with their life stories and problems while *under the influence* of their disease. We can take great comfort in knowing we are not alone, that our life problems and our suffering are not unique. We may not be able to entirely overcome our distorted perceptions of other people, but we can see that this failing is our human condition and not our spiritual one.

On Our Knees or In Our Own Way

Cultivating humility calls upon growing resources of inner strength and spiritual wisdom, as we comprehend our place in the grand scheme and design of the Universe. We don't have a right to put our own needs or desires ahead of others. Each human has a right to pursue life, liberty and happiness and this human birthright is equally applied to all.

If being rich or famous distracts you from your primary purpose, staying sober from your addiction/dysfunction/neuroses/co-dependence, then it's not God's will. We check in with our Higher Power on a daily basis to make sure we stay involved in recovery. Getting sidetracked by the clamor of work, the pursuit of a relationship or the distractions of others' problems can keep us from the contemplation of our Higher Power's purpose for us.

We will face certain tests of our ability to be humble. We'll go back to thinking we know what's best for us. We were hurt, abandoned, rejected, neglected and abused, and our ideas about what was good for us became confused and distorted. Our lives were hopelessly mangled and our insight and knowledge were woefully inadequate.

What's going to happen then? If you can get yourself out of the way, I can tell you from experience that your life will unfold into something miraculous. Our Higher Power supports us through the challenges of humanness as long as we apply the principles of the program to the best of our ability at any given moment. This doesn't mean we take what isn't ours and God says go ahead. If we pray, meditate and do affirmations, people, places and things manifest to teach us something about ourselves. The more we direct our attention to working the Steps and practicing the principles, issues that once plagued us seem to lessen and then vanish. Approaching each life lesson with an open mind and heart is an opportunity to express our faith in a Divine Purpose. There are no coincidences. What might appear as a setback could, in fact, be the greatest thing that ever happened. I have learned not to judge the appearance of a situation in my life. I now know its presence is there for a reason. This is a fact for me and many others who are in recovery. Just ask them. Those that have truly worked the Steps – not just people who sit in meetings and share. But we have to become humble, and get down on our knees symbolically, if not physically.

There is a story told in the Bible that Jesus once said a rich man had as much chance of attaining heaven as a camel had of passing through an eye of the needle. Many interpretations of this passage abound, but in Jesus' day there was a long wall with doorways (gates) where people could pass through to the other side of the wall. It is thought that an eye of the needle was a four-foot high gate in this long wall through which people could pass easily, but camels could not pass unless they went down on their knees and crawled through the gate to the other side. The symbolism here emphasizes our willingness to accept the limitations of life as they are presented to us on a daily basis. The grandiosity of our former life doesn't represent anything other than a shallow defense against perceived assaults to our pride (ego). Our true strength is in our humility. Without humility, one cannot reap all the benefits of recovery.

In recovery, humility equals *teachability* for the simple reason that a person must truly let go of their old perspectives and rigid beliefs to give recovery a fair shot. There is no other way. Clinging to broken tools, skills, and strategies, including our deluded egos, will keep us in the same anguish forever. Humility heals many common ailments of self-pity, dependence, defiance, and an overblown estimation of our presence here on Earth.

The Business of Life

As you go through the Steps, mindfully working the exercises and inventories in the Recovery Companion Workbook, you have taken in a lot of information about your life circumstances, the way you think, what you believe and how you behave. Hopefully, you have experienced awareness into why you have been on a self-destructive path for so long.

To achieve serenity, it is necessary to attend to what life puts in front of us. At the same time, we adhere to the laws of our particular social structure. It means the rules apply to us – there are no special cases. We suit up and show up. It may be mundane and boring as hell but, oh, well. Mundane matters such as getting a job, taking care of your children, paying bills or taking out the trash, become matters of extreme importance that hold the power to literally save you.

If we are vigilant in the small things, our spiritual consciousness will be raised. We have fruitlessly attempted the grand and desperate gesture, self-seeking for love and appreciation, indulging our full-blown fantasies of being on top, the best and the smartest. Or we have neglected our responsibilities, indulging the devious twists and turns of our co-dependence, addictions and neuroses. Growing up means coming to terms with reality. As we develop the skills to arrive at an accurate assessment of our character flaws and self-defeating patterns, we won't want to go back to our painful delusions. We are going to be pleasantly surprised that most hurdles are surmountable.

By achieving some measure of humility, it is now possible to attend to the business of life.

Acquiring Character Assets

We prepare ourselves to accept what our Higher Power has in store for us. Praying each and every day, we listen for an answer to how we can acquire the qualities and character assets that will lead to true happiness. If you want a life full of stress, competition, drug and alcohol addiction, strife in relationships, dysfunction and neuroses, constant battles with any and all, then you may opt out of seeking humility. However, if you seek a larger life, an expansion of your soul and spiritual understanding, then you willingly choose humility,

Many people resist the notion that humility is a requisite tool for a spiritual conversion and our Higher Power may be forced to even greater lengths to get our attention. The law of natural consequences subjects our *sensitive* natures to further humiliations, defeats and failures. Even if we manage to succeed by sheer self-determined will, the glow of victory is usually fleeting. Without deeper meaning and purpose, short-lived successes are not able to sustain our fragile egos for long. We feel that there must be something more.

Out of the fertile soil of humility and a realistic perspective of our place in the world, we acquire a new sense of self-worth and self-esteem. We realize that this intuitive knowledge comes almost naturally. Our struggle with the demons of our childhoods, our self-destructive patterns, our fears and resulting selfishness may be painful but they have borne fruit. We are blossoming and growing in the sunshine of God's Grace.

Our diligence in working the Steps enables us to transcend to another level of spiritual awareness. Continuing our footwork, we realize that our Higher Power is creating opportunities, or bringing people into our lives or making it easier to stop indulging in former negative behaviors.

Removal of Shortcomings

Can God really remove our shortcomings? I am a walking example of that. But the thing is – we don't get to choose which character defects our Higher Power is going to remove. When we improve our spiritual condition, many shortcomings are automatically taken from us as we work in a spiritual partnership with our Higher Power. That's a real trip. For example, I had smoked cigarettes since I was a teenager, over 27 years. In 1998, I experienced heart palpitations and felt that my smoking might be a factor. Many times over the years I had rationalized my nicotine addiction with illogical arguments. If you're a smoker, I'm sure you're familiar with how we minimize the effects that smoking has on our bodies and health. Finally, the voice of reason got through the smokescreen and I felt strangely calm and anticipatory. I knew I couldn't stop smoking without God's intervention. So I prayed, "God, if you want me to stop smoking, make it easy." I knew if it was too difficult I wouldn't be able to do it. A month later I had stopped smoking. One day I just put down my cigarettes and found that quitting was manageable. I didn't use a patch, I didn't take a pill, I took a dose of spiritual reliance. I haven't had a cigarette since.

In asking God to remove my shortcomings, I have faith that my Higher Power knows best what those shortcomings are, which are most destructive and which need to be eliminated. Did I have shortcomings? Many. Were they removed? Many of them have been over the years, some without my conscious knowledge. I can only tell you that I am transformed from who and what I was before I got sober. Everything is different. I am still the essential Linda with all the talents and abilities I had before recovery but now they are so much better. For example, I stopped singing for years during marriage to my first husband. Then I got sober and singing jobs started coming to me. I had always performed in plays and musical comedies but I began singing in nightclubs and bars. I wasn't bothered in the least by others drinking because the Big Book tells me I can be around alcohol as long as I have a reason for being there – which was entertaining.

Do I still cuss? Yes. Do I have moments of grandiosity? Hell, yes. We are not perfect but in progress.

I slammed headfirst into one defect that I had modeled after my father. A rageaholic, his ego was so fragile that many trigger words and actions by others were perceived as threats. My father would get into impulsive fistfights for no reason other than he felt someone had insulted him. My rage was provoked when authority figures tried to use the power of their position to tell me what to do and I would feel small and powerless. Through journaling and directed writing, I delved into the causes and conditions of my rage. My investigation, and subsequent awareness of why I became so full of rage, allowed me to think before I got myself into such an angry state when I felt powerless. What's more important, keeping my serenity or getting my way? My inner harmony feels so much better – I think I'll keep it.

Life's In Session

When I became newly sober, my sponsor kept spouting on and on about how the will of God was for me to stay sober and help another alcoholic. This was the sponsor that I fired after the 5th Step disaster, right? Pat kept repeating this over and over…blah….blah….blah. I guess it sounded good. But the limitations of that definition of God's will for me actually hurt my feelings. Pat was plugged into her punitive, harsh and patriarchal God. I wasn't buying it. In her version of God's will for me, I was hanging around meetings 24/7 and never getting out and living life. Is that all God had in store for me? What about falling in love? Getting my child back? Finding a job that I love? Living in a home? Having money? Finally, I got ticked off and realized that she may have been right during those first months of sobriety when I didn't know my ass from my elbow. However, God's will for me is a whole lot more – as it is for you.

My life is predicated on the premise of my sobriety and adherence to my recovery program and must be the constant factor governing all other actions. In sobriety, everything else is possible. I can become anything I choose, as long as it's God's will. I can have anything I want, as long as it's God's will. I can do anything I want, as long as it's God's will. Many times it's just the mundane stuff. I do more battle with my own nature than fire-eating dragons in a given day.

Practicing humility in our daily lives does not mean we stop striving to better our lives, or become doormats, or hide our light and talents under a basket. We can be proud of our achievements, the strides we have made in the program and our new lives. Our Higher Power has brought people into our lives that have a positive effect on us and to whom we can express our gratitude.

As the Big Book says, "we have been rocketed into the 4th dimension." This is entirely true. Appearances are deceiving. In the material world of self-seeking, humility is considered a liability. Then why does true greatness always walk hand in hand with humility?

Humility requires us to reinvent ourselves in a new spiritual design.

There are many who won't, or refuse to believe, that the humbling of the ego is necessary to profoundly change one's life. We lessen our need for the approval of others as we joyfully seek guidance from Divine Intelligence to become a resilient, stronger self that can withstand the naysayers and the disbelievers.

Chapter Ten

STEP EIGHT

*Made a list of all persons whom we had harmed
and became willing to make amends to them all*

Fresh Starts

Going back through your 4th Step inventories and resentments begins a selection process that assists you in listing those you have harmed. It may be difficult to single out those to whom amends need to be made because many times harm went both ways. It is not your job to <u>take another person's inventory</u> even though you feel that he or she should also make amends to you. You may question the necessity of taking this Step; the other person did more harm, the harm was minor, the harm was mainly to yourself as you were self-destructive, the harm was unintentional or the harm was justified.

You cannot make a fresh start based upon new spiritual principles with old ideas tripping you up at every turn. Your awakening from denial and delusion is pointless unless you take action. First, is it essential to recognize how we hurt others, and secondly, the nature and extent of the wrongs committed. Though we were emotionally and spiritually sick and may still be, our spiritual progress depends upon our ability to take direction from those who have already passed this way. Millions of people from all walks of life have taken these Steps to recovery.

You may have stopped the offending behavior or a crime committed is decades old, but excusing yourself from correcting these wrongs is setting yourself up for failure. Perhaps a more thorough re-examination of our character defects, as outlined in Steps Six and Seven, is indicated. We must account for our past wrongs and our part in them. This is not meant to be unduly burdensome. The road to redemption requires us to acknowledge and move through the pain of the past in order to cleanse our hearts, minds and spirits.

Accountability

It is very easy to negate our part in the problems that plague us by blaming others, or refusing to take responsibility for all the trouble we encounter in our lives. Unwittingly, you may attempt to lessen your accountability for any wrongdoing, minimizing and rationalizing the severity of your actions. Your 4th Step does not necessarily include those *you* have harmed because you may have no resentments or anger in connection with those people. In order to obtain a more complete list, you need to continue your honest investigation of the past, praying for guidance and compassion. Your willingness to admit that you have something in your past to remedy will bring to your consciousness the persons or institutions to be included on your list. In most cases, our actions were a result of fear, dishonesty, self-seeking and selfishness, and we can apply this reasoning to those we have harmed.

Some may have a self-destructive pattern of blaming and criticizing themselves for things that are not their fault. This lack of self-esteem distorts our perceptions, or could be construed as pride in reverse. This is particularly true of severe co-dependents. Co-dependents have difficulty distinguishing themselves from others which is crucial to establishing and maintaining proper boundaries. However, if you have been *playing* God and trying to fix another, then you owe them an amends for that behavior. It is not up to you to decide what needs to be altered or repaired in another person unless you are participating in an intervention with clearly defined boundaries, and you are prepared to stop enabling that person. Please refer to your Workbook on the section on Cognitive Distortions (Step Two) for further help recognizing the thought processes of personalization and other mental roadblocks that prevent us from seeing the need to make amends.

We take a balanced approach toward this Step, not castigating or flogging ourselves for our wrongdoing, but softening our hearts and souls to admitting that there was harm done to strangers, acquaintances and those we cared about. It is now time to take responsibility rather than fruitlessly blaming ourselves. Blame and shame so often immobilize us into paralysis until we are stuck doing nothing to reconcile or resolve the issues at hand.

What is Harm?

Our lives as addicts, alcoholics, co-dependents and our practice of other forms of dysfunctional behaviors and neuroses have left indelible marks on the lives of those who have been involved with us. Often, we were unpredictable, demanding, unreliable and unable to comprehend the damaging effect we were having on others. In working the Steps and acquiring a deeper sensibility, we may now realize that we have blown through people's lives with our character defects at full throttle causing disaster and upset at every turn. Some of the time we were hurting ourselves but think, by hurting ourselves weren't we also hurting those who loved us? By seeing us in the disordered states of the addiction and dysfunction that consumed our lives, those that cared about us were frustrated in their attempts to help us and ultimately, they have either left us or enabled us.

Some of you may have done irreparable damage to the lives of loved ones or strangers. You may have stolen, cheated or lied to get your drugs, booze or other mind and mood altering substances or behaviors. You may have spent time in jail, may be in jail now or participated in unsavory and criminal acts the authorities are unaware of. Some of you may have committed manslaughter or murder while driving drunk. Some of you may have abandoned a child or embezzled funds from your place of work.

Others may have committed seemingly benign offenses that had reverberating repercussions later on. Some possible areas of harm are:

Relationships – Here we have much to examine. How have you treated those you claim to love? With disdain and disregard? Thoughtlessly? Seeking to control them? Have you regularly engaged in the condemnation of others while ignoring the examination of your own misconduct? Have you been truly giving or are you always seeking to get what you can out of relationships? Have you gossiped behind somebody's back, indulging in character assassination of co-workers, friends and strangers?

Financial wrongdoing – Did you squander your money or other people's money on your addictions and/or compulsions and turn a blind eye to your fiscal responsibilities, such as paying rent, bills, or utilities and causing concern and anguish for your loved ones? Or left unpaid a debt that was your obligation to resolve?

Parental obligations – Shirking your parental responsibilities by not providing your child(ren) with proper housing, clothing or nutrition, or being critical or excessively punitive with your child. Not protecting them from potentially harmful family members or others in the periphery of your family who had access to your children. These acts require amends.

More Than an Apology

An apology is never sufficient without the contemplation of the harm we actually caused that person from **_that person's point of view_**. A shallow, lip-serving statement that "you're sorry" will ring false and maybe cause further damage to the relationship or your spiritual condition. Making amends is more than apologizing for what you've done. In the rush of daily living, people apologize all the time without really caring how the offense affected the other person. On some level, this could be construed as making light of their offenses. If we find ourselves apologizing over and over again for the same reason, then we have a problem that requires much deeper investigation of our behavior and its effect on other people.

Making a true amends begins with admitting you committed certain acts, or spoke certain words that harmed another human being **_regardless of what they did to you_**. Next, you must process the feelings that you have about the harm you did to that person. You may have feelings of remorse, anger, guilt, shame, fear, self-pity or horror. You may also try to minimize, justify or rationalize what happened. But first, it's important to write out what happened and what you did to that person. You need to look at the sick and twisted scenarios of your life and make amends for your part in them. There's a wonderful saying in recovery: <u>You can't save your face and your ass at the same time</u>. It's humbling to acknowledge that we harmed others and have to make amends, but we can't get well unless we do. This is one of those Steps that lead to an action Step. Before the action is the commitment to act.

Those Not to Be Included

Do not include anyone who sexually, physically or emotionally abused you as a child. You were not responsible for those acts committed against you. In fact, you are going to have to find a way to forgive those who have done horrible wrongs to you.

We are not obligated to make amends to our parents. They were responsible for our well-being when we were children. However, parents may be included under certain circumstances. As an adult, you may have mishandled their financial matters, physically and emotionally abused them or committed other harmful acts towards your parents. You may have stolen money from them to fuel your addictions and dysfunctional behaviors or taken advantage of their love to manipulate and abuse them. In these cases, you do owe them amends and reparations.

If you were in a relationship as an adult where you suffered physical battering or emotional and mental abuse, then you are not required to make amends to that person. It is imperative that you examine this relationship thoroughly for co-dependence and other erroneous beliefs that kept you trapped in this situation. However, if you believe that you provoked someone to violence against you by hitting them first, or committed other acts or engaged in behaviors calculated on your part to get a reaction from that person, then you would owe them an amend. Whether or not circumstances warrant amends from you, it is still important to get help for the damage caused by staying in this battering and abusive relationship. Once you have processed the feelings about this relationship it is also healing to make amends to yourself.

Amends Toward Others

The United States is a very punitive country. We incarcerate more people than anywhere else on the planet. Our Puritan roots reach across the nation demanding blood and retribution rather than offering much understanding, forgiveness or rehabilitation.

Are some acts so heinous that they cannot be forgiven?

No, all acts can be forgiven by our Higher Power. No matter what we have done, Divine Spirit loves us unconditionally. It doesn't matter that our human self has committed terrible deeds, our spirit self is perfect in the eyes of God.

Many people will be shocked to hear this but I don't believe that God punishes finite sins with infinite punishment. That would be excessive, cruel and unjust. For finite crimes committed, we are punished through the means available in the temporal world. In many instances, we pay through the laws of natural and spiritual consequences or in our conscience, which becomes burdened and consumed with guilt and shame over actions that have hurt another. We pay by becoming isolated from our fellow human beings with feelings of worthlessness and a loss of self-esteem, and these, in turn, feed our addictions, dysfunctions, self-pity or depression. Guilt and shame over our actions lock us in a stalemate that requires some kind of resolution, either by making amends or, if it isn't possible to make amends, forgiving ourselves.

Step Eight makes it possible to ascertain the nature of our spiritual responsibilities. We are asked to account for our motives and past actions using moral and spiritual principles. We may be tempted to try and find the easy way out especially when we're put on the spiritual hotseat. Lukewarm intentions and lackluster attempts to work any of these Steps simply won't work. A favorite saying in AA is half-measures avail us nothing. Not half, but nothing. Many people think that's not fair. Surely, doing anything at all should be rewarded with some small success. Only it doesn't work that way. Sobriety has to be our number one priority and the top requirement is the willingness to go to any lengths to keep it. Sometimes that isn't easy. If this program were easy the gains wouldn't be as great. It's too much work. I understand that. So why are we doing it?

For me, I wanted sobriety more than I wanted the nightmare of my old life back. It was my time to face down my demons and take courage from something or someone else for a change. Though it felt as if I were hobbling through the steps, I felt a Presence working in my life. Making amends was not easy but it's something I had to do because it had the power to alter the course of my future. Did I want to do this? No. I did not. Did I make amends to every single person I harmed. No. I did not.

The person I harmed the most was my son. I had the responsibility to care for him and he didn't ask for a drunken mother. Did I say I was sorry to him? He was 4 years old and it is highly doubtful he would have understood what I was saying. But I did tell him that none of it was his fault. How did I make amends then? I have tried to be the best mother I know how. Was it perfect? No, I made many mistakes, but by being there for my son, guiding him in spiritual principles, making him feel he would always have my love and support, I have made the best amends I can.

Balancing the Spiritual Scales

In the 8th Step, we are being asked to balance the spiritual scales of right and wrong by making amends for wrongs we have perpetrated on others and to forgive those who have wronged us in return. This is an opportunity to set matters right again to the best of our ability. This is all our Higher Power asks of us. There may be things we have done that cannot be repaired because of circumstances beyond our control, such as the person is dead or living too far away, or a child we harmed is already grown. But you can always find a way to make amends. Perhaps by contributing to a charity, or donating your time to a cause that helps others, or by helping another person if you cannot help the one you have harmed.

Transgressions and resentments that are described in Step Eight fall into several categories, some of which I have included below:

> *Those we have harmed who have not harmed us.*
> *Those we have harmed and have also harmed us.*
> *Those we have harmed and whom we resent.*
> *Those who have a resentment toward us that we have not harmed.*
> *Those we have harmed but to make amends would injure them.*
> *Those we have harmed but to make amends would injure ourselves.*
> *Those we have harmed but now live far away.*
> *Those we have harmed physically.*
> *Those we have harmed emotionally.*
> *Those we have harmed financially.*
> *Those we have harmed mentally.*
> *Those we have harmed who are now dead but not because of us.*
> *Those we have harmed who are now dead because of us.*

Our offenses against others require our attention and genuine humility. Without humility, it is doubtful that we will make the necessary provisions for redress and reparation of the thoughts, words and deeds that plague our relationships with ourselves, with others and with the world.

Forgiving Yourself

While contemplating the wrongs you have committed you may feel deep remorse and regret, depending upon the severity of your transgression. You may try to make amends to someone who is simply not prepared to forgive you for what you did. Without needing to ask, your Higher Power has already forgiven you. Over time, you will learn how to forgive yourself.

If you are sincerely working this program of recovery, you have seen how sick you were, physically, emotionally, mentally and spiritually. Would you deny a sick person forgiveness? Your healing continues with forgiveness of yourself and others.

Forgiving Others

We may not be prepared to forgive those who have harmed us. It is a lot to ask. This could hinder your ability to make amends to others. If you have committed relatively small offenses toward others, yet have suffered greatly at the hands of your families, friends, and others, to forgive seems an insurmountable task. Why should you forgive them? Why should you make amends to these people?

Very often, it is those we love the most that hurt us the most and become the ones we find the hardest to forgive. Love turned in on itself becomes bitter, angry and distrustful, ruminating over imagined slights, assaults to our ego, and the pain of love not returned in the ways we expected. It is in your unfulfilled expectations where you find most of your pain. As we toughen our hearts against those we love so that we don't get hurt again, we have missed the chance to love without expectation. To forgive is to heal.

In acknowledging our wrongs, we may expect that others in our life recognize their wrongs against us. But this is usually not the case. Forgiveness is accepting that those we forgive may never admit their wrongs toward us.

Lack of love is always our dilemma. As we are hurt by those unable to love us, those same people are unable to love themselves. Just as we were incapable of loving ourselves and caused harm to others. How could we hurt another if we truly love ourselves unconditionally? It is not possible. Therefore, those who have wounded us have also not loved themselves and require our love to begin a healing process just as we are learning to be healed by loving ourselves and allowing others to love us. We receive healing on a daily basis by the love we experience from those in our 12 Step programs and by our Higher Power, and the more we see demonstrations of this love in our lives, the easier it becomes to love and forgive someone who has done us grievous harm. Most offenses are committed out of fear, ignorance and self-hate. Fear is lack of faith and love. The circle goes round and round endlessly creating disasters that range in severity from misunderstandings to atrocities.

But we cannot forgive others prematurely before we have processed the events and the losses that resulted from the behaviors of our caretakers, parents, family, and other significant people in our lives who shaped the internal image we have of ourselves. As we change the way we see ourselves, feeling more competent in our decision-making processes, more self-assured in our recovery, and become more humble in our response to life, we may be able to find the generosity of spirit in our feelings toward others.

In order to maintain the integrity of the process, take the **should** out of forgiveness as it leads to dishonesty and detaching from our deeper feelings. Don't forgive someone because you are being subtly forced by others to do so. Take your time. Don't do it to be a **nice** person. It could literally take years before you are ready to forgive. That's okay.

You might be ready and willing to forgive someone but you don't want to continue an association with that person because they are toxic and damaging to your continued emotional growth and recovery. Someone else may feel that way about us. In the same way, we can't expect others to forgive us. If both parties decide they wish to salvage the relationship, forgiveness on either side is a process of reconciliation and renewed trust.

Sometimes the person you are ready to forgive is also someone you need to make amends to because there was harm on both sides. You have been hurt and you, in turn, have hurt the other person. Sometimes it is not. You may forgive someone who harmed you during your childhood that you did not harm (such as a parent/stepparent) but you don't owe him or her amends. For those you have decided to forgive, include them in your prayers, meditations and affirmations. Hold them in the light and release them with love.

This Step gives you a wonderful opportunity to walk in the sunlight of the Spirit with your eyes turned toward the unending landscape of redemption and grace.

Chapter Eleven

STEP NINE

Made direct amends to such people, whenever possible,
except when to do so would injure them or others

Closure

Unresolved problems with people, places and things are like a minefield waiting to blow up in our lives. Better to face some of these amends head on. It's dangerous to excuse ourselves with the rationalization that since we are doing so well it won't hurt to skip over lesser offenses, others weren't hurt that badly, or we're not strong enough to confront those we have harmed in the past. Yes, in some areas, we may be improving but if we delay or skip this Step we will find that the full benefits of recovery are elusive because our hands-on experience is incomplete.

Depending upon the wreckage that you have brought upon others, the more difficult and complicated this task may seem to you. We take it slow to be sure that our footing is solidly anchored on the new ground of the character we are building through the guidance of our Higher Power. We have brought our darkest fears to light and are now required to act upon what we have found. We can finally close the books on past wrongs we have committed, whether they were meant maliciously or not, and get on with the business of living with our conscience absolved and free of recrimination.

Vulnerability Leads To Intimacy

It is illuminating to get a reality check from the people that you interact with on a daily basis. Ask them how they see you. Ask them if you are hurting them in some way by your behavior. This requires you to become vulnerable to those you love and, in forfeiting the dubious protection of your ego defenses, find a greater intimacy and closeness with those important to you. The risks we take to discover how we are perceived by those we care about are a necessary part of recovery. Only in exposing our innermost fears and unguarded selves will we find the true meaning of intimacy. Misconceptions about how we are seen in the eyes of others can destroy relationships that we hold dear.

This is a great beginning. Even if you are in jail, rehabilitation, a half-way house or other facility that keeps you under constant or intermittent supervision, you can still go to 12 Step meetings. If there are 12 Step meetings in prison, keep close counsel with your spiritual advisor and take heart that all is not lost. Some of us have committed more damaging transgressions against others but if we are straightforward in our efforts to compensate for prior actions by transforming our lives, then we are doing our best.

The Investigation

Below we will examine how to handle certain types of situations where amends may, or may not, be needed.

- ***Those we have harmed who have not harmed us.***

1) We write down what we have done to the other person because we were selfish, self-centered, dishonest or afraid.

2) We go to that person with a detailed accounting of how we have harmed them and, absent of any personal agenda or motive for ourselves, transmit to them the desire that we are now willing to make amends in whatever way they deem we should and that we can make within our power to do so.

- ***Those we have harmed and have also harmed us.***
  Repeat Steps 1 and 2 above.

- ***Those who have harmed us and whom we resent.***
  See below.

- ***Those who have done nothing to us and whom we resent.***

With varying degrees of success, we resolved our conflicting feelings about those we resented or still resent, who may or may not have done us harm, by realizing that they, too were spiritually and emotionally ill. But we are human, and resentments may resurface time and again, necessitating further examination and subsequent action. Resentments and accompanying anger are major deterrents to continued recovery. We work on forgiving the person, place or thing that we resent, praying for guidance and compassion from our Higher Power. Some say that having a resentment is a criterion for making amends and that we need to go to that person we resent and apologize for resenting them. If we can't do this right away, it's okay. As we look further into why we hold tightly to certain resentments, we may see that it hurts us more than it hurts the person we resent.

- ***Those who hold a resentment toward us that we have not harmed.***

First, we examine how we may have provoked this person. It may seem strange, but as we make peace with the world around us, resentments toward us may lessen. People with no valid reason for their resentments against us have issues to work on, and may discover that resentments are unproductive. If we have not provoked this person, then they too suffer from spiritual deficits to a more or less degree than we ourselves do. We don't judge but pray they find peace.

- ***Those we have harmed but to make amends would injure them.***

How can making amends be injurious to another? When we have harmed them irrevocably and our presence would make them anxious, fearful, panicked and terrified, or pain them even greater. For example, if you have raped someone and want to face that person, admit your crime and apologize, you may end up causing more harm than good because they may still be traumatized. Or you may have information about a situation that the other does not have that could hurt them. If so, it is best to keep silent about offenses that may expose the injured party to information that would be painful. You may want to make amends to the parents or relatives of someone you have harmed, or someone killed, as in a drunk driving accident. Under certain circumstances, writing a letter may be the right thing to do and could help the other person to resolve their pain and find forgiveness. Conversely, it might be too traumatic for the other person. If you pray for guidance, inspiration will be given about what you need to do.

- ***Those we have harmed but to make amends would injure others.***

Making amends must be weighed against committing further offenses that would impact the lives of those who depend on us and are innocent of any wrongdoing. An example: if a person was unfaithful with a brother's wife or sister's husband. To admit the infidelity could cause irreparable harm to all family members. Children, parents, other siblings, cousins, aunts, uncles, and close family friends. What can be done in this situation? Sometimes the truth will come out on its own, and perhaps it should. Sometimes this kind of pain is unavoidable depending upon the offenses committed on our part. We can try to make amends but, until time has passed, it is doubtful they will be accepted.

Certain harmful acts have grave repercussions and can cause us to dwell in a tempest of guilt and shame. This helps no one, whether or not the truth comes out of its own accord, or you decide it is best to admit the truth. Feeling remorse is a healthy response to those actions we have committed that are reprehensible, but if it destroys your life, leading you back to your addictions and dysfunctions, then those actions have taught you nothing and cause further damage. Making amends must be carefully examined for potential harm to others because we cannot alleviate our burden at the expense of another. This would compound the original injury. If you have robbed a bank and escaped apprehension by the authorities, but are now responsible for the care of your family and their financial well-being through legitimate means, then to confess might injure **others**. All such amends must be examined with another person who has sufficient time in recovery and a thorough understanding of all the possible ramifications. Perhaps restitution could be made anonymously or through an intermediary. Admitting to offenses that present harsh consequences may be distasteful and frightening but we must really believe, and have it supported by another, that keeping silent is in the ultimate best interests of those for whom we are responsible and not just a way out of our amends.

- ### *Those we have harmed but to make an amends would injure ourselves.*

Injury to ourselves does not mean the amends process itself.

In a rare instance, it may be that someone in recovery has been psychiatrically diagnosed with a mental condition that would place immense pressure on their psychological well-being to face, in person, those s/he has harmed. In that case, the recovering person must find another way to resolve their trespasses to substantiate to themselves that they are committed to their participation in an honest and ongoing recovery program. If this resembles your situation and you have already done the 5th Step and disclosed your wrongdoings to another, then consult with that person for direction while continuing to pray and meditate for the right solution. It may happen that a way through your dilemma will appear.

Another reason for not making amends to someone you have harmed is if harm was reciprocal and violent from that person. Keeping yourself safe is important. It would produce more harm than good to place yourself in a dangerous situation, emotionally or physically, by making amends. For example, let's say you resent someone because they physically abused you as an adult and you feel sorry for your resentment and want to clean the slate with the person. They could misconstrue your true intentions and use it as an invitation back into your life or become menacing and physically threatening again. We avoid setting into motion a likely confrontation and pray for the other as our amends to them. We ask for change on a spiritual level that will manifest that person's highest good. If we find that making an amends to someone who has exhibited resentment and hostility towards us will produce more animosity than healing, then we must delay our amends until we have prayed for this person. Then we wait and see. If our Higher Power guides us in the direction of making amends, we will know it and, if not, we will know that too. Again, balance is sought in all spiritual matters and we must be careful that we are not seeking perfection – because that is not possible.

- ### *Those we have harmed but now live far away.*

For those who have moved away from us – perhaps it is best to let the matter rest – unless it is a very serious matter. A slight resentment can be resolved with prayer and good works on our part toward any other person. If it is a more serious transgression, resolution is probably needed on both sides to move forward. You could try writing a letter using the above Steps 1 and 2 as your template for making your amends.

- ### *Those we have harmed physically.*

It is probably best to stay away from those you have harmed physically, if possible, as they may feel threatened or frightened if you approach them no matter how benign and repentant your demeanor. Let time go by and, if indicated by your Higher Power, you may be granted an opportunity to make amends. If those people are your children, then you must earn back their trust without expecting anything in return. Abusing your children makes it extremely difficult to take up the reins of parenting again even if they know you're in recovery. Distressing memories and unresolved guilt from broken promises must be acknowledged in order to build trust with your children. Do your best to rein in your temper and show them you will not abuse them physically or emotionally ever again. It is beneficial to take parenting classes especially designed for those who are addicts, alcoholics and dysfunctionals. You need to learn alternative ways of disciplining your children so they always feel safe in your presence.

If you have harmed someone else physically other than your children, writing a letter will be sufficient unless you have disabled them in some way. You could have put them in the hospital. You can offer to make restitution by paying for hospital bills or putting yourself in their service for whatever they might need from you. Restore what you have taken to the best of your ability.

- ### *Those we have harmed emotionally.*

If we feel we have left emotional scars on those we love, we must let time take its course, continuing in our recovery and demonstrating by example that we are changing, growing and maturing. When the time is right, we can make a face-to-face amends expecting nothing in return.

- ### *Those we have harmed financially.*

We make restitution as best we can, except when to do so would injure others. Injuring others includes taking away financial support from our loved ones or others who depend upon us financially. If we can possibly make payments, then we do so. If our financial burden is just too great, then we seek counsel from a financial advisor on the wisest course of action. If we owe money to those for whom we are financially responsible, such as our children, spouse or others, then we do what we must to ensure their financial safety by getting a job, paying the bills, child support or alimony. We do not run from our financial responsibilities but trust in our Higher Power to make it possible to honor them. We begin making what payments we can as part of the amends process towards those we have hurt with our financial recklessness and irresponsibility.

If we have stolen money or owe money to another, we offer to make restitution with reasonable payments that we can afford.

- ***Those we have harmed who are now dead but not because of us.***

We can make amends by treating those still living with dignity, respect and love. We can write a letter to the deceased, then read it aloud to them as part of our amends. Our sincerity will be demonstrated in how willing we are to help others through direct or charitable means.

- ***Those we have harmed who are now dead because of us.***

If we have committed a crime and have been convicted of it, then to serve our time with the right attitude of remorse and genuine regret for our actions is the proper course. If we justify what happened we can't move past it. When we actually say it out loud – we have hurt some-one, murdered someone, or killed him or her accidentally – then we can begin the reparation process for others and ourselves. Courts, trials and judges may dictate the length and severity of our physical punishment, however the more permanent punishment is in how we feel about ourselves. If we are unable to resolve these issues then we will become defined by them for the rest of our lives and help no one. You can never return a life; that is irrevocable and final. But you can make that life mean something. If working this program shifts your perception and alters your life in such a profound way that you want to become a different person from the one who committed this act, then tragedy can turn to redemption. We may not be able to make amends to those we have injured because we cannot return the loss of a loved one, but we can make different, better choices and salvage what is left of our lives.

Courage requires that we alter our course, work the program, pray for guidance, stay sober and stop the behavior that has the destructive potential to devastate lives. It requires that we help others and make our life an example of how the human spirit can prevail in spite of our past deeds.

After Amends Are Made

Perhaps those you have gone to with remorse and a plan for reparation, slam the door in your face and are not ready for an apology. We try to heal the wounds of our past dysfunctional behavior as best we can, and then we turn it over to our Higher Power.

No matter what crime or deed, act or omission has been committed, once we have done all we can to rectify our part in the matter, we are forgiven by our Higher Power. Think about this: if your child were a murderer, sitting on death row, would you still love him or her? I believe you would and you are only human. Should we expect anything less from our Higher Power? If

God is Infinite Love, then God/Goddess/Divine Consciousness can surely forgive and love us no matter what we have done.

If the person has asked us to do something specific, we plan with that person how we are going to make reparations, i.e. pay back money that we owe them, take more responsibility for children we share with this person, desist from behaviors that are harming the person in the future or staying away from that person if they so desire.

You don't get to choose how you're going to make it up to the other person. Making amends means that you ask them how you can make it up to them and abide by their decision.

In many cases the person will forgive you and move on, praying for you and releasing you with love. The other person may see the hurt they've caused you and make a return amends. If you are ready to forgive them, do so. If not, continue with your own amend, receive their forgiveness, acknowledge your wrongdoing and assure them that you won't behave that way again. Ask how you can make it up to them, creating a plan to do so. Do we need to forgive a person before making amends to them? It might be that you are unable to even make amends without the requisite forgiveness. The burden of resentment is yours as long as you want. Instead, pray for guidance, affirm a positive result and let the answers come.

There are many possible outcomes of this Step because, as we've stepped on the toes of others, others have stepped on our toes. But this remains our recovery program – not the other person's.

Living Amends

Each day that you remain in recovery abstaining from mind or mood-altering substances and behaviors, addictions, compulsions and neuroses, you are making amends to the world in which you live. This is the greatest gift you can give to yourself and others who interact with you on a daily basis. They're probably already seeing considerable changes in you. Your skin is glowing, you smile more often and seem better able to manage situations that were difficult before you began your recovery program. Each day you grow in wisdom, maturity and common sense, embracing your reality rather than running from it. Trying to do the best you can for you and your loved ones, you are making progress in spiritual living and making amends to those you have harmed.

These are indirect, sometimes called "living" amends, that we make for as long as we stay in recovery. We are part of the solution rather than part of the problem. Our new vision into the truth of our human existence, free of the ego defenses and the struggles they impose on our lives, gives us strength to go out each day and make a difference.

Aftermath

Sometimes the consequences of making amends may be severe, if our actions or omissions were serious. We must fully prepare ourselves for the aftermath of our prior acts. If we have decided to turn ourselves in for a crime committed in the past where we were not caught, then getting a good lawyer is required. If we are incarcerated and serving time for our crime, then we can make the best use of our time by connecting with other members of 12 Step Groups, going to meetings offered, obeying the authorities and becoming an exemplary prisoner. We can also prepare ourselves for a future in the world by educating ourselves. Helping others and giving back to society allows the pain of the harm we have caused to diminish.

As we continue in our recovery program, many of the problems of the past will become resolved. We will be shown a new path or a new solution will appear.

A New Way of Looking At Life

Addictions and dysfunctions are symptoms of a deeper psychological and spiritual disease that once permeated every moment of our lives. What we have discovered in our examination has tested our strength, courage and honesty and we have accepted certain irrevocable principles as truths in our lives. We are feeling comfortable in our skin, perhaps for the first time ever since we were small children. If you have come this far, a new way of life has opened up to you. Based on our work and effort, AA made some bold statements and promises that seem almost unbelievable.

What are these promises?

**We are going to know a new freedom and
a new happiness.**

**We will not regret the past
nor wish to shut the door on it.**

We will comprehend the word serenity.

We will know peace.

**No matter how far down the scale we have gone,
we will see how our experience can benefit others.**

The feelings of uselessness and self-pity will disappear.

**We will lose interest in selfish things and
gain interest in our fellows.**

Self-seeking will slip away.

Our whole attitude and outlook upon life will change.

Fear of people and of economic insecurity will leave us.

We will intuitively know how to handle situations which used to baffle us.

**We will suddenly realize that God is doing for us
what we could not do for ourselves.**

I have been the grateful recipient of all these promises in my life. Today I am able to build long-term relationships, to enjoy intimacy with another person and have been released from the horrors and feelings that used to dominate my consciousness. I keep my word. I feel relatively normal. I can guarantee you that this wasn't who I was 22 years ago. I have changed dramatically and the changes are too extraordinary for any human to accomplish on their own. I have known people who spent years in therapy and achieved few significant adjustments in their perspective and personality. There is no question in my mind that a Power was working with and through me to achieve these results. I am blessed. Why was I given this miracle? Am I different from you? No, I am not. I didn't work the program perfectly. I certainly haven't reached anything near perfection, nor will I ever, nor does my Higher Power expect perfection of me. I cried many tears, got angry, shouted to the heavens, lost jobs, went ballistic, was inappropriate, and screwed up many, many times. Still, I stayed sober.

We don't have to do anything in this program anywhere near perfect. Our willingness to go to any length to stay sober is sufficient and our desire to help others will bring us an inner peace and tranquility that we have never known. These promises are real. Unlike the fleeting and false promises of our dysfunctional lifestyles. Reality can be your friend.

Chapter Twelve

STEP TEN

Continued to take personal inventory
and when we were wrong, promptly admitted it

When Socrates claimed, "The unexamined life is not worth living," he understood that self-examination is a cornerstone of spiritual growth. Without the continued evaluation of our assets and liabilities, we will fail to grow emotionally and fall prey to our old nemesis – denial. Denial masquerades as an ally, buffering our delicate egos from painful realities with broken weapons of justification and rationalization. Denial eventually erodes our ability to adjust our thoughts and behaviors according to spiritual principles.

Unfinished Business

Some goals of recovery include acquiring the emotional maturity to grow ourselves up, the ability to make accurate appraisals of our thoughts and deeds, and taking responsibility for our actions and behaviors.

The disruptive influence of our family system may keep us recycling old patterns, issues, and conflicts that fuel resistance to change. When we change, the dynamics of our dysfunctional family of origin are threatened and family members, particularly those invested in the delusions of the past, will fight to maintain the status quo. Unfinished business from our family of origin could compromise the inventory process. Getting well may feel as if you are betraying your family. You might act on and act out of the presumption that you are powerless to change your circumstances just as when you were a small child and through your teens. It is essential to recognize when this is happening, how you respond, and prepare a plan in advance how you will react differently. We make a daily, conscious decision to go beyond our self-inflicted dysfunctional borders to determine the reasoning and motivation for our thoughts and actions.

Intention of the Personal Inventory

The intention of the traditional personal inventory is to investigate our motives, agendas, and problems, while we attempt resolutions to our everyday struggles according to the principles of the 12 Steps of Recovery.

We have a wealth of information from prior Steps to guide us in examining the potential pitfalls of thought, attitude and behavior. In each Step, we wrote about our inability to let go and let God, our resentments, anger, jealousy, envy, our character defects, the ways we self-sabotage, and how our lives were unmanageable. Petty jealousies, character assassination, and revengeful thoughts fueled by self-pity, self-centeredness and pride may derail our best intentions. In our 10th Step, we can observe our thoughts and actions under the new paradigm for living that we are creating in conjunction with Divine Guidance and Intelligence or, if you choose, God. God will continually give us clues, letting us know what does, and doesn't work in our lives. As my sponsor once said, actions we take that "move like ball bearings and butter" are usually the actions inspired by our Higher Power and the outcomes turn out to be advantageous for all concerned. Those actions and behaviors that cause resistance in the Universe, and in those around us, are usually based on agendas of self-will and fear.

Axiom for Peace of Mind

To achieve balance, we need to cultivate the ability to detach ourselves at any time from the chaos of conditions that surround us. The Twelve and Twelve of AA, states: "It is a spiritual axiom that every time we are disturbed, no matter what the cause, there is something wrong **with us.**"

I have wrestled with this simple wisdom many times, but for peace of mind I keep this certainty close at hand. I call succumbing to conditions and apparent circumstances, "getting all goosed up." We can get all **goosy** about any number of things – from family problems to politics and religion – and it won't do us one bit of good. The only goal we are accomplishing is the destruction of our serenity. Anger doesn't change anything, resentment and self-righteousness don't change anything, self-pity and blame don't change anything. To solve my anxiety-producing problems, I have to be willing to accept circumstances as they are, or be willing to change myself in accordance with my circumstances.

Two things happen when I choose acceptance: first, I am releasing the power of Divine Consciousness within me to manifest my greatest good; and two, I am reinforcing the lesson that I can't change people, places or things into what I would have them be. Acceptance takes you out of the driver's seat. Acceptance gets you out of the way of what's best for you and for others and gives you the energy to pursue activities that are productive and enjoyable rather than worrying about what someone else is or is not doing.

I remember when I thought being an alcoholic was the most despicable thing to happen to a person – having a disease with no cure. Now I realize that being a drunk was a magnanimous gift from a Power beyond my comprehension, revitalizing and repurposing my whole existence. How could I have known that when I was homeless, hopeless, lost, without recourse, drunk, and about to sell myself out one more time?

Higher-Powered

Once we allow our Higher Power to guide and direct our lives, we become able to <u>practice these principles in all our affairs</u>. We are momentarily able to transcend our ego and the pain of toxic shame and encourage our psyches to consider more pro-active solutions. The practice of the 10th Step instills more and more competencies and reveals the actualization of our Higher Purpose. We are no longer slaves to fleeting emotions and negative thought patterns. We discover that the false reasoning of the ego is self-limiting and self-serving. We are now in the rarified zone of making decisions that are realistic and, at the same, manifesting life-changing outcomes for all concerned. We have been set free from many of the dysfunctional patterns of our childhood.

Qualities Necessary for Successful Living

Re-labeling our adversities and failures as challenges is a great step toward personal ownership of our problems. We can then cultivate the persistence necessary to eventually overcome them. This takes time and practice.

Change is not linear. We may have insights, epiphanies and moments of enlightenment, but translating them into action and behavioral change takes hard work. We make progress, we slide back, progress, slide back, again and again until, with the continual application of our new principles and beliefs we actually remain in a state of relative calm, serenity and acceptance.

Emotional excesses of the past must be eliminated. Anger and resentment, self-pity, over-blown pride and grandiosity, are obstructions to successful social interaction and internal balance. Our footing is to be found in admitting the wrongs we have committed and making peace with others and ourselves. We incorporate courtesy, kindness, justice and love, into our daily strategy for living. Thoughtfulness and consideration are the lubricants keeping the engine of social interaction and exchange running smoothly, transferring positive attitudes from us to those around us. We foster our willingness to forgive others for their transgressions against us, rather than holding onto grudges and reliving past hurts and wrongs.

At some point, we will be astonished that social transactions that used to be confusing have become clearer. We will recognize boundary violations and respond accordingly. We will pay attention to our feelings and express ourselves truthfully and without rancor. Self-realization requires that we travel the road of forgiveness, tolerance, and patience, although many with whom we interact will be emotionally and spiritually ill.

Types of Inventories

Our personal accounting consists of writing out our inventory, much the same way as in the 4th Step. We also check in with our sponsors, counselors, therapists and other 12 steppers, to confirm our observations in these troublesome areas of our lives. If we feel pressured, confused, or upset, then we get to a meeting, or call someone on the phone immediately.

Spot Check

The spot check can be done when we find ourselves in emotional turmoil. In our first few months of recovery this might happen several times a day. We don't wallow in morbid obsession over these occurrences but encourage constructive reflection, if possible. We use the spot check to alert ourselves to the presence of discordant energies and begin to enlist strategies to resolve these issues. Can you see where you veered off-course? Can you make an amends to circumvent the potential problem? If your ego defenses kicked in, where can you find a voice of reason? Should you call your sponsor or spiritual advisor, a sober friend? Can you find a place to calm down? Can you take 10 deep breaths before you renew the disagreement or confrontation? Can you give someone else a time-out? Can you get to a meeting?

The Nightly Inventory

At the end of the day, we relax and let our minds and hearts replay the more important events of the day. We review our thoughts, actions, attitudes and behaviors. We could make two columns – one for progress we've made and the other for emotional disturbances arising out of negative issues. We write out what happened, why it happened, to whom it happened, our various reactions and dilemmas, if any exist. We continue to examine our part in any altercation with another. We see where we were selfish, self-seeking, dishonest or afraid. Then we resolve to correct our wrongdoing.

In the positive inventory, you recognize progress in changed behaviors. There may be many areas where you are making significant headway. It is helpful to compare old behavior with new skills and new behaviors so that you may record your successes. Give yourself a mental high-five as you realize you didn't react with anger and resentment to frustrations, but rather had the patience to work your situation out successfully. Over time, you will be able to comprehend the rationale in maintaining your efforts as you are reap the rewards of satisfaction and inner peace.

Outline a goal for achieving competency and control over errant emotions and behaviors. Admit when you're wrong and move on. If someone doesn't forgive and forget, so what? You've cleaned your side of the street. Leave the results to your Higher Power. With an attitude of gratitude, we thank our Higher Power for the blessings we now enjoy in our life.

Meeting with Sponsor/Spiritual Advisor

At certain times throughout the month or once a month, it is wise to meet with your sponsor or spiritual advisor to set more behavioral and emotional goals and agendas. You can go over the persistent patterns that have resisted your best efforts and ask for guidance from your sponsor or spiritual advisor. Sometimes another person can see our behavior more objectively. The point is to be open-minded and to refrain from ego defensiveness.

The Easier, Softer Way

I've had many experiences with the easier, softer way, and I can attest that it seldom produces the desired results in one's life and relationships. This doesn't mean that life has to be a struggle. Our thinking makes life a hell or heaven, not circumstances. Circumstances are challenges to be met with all the behavioral skills we have accumulated in our arsenal up to this point. Behavior will dictate the quality of your life. That is a fact. If we don't take care of the business at hand today, it will be there tomorrow and more will pile up in a heap of complications. Do the hardest thing first – get it out of the way – breathe a sigh of relief and enjoy the rest of the day.

If we have to make amends, or apologize, or change our behavior, then we do. Trying to circumvent the obvious solution only causes more adversity. That supposed *easier* way usually puts us on a road full of potholes, with two flat tires, in the middle of the night, with cell service down and a nice stranger driving up to rescue us. Why didn't we take the highway? Why didn't we check that our tires could make the trip? Why didn't we prepare? Reckless behavior can produce irrevocable mistakes. That nice stranger could be intending serious bodily harm. How can we trust ourselves, when we can't be trusted to take care of ourselves?

It's never easier to take short-cuts, delay making an apology, or to keep doing the same thing over and over expecting different results.

The essentials of character building, justice, conflict resolution, making amends, maintaining serenity, integrity, and willingness are the keys to developing a new moral structure. Do unto others as you would have them do unto you. Look out for your neighbor and your Higher Power will look out for you. ***Make a list of things you're grateful for and look at it often.***

Getting A Real Life

People with semi-normal to normal lives have much of the following:

- self-esteem
- a healthy evaluation of their self-image
- can adapt to the circumstances around them
- can experience joy and spontaneity in their interactions with others
- can reveal their authentic selves to those who become close to them
- do not rush into relationships out of fear of abandonment
- don't stay in relationships where their boundaries are violated
- self-respect
- a lot of laughter
- ability to love unconditionally
- make love with someone who truly cares about them
- work reasonable hours
- enjoy time spent alone
- enjoy time spent with others
- can reveal themselves to others who they are without shame
- can be vulnerable and risk trusting significant others
- feel they are good enough to be on the planet
- can accept love and compliments
- have healthy expectations for advancement in their lives
- take care of business
- take care of their health
- handle problems without going crazy
- keep drama to a minimum
- stand up for themselves
- make reasonable demands
- are not overly needy for others' approval and love.

I had no idea! Wow! Naturally, no one is completely normal, but I have days where I'm almost there.

Chapter Thirteen

RELAPSE PREVENTION

The recovery field has grown by leaps and bounds since the inception of the 12 Steps of Alcoholic Anonymous over 70 years ago. It is widely recognized that relapse occurs and it is imperative that we continue to develop skills, tools, techniques and strategies to reinforce our newly created schemas of recovery.

The relapse prevention field is extensive, the literature written vast, and it is beyond the scope of this book to provide an exhaustive relapse prevention program. However, I feel it is necessary to include major elements of treatment issues that have been incorporated into the recovery field. It is useful to recognize internal and external cues that jeopardize our sobriety and how we can best maintain our ability to stay physically and emotionally sober.

The Dry Drunk

In Alcoholics Anonymous, we are alert to the signs of impending relapse by noticing behaviors that take us out of recovery. When we start feeling <u>restless, irritable and discontented</u>, it is time to act before we give in to our addictions. This is referred to as being on a <u>dry drunk</u>.

Someone on a dry drunk is not actively drinking, using drugs or other mind or mood altering substances or behavior, but they are also not acting in a manner that suggests serenity, acceptance and adherence to the 12 Step recovery program. I'm not saying we don't all have a bad day, get angry or upset, or even emotionally overwrought. I am describing an intensifying mental and emotional condition lasting from one hour to several days that precipitates a relapse. For example, you might find yourself in a constant state of resentment or anger. You may blame others for your problems. Next, you stop praying and meditating. You become more selfish and self-seeking. Nothing is going right in your life so you're restless. People are not doing it your way so you're irritable. You fantasize about former destructive behaviors and *romanticize* their effect on your life so you're discontented. You have a hard time remembering what it was like when you were deep into your addictions, dysfunctions and neuroses. You become cranky, easily distracted and unfocused. Any of these behaviors, feelings and attitudes will eventually lead to a crisis in your life. For an addict/alcoholic this will lead back to the drugs and alcohol. For others, it will end up in relapsing behavior such as binging/purging, gambling, debting, sexing, using pornography, working addictively or obsessing on others.

When your behavior starts to reek of old ideas, we call this <u>stinking thinking.</u> You find yourself plummeting into a dark vortex of unproductive feelings, becoming resentful, angry or irrationally upset. What you do next will determine whether or not you'll stay sober, physically and emotionally.

Relapse Prevention

Relapse prevention is an area of rehabilitation that is highly emphasized as the first line of defense against factors, both internal and external, which could cause you to go back to self-destructive behaviors. You need to discover what emotional, mental, and physical <u>triggers</u> could weaken your intention to stay sober from alcohol, drugs and other addictive uses of mind or mood altering substances or behavior. Your response to life and how successfully you navigate through tense family and social environments, will determine your ability to continue on the path of recovery. I sang in bars in my early recovery and it didn't bother me at all. It was quite interesting to watch other people get drunk and make idiots of themselves for a change. I shuddered in remembrance of all the times it was me on the dance floor, falling on my ass. Not a pretty picture, huh?

Relapse is considered a part of recovery. However, I never relapsed so I don't consider it a part of recovery. Relapse may happen but it happens for a reason, not because it is part of recovery. Recovery has a very clear boundary – one is physically sober from all harmful addictions that include drugs, alcohol, prescription medication, cocaine, heroin, sniffing substances, or other mood or mind-altering behaviors such as eating disorders, gambling, pornography, sex, spending/debting, and work, and, in cases of neuroses or dysfunction, one is relatively healthy from co-dependent behaviors and relationships. You can determine your sobriety from co-dependence and other addictions (not just drugs and alcohol) by your ability to stay serene and balanced even in the face of someone else's problems. You no longer have to be part of the *drama* or chaos created by those around you because you have found it more important to maintain your spiritual equilibrium. You've made a conscious decision not to give that up for anyone. You're sustaining a feeling of self-worth and self-respect.

What can obstruct our recovery progress?

Isolation – Loneliness - Self-pity - Anger - Resentment - Complacency - Stress - Social Pressure - Obsession - Family Pressure - Depression - Frustration - Elation - Happiness

Triggers for Relapse

Self-efficacy is a person's feeling of confidence in their ability to cope with situations or tasks at hand. Much of your resiliency and ability to adapt to the threat of relapse will be in direct proportion to your coping skills.

Duress, pressure and stress from our families, employers, significant others, husbands, wives, children and the general population can overload our circuits and leave us feeling depleted and unable to manage our lives effectively. Paradoxically, feeling great – celebrating a promotion, birth of a child, or other significant life passage, may make us feel ebullient and capable of handling a small dose of our addiction. This is how the mind lies and sets us up for a fall. Feeling good or feeling bad can incite a response to our emotional states with a drink, drug, gambling bet, spending spree, food binges, or an inappropriate sexual encounter.

Triggers are people, places and things, smells, thoughts, feelings, colors, and sense memories that we became habituated to during our destructive use of drugs, alcohol and other dysfunctional behaviors, and can set off an extreme urge or craving to indulge in these behaviors or addictions again. These triggers need to be intercepted with opposing thoughts or actions to stop the potential for relapse.

It is crucial to your continued recovery to plan for any possible relapse trigger – good or bad. It could happen in an instant. You're going along fine, everything's okay, and then all of a sudden a feeling comes over you; sadness, self-pity or hopelessness, or in the contrary, you feel wonderful, elated and super-confident. Or someone says or does something that makes you feel toxically shamed and brings you back to the way you used to feel about yourself, less than and damaged (this is my particular trigger). You may wonder if it's worth it. What good is seeking healthy alternatives? What good is becoming more spiritual when most people wallow in their emotional and mental garbage? You might as well join them....blah...blah...blah.

Two factors may determine the outcome:

One) **Your level of motivation to abstain from your drug and negative behavior of choice.**

Two) **Intervention from your Higher Power.**

Sufficient motivation is needed to practice the skill of taking the time to reconsider the negative consequences of indulging in addictive behaviors of the past. You can overcome reactive thought patterns with effective, new ways of coping. For example, I play the **_movie_** of my addicted, drunken life and although the movie contains 35 years of dysfunction, in one minute

I am completely convinced that I am an alcoholic and I'm not willing to test the theory that I may not be.

A stimulus or trigger can be anything, as mentioned, but most often it will be a familiar place where we've used drugs and alcohol, engaged in our addictive behaviors, a person we used with or a situation that echoes our dysfunctional past. This stimulus or trigger will cause a thought to enter our heads – an automatic thought about the stimulus presented and we could act upon that thought automatically **if we don't stop ourselves.**

It is crucial to take a moment to interrupt this automatic thought by detaching ourselves and mentally observing the thought. This moment of detachment displaces our simultaneous thought/reaction cycle about the stimulus or trigger we've been exposed to hundreds of times before. When we practice identifying the negative thought, detaching from that thought, and then choosing another thought about the trigger, we find we are also replacing and changing our feeling about that stimulus. We soon become adept at responding to life by using a potent coping skill to replace undefined urges masquerading as feelings.

Feelings and urges are distinct from one another. A feeling is deeper than an urge. An urge is momentary. Feelings are guideposts to inner states of being that allow us to investigate and discover ourselves. When we react to stimuli with automatic thoughts this can result in a temporary urge that could lead to a relapse. Our thoughts need to be monitored so that our belief systems can be altered over time and we don't allow automatic reactions to influence our feelings.

In many cases, when we are found wanting in resolve, our Higher Power is there to intervene.

A fellow AA member once related a story about wanting to drink again. This lady had been on the brink of pancreatitis before her recovery. She prayed to God for help and she ended up in AA. She had been sober for several years, when one evening she came home from work and craved her once favorite drink, vodka and orange juice. However, she had no vodka. As she was thinking about where she would go to get the booze, she fell asleep and woke up the next morning, fully clothed, still in her living room chair. She no longer had any desire to drink – no craving and no urges. Is this coincidence? Luck? Happy chance? Or Divine Intervention? Who knows? She didn't drink.

Reasons for Relapse

Research has found that the majority of relapses are caused by negative mental and emotional states such as those outlined above. Secondly, social pressure from acquaintances, families and friends is another factor for relapse. Third, conflicted relationships can be fairly predictive of our ability to stay physically and emotionally sober. If these areas of our lives are troublesome, then they must be transformed by utilizing the coping skills we've been practicing. We're frightened of doing something new, for fear of abandonment by our loved ones. We face the unknown when we start tinkering with the dynamics of long-standing dysfunctional relationships.

You may think that your mom wants you to stay sober but, if there's been a lot of drinking in your family, unconsciously she may want it back the way it was when everybody was dysfunctional. Getting well will change the landscape of your relationships with everyone who knew you when you were an addict or a dysfunctional, neurotic mess. Be prepared for their resistance to your new life in recovery. That's why it's so important to hang out with your 12 Step groups and other recovering people.

My first sober New Years was spent with my mother, my younger sister and her friend. We went down to Oceanside for my uncle's birthday. My mother and uncle were heavy drinkers, and my sister and her friend were getting a head start on the festivities. Everyone was getting drunk at my uncle's house but I was okay with it. Until we got back to the motel. There was a bar within walking distance which was apparently a New Years' Eve hotspot. The place was jammed, music blasting, glasses clinking, champagne bottle corks popping, and I was sitting at a table with my drunken mother who was yelling above the din telling me why I should have lived with her when I was a child, while she kept getting drunker along with the whole room. One minute I was fine, the next moment, I was gasping for air. I felt consumed by my mother and her sickness, the room of full of drunken revelers and I had to get out. I shouted over the noise to my mother that I wanted the room key, which she wouldn't give me. She shouted in response for me to wait – she'd go back to the room with me. I jumped up and ran out of there like my hair was on fire. I couldn't stand one more second - let alone five minutes. I got the hotel clerk to give me another key, and the blessed silence of the motel room gave me back my sober piece of the world.

I share my story with you to illustrate that not everyone in your family will want you to get sober and healthy. If they're still sick, they want you sick. That's the nature of the disease. Selfish, self-seeking, dishonest and afraid. If they're still sick it can't be any other way. So we don't judge them. We pray for them and try to forgive them.

Recovery Plan in Case of Trouble

When you feel the first signs of your former insanity assaulting you, it's time to get on the phone with another member of your 12 Step Group (keep those numbers handy), start praying for guidance, or get out of the house to a meeting. You might also go out to a movie, go to the library or visit your neighbor. I can assure you that whatever it is you choose to do, your Higher Power will protect you from relapsing. You are now in a partnership with a Divine Protector and together you will find a way out of your recovery dilemmas.

Don't rationalize that you're feeling okay and it will pass!!! Don't take the chance!! Call someone if you're feeling down!! Share your feelings with someone on the program!!!!

This is all part of our responsibility to take personal inventory. Take a daily inventory of feelings, goals, plans, meeting schedules, job and family responsibilities. We can get caught up in busy lives and neglect certain aspects of our program that were the cornerstones of our earlier recovery. Everything else must take a back seat to our recovery. That's the bottom line. We will explore more options and plans when dangerous relapsing thoughts occur in the Recovery Companion Workbook.

Social Skills

Certain areas of our life will require an overhaul so that we may become more adaptive to a normal lifestyle. We may be developmentally challenged because we did not go through certain necessary phases to attain maturity. We now need to learn a different way. There are several ways to go about learning new social skills. This includes going to meetings, sober dances, and recovery retreats and functions. Volunteering at a favorite meeting. Greeting other members at the door. Calling someone first that you don't know very well. Group therapy.

Anger Management

Many of us have anger issues and the more stressed out we get, the harder it becomes to respond with alternative styles of communication. We are used to reacting in annoyance and anger but those kinds of responses have us sliding back into our disease. Much of our anger is chronic. Stress and blame are two culprits in the recurring theme of the constantly angry person. What can we do? There are anger management seminars, programs and books that will help you become more effective at managing your anger. Keeping an anger journal is one way of understanding what makes you angry, how it escalates, whether stress or blame is the catalyst and what other responses can be substituted rather than anger. Becoming aware of your anger rather than repeating an unsuccessful way of coping with life is important to maintaining sobriety.

Job Skills

After years of performing at a fraction of our capabilities, we have neglected our growth in many areas. These could include continued education in our particular career or occupation, updating our computer knowledge, or creating ways of marketing ourselves in the form of resumes and cover letters. Perhaps we never developed ourselves for the job market, have no skills at all, and need training to compete. You could begin by utilizing available educational resources. Also, make sure that your job goals are realistic. Rather than putting too much pressure on yourself, it may be wise to take a less demanding job for the time being. If you are already in a high-stress job, you might consider downsizing your career until you have a firm handle on your recovery. Your job may have contributed to your addiction and dysfunction.

For those who are being reintroduced to the employment market, it's useful to get help in rewriting your resume. You can find assistance at the local community college or job center at the unemployment office. There are online resources that offer training in Excel, Microsoft Word and Power Point and other software programs. The local unemployment office may offer classes in designing the best resume for a job in your field of occupation. There are other resources in every community that could be valuable to your cause. Reach out to others and help yourself.

It's been said that, "You never get a second chance to make a first impression." When going on job interviews, appearances are important. Grooming includes properly cut hair, being properly shaved, if applicable to you, having clean or polished fingernails and wearing the appropriate clothes for the position. These are some of the ways to show the potential employer that you are prepared to do a good job and willing to undertake the training necessary for job success. If you don't get a job quickly, go easy on yourself. It will happen. Trust in your Higher Power.

When you're able to harness your newfound energy, it's time to become <u>self-supporting through our own contributions</u> as we say in AA. In acquiring job skills or advancing yourself in the job market, you are becoming more self-sufficient and more confident in your ability to sustain yourself. Each small movement forward is a victory over former dysfunctional behaviors, and though progress seems slow at times, everything is exactly as it should be for your ultimate good.

Parenting Skills

No, there isn't a manual on the care, feeding and discipline of our children, but we can be pretty sure that our parenting skills are largely modeled after the way we were parented. Since we're changing our whole life because of the mistakes of the past, it is only reasonable that we should make a new start with our children. Most likely, we don't know how to parent, either over-indulging our children or being too strict and punitive. Trust must be reestablished between you and your children over time. Keeping your children safe from negative outside influences is the first step toward proving your competence as a parent.

The nature of the relationships that your children have with significant people in your lives may change dramatically depending upon the prevailing circumstances of these relationships. The emotional and psychological safety and welfare of your children is your first priority and needs to be used as a guide for deciding who shall participate in your newly defined family system. You may feel that until you are stronger in recovery, family interactions with grandparents, uncles, aunts or any dysfunctional members of your family should be limited or supervised. Family members may, in turn, become angry over your new requirements for their presence in your children's lives. They may attempt to manipulative you into feeling guilty about your newfound boundaries. You need to continue doing what you consider best for your children. So often we have been distracted by our addictions and need to build trust and a sense of safety regarding our children.

Parenting classes can be instrumental in acquiring parenting skills, tools and other ways of interacting with our children. Again, there are resources in your community that may be available to help you enroll in classes.

Individual and Group Therapy

Another statistic from thousands of AA members indicates that 62% choose to engage a therapist for individual counseling and many attend group therapy. This is in addition to, and not instead of working the 12 Steps, attending 12 Step meetings and getting a sponsor. You can find 12 Step counselors or therapists who are well-versed in 12 Step ideology. Individual therapy provides one on one professional support. Therapy engages us in a deeper way, probing areas of particular significance to our recovery, while our counselor serves as an additional support person.

Group therapy is another excellent tool that enables us to relate to others and makes us aware of how we are being perceived and understood. This can be a useful tool for improving interactions with others. It will be difficult to accept the way others see us at times and may bring out our defensiveness. If we don't acquire the objectivity and insight necessary to honestly evaluate our personality or behaviors for their effectiveness in our lives, then we don't have any power to change. It doesn't mean that we have to give up our individuality or eccentricities. But our continued personal inventory requires that we remain on the path of self-discovery, assessing if our eccentricities are liabilities that prevent us from being of service to others, or limit our potentiality because of stubbornness and a mulish refusal to change.

It should be remembered that insight alone may not affect behavior. You have to ***do something different*** in order to get a different result. Risk = reward. We took huge risks in our addicted and dysfunctional lives, putting ourselves in harm's way and living in an unsafe world. It shouldn't be so frightening to take a small step toward changing a behavior but it is. Knowing what will happen, even if it's painful, is its own crazy comfort. Group and individual therapy challenge us to reach beyond the familiar to reinvent ourselves.

Assertiveness Training

Many of us have a difficult time saying "no." No is a very powerful word and delineates our physical, emotional, ethical, moral and personal boundaries. "No" tells someone we have our own viewpoints and will stick up for ourselves. In dysfunctional homes, we are often robbed of our personal identity and lost who we are in the process. Many of us are chronic people pleasers and become unsure what it is we really want out of life in the face of opposition to our ideas. This is another dangerous trap for relapse. In trying to please too many people, we stop focusing on ourselves, our issues, our problems, our growth and our viewpoints. You need to know who you are, your authentic feelings, your true nature and personality. Your authentic self does not have to continue to be the construct of a dysfunctional childhood or addictive lifestyle.

Others have the opposite problem. Instead of being a people pleaser, you may feel that you are entitled to have your way regardless of the consequences and other peoples' comfort, viewpoint or wishes. You also need assertiveness training to learn new ways of getting your point across and your needs met, without violating the rights of others.

Dysfunctional Relationships-Lack of Intimacy

In working these Steps, we uncovered many aspects of our inner selves and started an honest dialogue with ourselves and with others. We are now defining ourselves as people who deserve love and intimacy with another. However, our biggest challenge is usually in our relationships or lack thereof. Most of us were involved in dysfunctional relationships because we internalized unsuccessful strategies that pushed people away rather than nurtured closeness.

Emotionally healthy individuals are characterized by their ability to **sustain** intimacy in mutually satisfying relationships.

There are many different ways of fooling ourselves into thinking we're having relationships – when we're not. We choose people who are incapable of intimacy, sabotage those relationships that could possibly become intimate, or run away from someone and then run to them in an endless dance of fear of real closeness. The quality of our relationships will be determined by our ability to be vulnerable with another, to accept ourselves and to be accepted by the other person.

Intimacy is destroyed by rage, criticism, sarcasm and withdrawal. Many of us default to these relationship destroyers when we feel threatened by closeness to others. We may not even be aware that we're keeping others at arm's length by behaving in this manner. False beliefs keep us from loving ourselves and getting close to those who could love us. In recovery, we learn to overcome this behavior by, first trusting in our Higher Power and then, trusting in others. These are the first steps on the road to developing relationships with those who are capable of intimacy, trust, vulnerability and love.

The Pain of Recovery

You can't do the healing without the feelings, nor can you do the leaving until you finish the grieving. The means for accomplishing these emotional goals will be different for everyone. Group or individual therapy can be a safe place to explore the pain of your past while being supported and encouraged to remember the incidents that contain your most traumatic memories. It's necessary to grieve the losses and process the sadness.

My anguish was immense at times, but I knew that it was inevitable. Our addictions are designed to keep us from feeling the hurt, so it seems logical to assume that, if you are seeking recovery, then your emotional and mental suffering was extensive and left indelible and sometimes visible scars. The past is not resolved until we exhume these feelings, cry, grieve, and then release them. Otherwise, we are destined to engage in what Freud called "repetition compulsion." We are subconsciously driven to choose partners whose personalities and dysfunctional characteristics repeat similar, and sometimes identical themes from our childhood. We reenact these themes because our subconscious is determined to overcome the trauma we experienced. We are trying to empower ourselves only this method rarely, if ever, works.

My delusional infatuation with Colin recreated my original scenarios of abandonment and rejection. It was a recurring pattern with many other men in my life. In my search for an answer, I realized that much of our pain is not because of present circumstances, but instead we are actually *re-feeling* the distress of our dysfunctional childhood relationships. I have since resolved many of the issues from my childhood and I experience very few painful episodes in my life today.

Grief Work

Grieving the past is essential. I highly recommend grief work for resolving the pain of our dysfunctional lives. Many of us have lost much – our families, our children, our integrity, our good feelings about ourselves.

Grieving is the process of acknowledging the losses in our lives and promises left unfulfilled. Promises we made to others that we were unable to keep because of our spiritual illness, addictions, neuroses and dysfunction. The losses are many, but from the wreckage, we can emerge whole and complete within ourselves – as the phoenix – who rises from the ashes to regenerate and reinvent itself into a new era and a new way of life.

In some cases, we may even grief the loss of our addiction and dysfunction of choice. Our addictions are familiar coping skills that brought fun, comfort and companionship in the lonely and harsh world that we perceived. Grieve the losses and welcome the new – as winter turns to spring – we will blossom.

Goals & Pursuing Interests

It is always beneficial to incorporate goals and projects into our daily lives. When we feel better about ourselves, we are often stimulated to become more productive and useful to ourselves and others. It is very important to develop other interests and hobbies that replace old, dysfunctional behaviors and focuses.

During one particularly bad time in my sobriety, around Christmas, my 12 Step counselor pointed out that I get to choose who and what is in my life. I didn't need to feel obligated to my mother to show up on Christmas day, or stay when she got drunk and abusive, or take back my inappropriate boyfriend out of loneliness. I could replace troublesome people, places and things with positive and life-affirming activities and people. My therapist was giving me permission, which I somehow needed, to do what was right for me and my ultimate growth. Over the years that guidance has been invaluable.

Chapter Fourteen

STEP ELEVEN

Sought through prayer and meditation
to improve our conscious contact with God, as we understood God
praying only for knowledge of God's will for us
and the Power to carry it out.

<u>Spiritual Intervention</u>

Every day is a miracle of intervention freely given by the Higher Power we have invited into our lives. One day at a time keeps us in the moment and working on what's in front of us, whether that's getting to a job or a meeting, working the Steps, processing our grief, or nurturing and protecting our inner child.

At a certain point in your recovery, you will be able to access the use of proactive coping skills, experience your emotions, and manage how you will express them. Some of the promises of the 12 Steps may have been realized and you are the grateful recipient of Divine Love, thankful for the exceptional people in your life, and the lessons they are teaching you, knowing that your Higher Power is doing for you what another human cannot. "No human power" is written in the Big Book of AA because it was understood that, as well-meaning as our families, friends, and sometimes even strangers were, they had no power to heal the spiritual bankruptcy that each addicted/dysfunctional person experiences. We were truly beyond the help of those who wanted the best for us.

<u>Interconnected</u>

The 3rd and 11th Step are closely interconnected. In the 3rd Step, we turned over situations, feelings, doubts, lies, fear, anger and our need to control people, places and things. Hopefully, it has become apparent that when we hold on to toxic and negative situations, feelings and people, we become filled with anxiety, worrying about everything and everybody. We can't stay sober under those conditions. Our anxiety levels alone will cry out for relief and seek the familiar comfort of our addictions. So we have turned many things over to the care of our Higher Power.

After a few months of sobriety, many recovering people experience a distinct and clear image of a Higher Power acting in their lives and rely upon this Power as a source of strength. So actually asking to know the will of God is not as outlandish as it may have been in the beginning of our sobriety. If we aren't quite there yet, we can use the 11th Step to support our efforts at prayer and meditation. The distinction of Step Eleven is that now we take an active role in quieting our minds and listening to the voice of intuition to gently direct us toward the will of God in our everyday affairs.

Right before I went to my first Alcoholics Anonymous meeting, I didn't know what to want, so my will didn't clash with God's. As you may recall from a previous chapter, I sought the will of God without even knowing it. My prayer was, "God put me where you would have me be." In the first few months of sobriety, I experienced emotional upheavals and cried almost every day, while at the same time feeling the exhilaration of discovery and serendipity. Some days I felt blissful, and at other times grief-stricken from the losses I had never allowed myself to feel. I was able to accept that everything was exactly as it was supposed to be.

When we begin to feel better and our lives improve, sometimes we want to take back our lives because it seems as if we've got a handle on things now. Uh-oh. This is the first sign that we're doing a solo. Our sneaky EGO (Edging God Out) has tiptoed up to the back entrance and found the door unlocked. Before you let your ego break down the healthy boundaries of your recovery program, remember how you got this far. By turning it over and trusting in a Higher Power that has an all-encompassing vantage point. We mere mortals just can't see the whole picture. Feeling better can sometimes lead to taking back control. The trick is to feel better while letting our Higher Power lead us through the next challenge.

I have come to recognize that I am a co-creator with Divine Source. God sustains me with the necessary power to do anything that I choose when I am in right alignment. God cannot work alone . . . isn't this the whole point of having created life? To connect and co-create. The human race, through singular individuals, has co-created electricity, mathematical concepts, space travel, and the Pet Rock. Quite a partnership. Through God, we create the love necessary within ourselves to heal our wounds and the wounds of others. Love is the universal language of the planet. Everyone can understand it and everyone can speak it. It has the power to connect us.

Prayers vs. Affirmations

When I redefined my concept of God/Goddess, many aspects of my inner life were shown to me. I acknowledged I had very low self-esteem, weak boundaries, had come from a highly dysfunctional family and that old ideas had gotten me nowhere. So I decided to continue doing affirmations. This is what is so wonderful about the 12 Step program. You can create a God of your understanding and you can choose how to communicate with that Higher Power.

Don't get me wrong. I still pray. At night, as I'm drifting off to sleep, I love that time where I speak to God, thanking Its Divine Presence in my life and asking for guidance. I always give thanks for my sobriety. In the morning, I may listen to my meditation tapes of ocean sounds and water flowing which puts me in a slight trance. I connect with my Higher Power and messages come to me from Divine Source.

At other times, I use affirmations rather than prayers and have for over 22 years. I continue to read and incorporate the dynamics of metaphysical principles into my life and my life is better. Affirmations instill an attitude of expectancy. Affirmations always use present tense, utilizing the material of the Universe, spiritual matter, to manifest what we have proclaimed to be true. Affirmations are used to change our belief system at the subconscious level. *Change your mind – change your life.* This is what I constantly tell people because it has had dramatic effect in my own life. Affirmations, done repeatedly, until the mind accepts what you are telling it, will work to improve your life. In AA, there is a similar saying: **Act as if.**

How does this help others? If you do not have your spiritual, material, mental and emotional domains in harmony, you cannot help anyone. The Big Book states that we are unable to help anyone until *"our own house is in order."* This house includes all our beliefs and attitudes, our psychological, emotional, and spiritual health. Otherwise, we continue to exhibit the symptoms of the disease rather than passing on the knowledge to others of how to overcome the spiritual sickness that keeps them from recovery.

What's in a Brain?

Many metaphysical teachers believe that the chemical make-up of our brains is influenced by our thoughts and molded by our beliefs. While we cannot grow new brain cells, we can increase the number of dendritic spines that connect our brain cells. Dendritic spines are located in the synapses of the brain that are part of the downstream nerve cell. They are small tendrils reaching out to other dendritic spines, allowing us to increase our memory and learning capabilities. Increasing our dendritic spines, through learning new information and furthering our education, can actually raise intelligence quotient (IQ). The brain's plasticity has been well-documented.

In the case of addiction or other repetitive behaviors, our neural pathways become like well-traveled roads, familiar to our brain cells, so it's difficult to alter their direction. These pathways led to pleasure centers that were activated when we practiced our addictions. Even in recovery, these centers may still clamor for stimulation and distract us from sobriety. Perhaps your craving for harmful behaviors and substances has not been entirely eradicated, but the brain is flexible and we can redirect it in positive ways. It would seem plausible that when incorporating the 12 Steps into our lives, we are causing harmful brain connections to wither from lack of activity.

It takes focused energy, the practice of positive affirmations, going to meetings, talking to our sponsors and spiritual advisors, going out to coffee with recovering partners, and other uplifting activities to redirect these brain passages.

Though scientists understand some of the workings of our brain, much remains mysterious, uncharted territory that responds in surprising ways. The phenomenon of recovery cannot be dissected under a microscope because it is more than just brain circuits being rewired. It is a spiritual process beyond our comprehension. Ultimately, our connection with our Higher Power and our reliance upon Its presence in our lives will determine the quality of our recovery.

Conscious Contact

When we consciously choose to maintain an ongoing relationship with our Higher Power, we develop a belief that somehow our paths will be illuminated and the lessons we need will be put in front of us. We trust in this Divine Source to give us the tools and strategies to overcome obstacles and maintain our spiritual equilibrium.

It is very easy to go negative when political parties rail against one another, when economic markets fail, when the stock market goes up and down like a seesaw and jobs are lost by the millions.

DON'T LET OUTER CIRCUMSTANCES DICTATE YOUR INNER WORLD.

We are accessing a dimension of the Universe through our faith in Its power to change us at depth. We are reaching beyond our senses to an inner realm of the unknowable. In our newfound faith we practice the presence of our Higher Power in our lives to do for us what we cannot do for ourselves. Working through the process of grief and self-parenting, that horrid emptiness that haunted us for so long is alleviated. This change in our belief system creates a new paradigm – that we are children of a God who wants our greatest good, loves us uncon-ditionally, and that we are worthy of this love. The result of receiving unconditional love from our Higher Power is that we start feeling unconditional love for ourselves and then for others. This love ignites a chain reaction of revelation – that we are worthy of self-respect, deserving of many good things and life can be enjoyed. Our growing self-esteem teaches us to delineate our emotional and physical boundaries more accurately. So many wondrous changes are happening in our lives that we never thought possible!

Spiritual and Psychological Evolution

As a result of the ongoing participation in our spiritual and psychological evolution, we have sudden flashes of insight and cognitions. Epiphanies. They come cascading into our consciousness, one after another, as we finally comprehend the meanings and motives of so much of our behavior and the behavior of others. This is one of the promises fulfilled, "We will intuitively know how to handle situations which used to baffle us." We are less concerned for ourselves, less obsessed over outcomes as we practice leaving the results to our Higher Power. We find a new strength in forgiving. Forgiveness is one of the main KEYS of spiritual growth and continued recovery. It begins with unconditional love and then forgiveness of ourselves and others. If you have been working some of the exercises in the Recovery Companion Workbook, then you are able to access another KEY of spiritual equanimity. That of acceptance.

Acceptance

On page 449, the Big Book of Alcoholics Anonymous contains a story about a recovering doctor. The Big Book is filled with many stories, but if you're frustrated with God's answers and think that events aren't moving fast enough to suit you, the more experienced members of the program will likely say, "page 449." It will sound like gibberish to you, but reading it may alleviate your discontent. The doctor states:

"Acceptance is the key to *all* of my problems today. When I am disturbed, it is because I find some person, place or thing or situation-some fact of my life unacceptable to me, and I can find no serenity until I accept that person, place, thing or situation as being exactly the way it is supposed to be at this moment."

It is difficult to digest the suggestion that circumstances, people, places or things are the way they're supposed to be. How can that be? Someone is in pain, hurting, starving, being abused, molested, or other horrendous events are taking place somewhere in the world at any given moment. There are hideous and evil acts being perpetrated against the innocent and sometimes the guilty. These acts and events are beyond our control. We might be able to alleviate some small measure of the pain brought about by these atrocities, by donating time or money to a particular charity or cause, but we cannot know the purpose of anyone's suffering.

Acceptance is a spiritual axiom. Without it, we cannot achieve serenity or peace of mind.

We can only account for our actions and behavior, not the actions and behaviors of others. It is not our business – no matter how horrific the consequences of the world's indifference or insanity. Humans must change - this is true. But in whose time and for what reason? If we can just change ourselves, which in and of itself is a tremendous task, perhaps we can make the world just that much better.

Usually, we are challenged by people, places and things, frustrated when they are not behaving in the manner we prescribe or deem correct. Again, we are looking outside of ourselves for answers that can only come from within. Accept others and the world as it is, change yourself, and give your kindness and strength to others.

Knowledge of God's Will

Upon awakening, God doesn't hand out a memo with Its Will for the day. God's will may not be evident at first. Sometimes, we have to feel our way through situations and circumstances, sometimes going the long way round, and sometimes getting lost, to find a lesson, a person, or a reason to act. We are learning to be emotionally available and present for ourselves and for others.

The Power to carry out God's will is inherent when something is already God's Will. God gives us the necessary strength. God's will may appear unorthodox to many people. It does seem strange to endow a bunch of dysfunctional, addicted and neurotic people with the ability to receive spiritual healing and who are able to achieve spiritual insight and understanding. What kind of God is running this Universe, anyway? Yes, recovery in and of itself is an unorthodox method of practicing the presence of God in our lives.

Life is uncertain. We may be unsure what our Higher Power wants with us or from us at times. We may be filled with doubt. Though difficulties are inevitable, if we continue to place our trust in God as our loving Parent, we can find comfort in knowing that ultimately God's will is for us to love and be loved.

I have sustained many losses throughout my life. My mother, father and many family members were distant, physically and emotionally. I have tentative relationships with my sisters due to the drama of dysfunction and I've lost my brother to AIDS. But it seems as if I'm still okay. God gives us free will and he has given my loved ones free will. I cannot interfere with anyone's free will. But God has given me a choice. To find other like-minded people as friends and recovery partners. God has given me my husband who is my best friend and steadfast supporter. God always provides if we believe that He/She/It can be trusted to provide. God's will is sometimes just as simple as this: Get better, stay well and help others. That will get you through the day when all else fails. If you make a million dollars along the way – hey, great! If you're a movie star – bravo!! But our fundamental purpose is spiritual and requires us to follow a set of principles in all our affairs.

Following spiritual principles of love, courage, humility and faith, may run counter to logic and common sense. It would seem that the prevailing outcry is – ME, FIRST! Well, if you are so worried about yourself, where is the necessary faith to let God handle your affairs? Strangely enough, when I am busy focusing on the business of living, doing what's in front of me to do, taking one step at a time, solutions and answers appear out of the matrix of existence to assist and guide me. Instead of worrying, I get into solution. This keeps me stable. Spiritual people tend to stay balanced and are able to find their equilibrium even in the most trying of situations and in the face of difficult people, places and things. I'm not that spiritual yet. My modus operandi is to get upset, my brain and emotions buzzing at warp speed like an angry bee. Then I slowly calm down and apply the concepts of the program until I finally reach a place of acceptance and balance. I'm still crazy, remember?

Healing our Wounds

Much of the energy in our affirmations, meditation and prayers will be directed toward healing the wounds of our childhood and our continuing dysfunction. We are co-creators with Divine Source in our quest for serenity and release from painful trauma of the past.

There are many resources to support our spiritual journey and psychological health:

- Inner child work
- Processing our losses/grief work
- Healthy relationships and recovery partners
- Creative visualization
- Affirmations
- Meditation
- Meetings/sponsorship/fellowship
- Spiritual and self-help workbooks
- Therapy
- Churches – spiritual & religious organizations
- Charitable organizations

As we go about our daily lives, we have the ability to make positive choices and God gives us the power to continue the journey toward health and happiness.

Religious Organizations

The Big Book talks briefly about conventional churches and of drunks going to them to get saved, and the failure of these interventions. Spirituality is not religion – nor is religion, spirituality. Both may reside together, but not necessarily.

Spirituality is found everywhere and in everything and is the stuff that stars and people are made of – a belief in One Presence, Universal in scope and personal by nature, that is accessible to all without adherence to certain doctrines or dogmas.

Religion, by its own definition, is organized and has dogmatic texts and teachings that a person must believe or acceptance into this province is prohibited. It's kind of like an exclusive country club that charges an exorbitant fee to join-you must pay or be excluded. In religion, you pay with your faith in the man-made rules of the religion which instructs you in the belief that somehow God supports, condones and encourages the separation of people into different and warring factions, and wants those people to fight for supremacy of their ideas and doctrines. The truth is no one has a monopoly on God.

If there are those who need religion and can obtain the depth of honesty needed to benefit progressive recovery, then an organized religion of your choice is indicated. But many in AA found that some religions did not care for honesty but instead, were founded upon blind obedience and submission. Submission is not surrender. Surrendering is humbling – submission is designed to humiliate and shame, the very basis of our problem. Being toxically shamed at our core is why we seek to destroy ourselves. Humility is essential, but does not require our toxic shame.

I have found religion in my recovery program and my Higher Power in the daily trials and tribulations of my life, and know that a Divine Consciousness is present within me and within all of us. I do not pretend to know what this Consciousness is and I don't profess having heard Its Voice from a burning bush.

Your spiritual beliefs, religious or otherwise, are your own to engage in, however you choose, as long as you follow the 12 Steps of Recovery. Adherence to a religious belief without working the 12 Steps has proven to be only partially effective. For many, going to church is a great spiritual comfort and available to anyone who wants organized religion in their lives. In addition to the 12 Steps, this is fine. Adherence to a particular religion is the right of every person as long as other people's rights to believe in their own religion or spiritual ideals are respected. We cannot wish harm on those who believe differently than ourselves because that is defeating the very purpose of our conscious contact with the Power that seeks to include all of humanity.

The Power to Carry Out God's Will

It is now known that through changing our thoughts we can change our reality. I have been the recipient of so many miracles in my recovery that I am astonished to be where I am right now. I was homeless, staying in a motel with a crazy, whacked-out druggie, standing outside the motel at 5:00 a.m. with all my worldly possessions, waiting to be rescued by another controlling man, and believing that it was what I deserved. How did I get here?

At each turning point, I was given the requisite power to continue. Though I was beaten down, abused, hysterical, rageful, doubting, mourning, and a crying mess at certain times, I didn't drink or go back to other destructive behaviors. The power to carry out God's purpose was supplied somehow. Part of staying sober was that I wanted to continue having the life that recovery allowed me even if it was rough-going at times. I no longer fought the feelings, or tried to divert from the course that so obviously suited me.

When we change our thoughts, we literally change our brain chemistry. But change is a difficult process. The 12 Steps give us a template for change that is inevitable if we take the risks inherent in the process. We can't dismiss making amends or ignore taking daily inventory. You can and will change if you work these steps and have faith in a Higher Power. There are many who have done it without belief in a Higher Power. They have used their 12-Step group as their Higher Power. Great! Hug a tree! Meditate to the Sun! Do a rain dance!

There are many available resources if you seek them out. The connection to God is there whether or not you are able to see it. This invisible thread links us to God and others in the dynamic flux of life, seemingly random, but always moving us in the right direction of our greater purpose. Some of the tasks of recovery will require discipline and faith. But if we develop these qualities to the best of our ability, we are protected.

Chapter Fifteen

STEP TWELVE

Having had a spiritual awakening as a result of these Steps
we tried to carry this message to alcoholics
and to practice these principles in all our affairs

The Spiritual And Moral Solution

The prognosis for most physical addictions is very poor. People seldom wean themselves away from physical or psychological dependencies, such as heroin, alcohol, binging/purging, anorexia, methamphetamine, cigarettes, crack cocaine, prescriptions drugs, marijuana, sniffing computer cleaner, and other drugs or dysfunctional behaviors. The degradation and disintegration of personality and mental functioning slowly steals the soul. The spirit dies many deaths before the body finally takes its last breath. In many cases, death is accidental; an unintentional by-product of life lived on the edge of disaster. Too often, others also suffer along with the primary user.

In some cases, death is more attractive. Death is easy; living as an addict is hard. The demoralization and horror that we experience at the hands of ourselves, while in the grip of our illness, is mind-boggling. Yet many persevere, exhibiting a high baseline tolerance for inappropriate and insane behavior, both their own and others'. One of my mother's former husbands, Clayton, was an alcoholic and had smoked marijuana throughout his life. He was also an artist, a gifted jazz pianist, but had abused my mother physically. Many years after their divorce, he got a lung fungus from marijuana use and had to wear a bag that was attached by tubing through a small incision in his chest. The pus and mucus from the fungus was drained into this bag that had to be emptied by a nurse, and Clay suffered deep humiliation about his condition. My mother visited him occasionally and knew he was severely depressed about his illness. One morning he called and asked if she would come to see him. A sixth sense told her to say no and she made up an excuse why she couldn't visit that day. Clay blew his brains out that afternoon. Could he have wanted to take my mother with him? It is a grisly supposition but one played out over and over in the lives of addicts and alcoholics. One thing is sure, the consequences of years of addiction were too much and Clay wanted to die.

For decades, the medical community has known they have no real answer to these incomprehensible diseases. The psychiatric community has spent many an hour scratching their collective heads, trying to use psychoanalytic terms to diagnosis something that defies understanding. Addictions are counter-intuitive. They isolate us even as we suffer the soul-ache of abject loneliness. Rehabilitation facilities have sprung up around the world, yet many who go to these places end up achieving only short-term sobriety, if any. Drugs are sometimes used to relieve the craving associated with withdrawal from alcohol and other addictive substances, but the studies are inconclusive on their effectiveness. The side effects also prevent some from taking these drugs. Regardless, the requisite motivation is still necessary for any drug or treatment to work.

There is no therapeutic answer to addiction. There is no pill we can take to relieve our addictions. Yes, we can analyze the problem, speculate on the origin or cause, such as, whether or not addiction is an allergic reaction or disease, but there is no human solution to what ails us that has been found to be effective for any significant length of time. While it may be true that most of us suffer from childhood trauma and are products of dysfunctional families, that knowledge alone is not sufficient to motivate us to sobriety, contentment, or peace of mind. We may have all the information in the world at our disposal, be counselors ourselves, doctors, lawyers, intelligent, capable, and well-to-do, yet remain mystified about why we do not have the requisite power to heal ourselves from the myriad of addictions that plague us.

Money, power and prestige have not cured us. Technological advances haven't made a dent in the growing number of people getting addicted to anything and everything. It seems likely that our growing materialism distracts us from our spiritual nature. Certainly, Earthly problems keep us occupied and busy from both the outcomes of our dysfunctional behaviors, and the source of our unease. We have "pooh-poohed" the spiritual answer as old-fashioned and passé, reluctant to view the world in any spiritual sense at all. We are blinded by glittering momentary pleasures and designs for bigger and better gadgets. As we become more alienated from our spiritual selves, the condition of our disease worsens.

We are then told that going to church, believing in the religions that our parents believed in and that we were raised in, also cannot alleviate our addictive behaviors or dysfunctions. The history of AA and the ***human experiment*** in alcoholism and addiction has conclusively demonstrated, through evidence and heartbreak, that belief in God alone does not effect change. Adherence to religious ideologies and dogma do not have the power to save us. Churches do not have sufficient power to relieve us of the burden of the certain death that awaits many addicts. Priests have died of alcoholism. Ministers and heads of state have succumbed to self-destroying addictions. The waves of destruction break on the shore of our resolve, and we do not have enough strength to fight the tide of addiction rushing in again and again. We only drown.

So, we are left with a puzzle that remains unsolved until we surrender old ideas. We are then presented with perhaps the only solution to our powerlessness – and it is based on spiritual and moral psychology. This spiritual and moral solution is a lifeline thrown to us as we churn in our despair and hopelessness. Addiction is a primary diagnosis. Without sobriety, attempts to treat underlying psychological problems will be unsuccessful.

The spiritual solution begins with a small portion of faith and continues with a moral and spiritual cleansing of our past transgressions. Confession, amends, daily prayer and meditation; the cumulative effect of these activities produce a spiritual transformation. As we are changed at our core, amazingly, we no longer feel alone.

An alcoholic, who eventually became a member of the newly founded Alcoholics Anonymous, consulted Carl Jung, a prominent psychiatrist in Europe. Dr. Jung believed this man to be an alcoholic of the hopeless variety and, through certain therapies, had been trying to induce in him a *change at depth* that had been successful with other alcoholics. But for our future AAer, this did not work. Jung stated that he had never seen an alcoholic of this type get better except in the rare instance of profound *"emotional displacement and rearrangement."*

It seems that this emotional rearrangement is possible with the application of the 12 Steps of recovery though they are inherently spiritual. The Steps also produce a psychological readjustment of our attitudes.

Divinely Inspired

For most, the spiritual awakening is gradual, a house built upon demonstrations of faith, a result of the trust you place in your Higher Power over time. For others, it may be a flash of awareness, a disaster averted by miraculous intervention or a deepening conviction that a Power greater than yourself is acting on your behalf.

Your spirituality and continued desire to establish contact with your Higher Power on a daily basis eventually enlightened you to a greater purpose. You found yourself behaving and thinking differently than you used to think and behave. You began a remarkable turnaround and slowly, as the dawn of each day brought relief instead of dread, you felt redeemed by working the Steps; your destiny was irrevocably altered. You took the road less traveled and, beneath its mountainous and rocky terrain, found a rich and productive vein of ore that turns to gold upon closer examination. You saw the results of your efforts to change and this encouraged you to become more willing to stay humble and open-minded.

I say irrevocably altered because even if you go back to practicing your addictions you have experienced freedom, if only for a moment. This usually ruins your addiction forever. No longer can you deny the truth about yourself, and the truth without freedom from your addiction will eat you alive. Denial is a lie – the truth is in the results. The broken homes, relationships, and careers attest to the failure of our humanness to conquer a problem that is inherently spiritual in nature.

We can let ourselves be swept up in the excitement of our new destiny and, if we make our best effort, not a perfect effort, we will experience Divine Inspiration. Intuition, common sense, experience, and input from our Higher Consciousness direct our course and our lives improve. Sometimes, we can't even put our finger on exactly what is making our lives fuller, richer and filled with meaning. It doesn't do much good to try and analyze. Miracles can't be dissected by the human powers of intellect. They are given by grace and managed by faith.

Grace Consciousness

We don't have to be more than human to experience Divine Grace. The human state is one of constant ambivalence, leaning toward one side or another at any given moment. We are moody, sometimes unpredictable. There are times when we are depressed or anxious. We are having a human experience. We are never absolutely sure of anything. We will never believe perfectly. Despite this, we are saved.

Grace is a state wherein we have been absolved from our transgressions and are no longer attached to the retributory law of karma. Grace cannot be earned. According to Merriam Webster Dictionary, the definition of grace is:

"1) Unmerited help given to people by God (as in overcoming temptation);

2) Freedom from sin through divine grace; and

3) A virtue coming from God."

Grace is inexplicable. We find it in an answer that is given or problem solved. It is shown to us in a fateful encounter that alters the course of our lives. It's in the strength that helps us stay the course and readjust our thinking. In 12 Step meetings all over the world, people are sharing how they are the recipients of these *coincidences* every day. I truly believe that despite our hesitation, grace already sustains us and lights our path even as we struggle up the hill of cynicism.

Not all problems can or should be cleared away. Life is a challenge and sometimes we will meet that challenge and sometimes we will fail. Divine Love intervenes, pulling us out of the wreckage and lifting our burdens so that may enjoy the comfort and solace that sobriety offers on a daily basis.

Unfolding Designs

Manifestation begins in the unseen dimensions. The unfolding of purpose and design is revealed in incremental doses of intuition and common sense, gently leading us further on our divined path. That's why faith is required. Faith is the conduit between inner states and outer manifestations. The exchange of energies between you and Divine Intelligence develops into a mutually rewarding experience. We have an effect on our Higher Power. It's logical. If all is interconnected, then primary Creative Force must be influenced by us as we are by It. But without faith, we cannot feel the Power becoming active in our lives. It is only through surrender and faith that we are movers and shakers in the world of events not yet occurring. These are spiritual states of being that keep the connection flowing.

Creation is the synergy between us and our Higher Power in an ongoing interaction between faith and manifestation in our material world of those things we need, and what God's love bestows: love for others, belonging, resolution of past traumas, forgiveness of past hurts and transgressions and understanding.

Though we are finite beings, we have the Infinite essence of the Creator within us. This creative force becomes stronger and the channels of faith open in ever-widening circles so that the wisdom of the Eternal can be received in the form of divine inspiration. That's why open-mindedness is another requirement. It seems to be that the God/Goddess Force needs a partner through which It creates endlessly, infinitely, and forever.

We effect changes in our circumstances by our own belief in manifestation. Once we realize the profound relationships between our Higher Power and our own ability to create the life we have always dreamed of, faith compounds with interest, and we are willing participants in the continuous wondrous experiment of faith and surrender. These two spiritual elements lift us out of the murky waters of our resistance and denial and give us the vision to witness Divine Reality demonstrating its Presence in our daily living.

Carrying The Message

From the very moment we become physically and emotionally sober from our addictions and dysfunctions, we are carrying the message of hope and faith. Even a person with one day of sobriety can turn to the man, woman, or child beside them and offer a helping hand. You are

God in action. God has chosen you to help another human being and you are sending out the message in waves and ripples through the fabric of the Universe. God bestows upon us that power. If not you, then who? You have experienced the fall from grace, the spiral downward, mentally, physically, and spiritually. Who better than you to reach out to another in a similar situation? You have the unique qualifications required to help another one like you. You are connected to every person who has ever felt like you. There are many of us out there.

Each day that you are part of the solution rather than part of the problem, you are carrying the message. You demonstrate this by living responsibly, doing the best you can, and stepping outside the comfort zone of your dysfunction and addiction. These are all powerful messages to others that you are getting better. Overcoming obstacles with acceptance and graciousness is carrying the message. Changing your thoughts and behaviors is carrying the message. For example, I don't drive drunk anymore, I am saner than I was yesterday, I have educated myself, and I help others. I have done a thousand things in the past 22 years that show others I have been saved.

Bill Wilson stumbled upon a vital recovery tool when he discovered that he could remain sober by helping another alcoholic. Helping another addict, alcoholic or other dysfunctional person is a critical part of the program for several reasons:

- It gets us out of ourselves. So often we are caught up in the petty problems of the day. Our ego is constantly demanding attention. As we give of ourselves to another, we find that the problems we thought we had, disappear.
- Builds our self-esteem by making us feel useful. Even if we only have one day of sobriety, our experience, strength and hope can lift someone out of their darkness.
- Gives us purpose. When we don't understand why we're even here or what is the meaning of life, by focusing on one tiny part of the Universe, a sick person who needs our help, we can re-ignite the spark of purpose and direction.
- Reinforces our learning about the program. Teaching someone else reinforces the concepts and ideas inherent in the program. We are actually understanding the Steps at deeper levels each time we reach out to another by being of service.
- It is humbling to share with another the story of our drunken, addicted, dysfunctional or neurotic journey through life. We reveal a proper perspective of ourselves and our place in the world when recounting to another our own missteps. As we share our experience of deliverance by the grace of a Higher Power, we know that we have been divinely guided and have accomplished something greater than we could have attained on our own.

When we help others, we inevitably help ourselves, reinforcing over and over again the message we are internalizing through our meetings, Step work, therapy and sessions with our sponsor.

Please bear in mind however, that unsolicited advice is usually discarded and not taken in with any seriousness. When another person's life becomes chaotic and painful enough, they may ask for your help and advice. We have to draw the line between enabling another person who doesn't really want help and only using us for what they can get, and those who are truly sincere in their efforts to work the program.

Anonymity

Anonymity is a choice. It seems that carrying the message and anonymity coexist in an uneasy alliance. People will judge you when you tell them you're in a 12 Step program – that you are a recovering person. However, for ten people that judge, there may be one that comes to you for help because you were honest about yourself. Those that do judge have no idea what a 12 Step program is or how it works. This is to be expected. I can only hope that more education and awareness of 12 Step programs will enlighten people and lessen prejudice and judgment. We are *sobriety in motion*.

If telling another person about your recovery status would jeopardize your job or well-being, then certainly keeping your anonymity is paramount. We are under no obligation to trust others who we feel can't be trusted or to show vulnerability to those who would harm us. If self-disclosure would violate your boundary or those of another, then maintain anonymity. This is a personal choice for each of us and we must gauge our comfort levels of disclosure. But if we find we're keeping silent because of our ego, or that we don't want people to look down on us, or out of dishonesty or fear, then our reasons for anonymity must be examined according to the principles of the program.

I usually tell people that I am a recovering alcoholic because my sobriety is very much a part of who I am today. This is who I am. From my recovery everything else is possible. However, when I go on a singing gig, I don't announce over the microphone that I'm an alcoholic. If I exchange pleasantries with the grocery clerk, I don't tell her I'm a recovering drunk. But if you have a conversation with me for any length of time, you will probably find out that I'm in a 12 Step program of recovery. I am proud of that. I'm excited that I got the miracle and I want other people to get the miracle, too. It's so much more satisfying to share this incredible journey with others who are in sync with me. If they aren't in sync, I like to let people know where I'm coming from. If that feels uncomfortable for you, then don't disclose. It's up to each individual.

Sponsorship

Carrying the message is different from sponsorship. Sponsorship should only be attempted once we have a firm grasp on the concepts of the program and have worked the Steps with a competent sponsor ourselves. We can be of service only to that point where we have worked through our own issues and have an understanding of how an addict/alcoholic functions in their disease on a daily basis. Naturally, we only sponsor those who are practicing complete abstinence, but the disease will still be prevalent in thought and behavior. Knowing ourselves is helpful in sponsorship, but what we do to maintain our sobriety may not work with another person. However, the fundamental concepts outlined in this book are applicable to any addict, alcoholic and dysfunctional person. We learn to be patient, loving and tolerant as sponsors because people learn at their own pace, and as long as they remain sober, this is their primary purpose. Anything is possible once we are sober.

Sponsorship is not therapy. The responsibility of the sponsor ends at the concepts of the program. Expanding upon these concepts, such as examining toxic shame, grief issues and re-parenting, may require someone educated in other treatment methods. A drug and alcohol counselor has studied additional treatment models of addiction and recovery that include cognitive and behavioral therapies, dual diagnosis, psycho-educational guidelines, motivational interviewing, and gender issues specific to men or women. A sponsor is not expected to know these areas of treatment. Being a sponsor and having a sponsor is a confidential relationship with another person in the program that includes self-disclosure, guidance through the Steps, and, most importantly, trust. Sponsors are integral parts of a recovery support team.

Sponsorship is tough. Not everyone wants the program. Even those who desperately need a program for living will put up seemingly insurmountable barricades and hinder our eagerness for recovery on their behalf. They spent a lot of time in denial and resisting reality. Reality is not a relative concept. It is very real. Gravity is a principle of physics. If you go up on a high building and jump, gravity and the harsh pavement will crush you. This is reality. Transmitting reality to those who are new in the program can be exhausting, but try we must, once we are ready to take on the mantle of mentorship. We mentor those who desire to live a new way. We let go of our expectations and receive the gift of our continued sobriety for being of service to others.

Being of Service

I have found the idea of being of service to be one that translates into other areas of my life. Going to my job is being of service, cooking and cleaning for my family is being of service.

Listening to the problems of others is being of service as long as it stays within acceptable boundary limits. Once our problems are being handled by our Higher Power, our time is now free to give of ourselves to others.

It is a high wire act, at times, to determine what kind of help is enabling and what help is being of service. When you feel overwrought by the demands of others, there is probably quite a bit of enabling and co-dependency present. It could be time to step back and take a look at your commitments and decide whether you have over-extended yourself as a sponsor, a friend, a mother, a father, a wife, a husband or employee. We might get caught up in the enthusiasm of service to others, especially women who, for the most part, are the nurturers of society. It's time to let go and let God if you're anxious or over-worked.

Practicing the Principles

Each step has an underlying principle that operates spiritually in our newly designed reality. It's a tall order to **practice these principles in all our affairs**. We will never practice them all at the same time perfectly. But we make strides and walk proudly in our efforts to try and incorporate these principles into our dealings with the world. In taking a journey through the Steps, we apply the principles into matters that use to baffle and confound us and find clarity.

Step 1	Honesty	Admitting that we are powerlessness to control or conquer our problems and addictions on our own, we surrender. Without honesty, surrender is impossible.
Step 2	Hope	As we realize that our worldview is distorted and unrealistic, we hope for better outcomes by inviting a Power greater than ourselves to enter our lives.
Step 3	Faith	We practice turning over our problems to our Higher Power and we are rewarded with ever-increasing faith in Its ability to do for us what we cannot do for ourselves.
Step 4	Courage	Looking at ourselves through the lens of moral behavior and spiritual principles takes enormous courage throughout the process. When we are receiving unconditional love from our support centers we find the strength to reveal ourselves.
Step 5	Integrity	In telling another of our spiritual and moral lapses, we solidify the intent to stop practicing our addictions and dysfunctions. Our core structure of sobriety becomes much stronger as a result.
Step 6	Willingness	Throughout every phase of our recovery, willingness is key.
Step 7	Humility	In revealing our transgressions and admitting our powerlessness, we have found that humility is not weakness, but strength in our vulnerability. Vulnerability is key to becoming intimate with ourselves and another.
Step 8	Brotherly/Sisterly Love	Our widening sphere of love includes everyone. We try to see the world without prejudice and judgment. Just as we are not judged for our missteps but have been redeemed.
Step 9	Justice	As we balance the scales of the wrongs we have committed in thought, word and deed, we clear away our Earthly wreckage as best we can and become an available conduit for spiritual guidance.
Step 10	Perseverance	We continue our spiritual self-examination. We maintain sobriety through a continual appraisal of our life situation and sober state. We build a new life using skills we are learning and developing.
Step 11	Spiritual Awareness	Our awareness gradually increases with each day, until we are in tune with the messages sent out from our Higher Power, directing our course.
Step 12	Service	We help others by maintaining our sobriety from addictions/dysfunctions/neuroses. We are not perfect but we practice spiritual principles and use available resources to help others and ourselves continue the journey.

Transformation

The butterfly undergoes numerous stages of change before becoming a creature in full flight sailing on a ray of sunlight, dancing in the perfumed air of a bright summer day. The butterfly has lived in the darkness of a cocoon, engaged in ***becoming*** its true essence. It achieves this metamorphosis naturally, without thought or pain. The butterfly just simply is. In many cultures, the butterfly is a symbol for the soul.

Humans are much more complicated than butterflies, yet no less beautiful. We have been presented with certain challenges and our growth, moral and spiritual, is not effortless. Our hard-won serenity is not one of nature fulfilling itself, but of a person who relies upon a Creator for assistance and direction. We have been endowed with an intellect and numerous emotions, needs and desires. They seem to be necessary for human development. Otherwise, there would be no need for a spiritual quest to transcend certain baser parts of our nature. All would be well, people would be wonderful, without vices, flaws and selfishness, and humanity would be skipping through the forests of the world, laughing and care-free. This just isn't so.

So give yourself a huge pat on the back for being brave enough to take this journey. Not everyone will have the strength to continue or even know that such a journey is necessary in the first place. They may already have a code for living handed down from generation to generation that works well and requires no modification. But they are going to miss out on the ride of a lifetime! They can succumb to complacency without dire consequences. No so for us.

We, my friends, are complex butterflies. It is necessary for us to have a spiritual transformation. Because of devastation and loss, nightmare addictions and dysfunctions, we have been selected for this journey. Though we might stumble, might resist certain ideas, let go only to take back, or deviate from the course, once we have come this far, we are different than we were before. We have been transformed.

May you all dance in the sunlight.

RECOVERY COMPANION WORKBOOK

RECOVERY MODEL FOR ALL

I believe the 12 Steps can work for many people because my life has been so dramatically transformed by application of this recovery program. There are many reasons why some people are more susceptible to addiction, dysfunction and neuroses, including family of origin, belief systems, trauma and violence in the home, genetics, environment, enmeshment, boundary violations and physical and sexual abuse.

Our first beliefs are transmitted through our family of origin. We start here. **If the feelings get too overwhelming or cause <u>flooding</u>, discontinue the exercise and move to the next one. It may be necessary for you to consult a therapist knowledgeable in family dysfunction.**

EXPAND UPON THESE EXERCISES AS NEEDED IN JOURNAL OR NOTEBOOK.

Family Systems

Normal Families
Normal family systems have strong but flexible boundaries. Parents and/or primary caregivers nurture, protect, encourage and respect all members of the family system. They are not excessively punitive or overly permissive in allowing inappropriate behaviors. Normal families communicate in healthy ways; anger is expressed in non-violent ways. There is little trauma and, if there is trauma, the family members communicate their feelings about the trauma to each other freely and without fear of retribution. Children are encouraged to be cooperative, independent and autonomous, and are supported in the ongoing, developmental process of separation and individuation from parents. Parents do not inappropriately burden children with their problems. There is minimal mental illness, addiction or abuse present in a normal family system.

Dysfunctional Families
In dysfunctional family systems these attributes are either non-existent or inconsistent. Abandonment occurs, either physical or emotional, together with boundary violations, enmeshment, violence, abuse, addiction and neglect. Children may be either physically or sexually abused. As a result, children internalize negative messages about themselves from their environment causing extreme emotional pain. As children determine, incorrectly, that they are flawed and defective, they develop unhealthy shame about themselves which has been called toxic shame.

Features of Dysfunctional Families

Use the reading to determine how your family may have been dysfunctional, and, if applicable, please describe your experience with any of the following features: neglect, abandonment, over-permissiveness, over-control, boundary violations, enmeshment, a sick, addicted, mentally or physically disordered family member.

_____
_____
_____
_____
_____
_____
_____
_____
_____
_____
_____
_____
_____
_____
_____
_____
_____
_____

What rules of the family system were used to maintain the dysfunction?

_____
_____
_____
_____
_____
_____

What was your role in the family system? _____
_____
_____
_____
_____
_____

Were there verbal or non-verbal messages about not asking and not telling what went on in your family system?   No _____   Yes _____

If yes, what did you understand about the *silence* rule?

_____
_____
_____
_____
_____

Trauma

Please describe any significant trauma in your family. Was there a sick or addicted parent, any major hospitalization or incarceration of a family member, or mental or physical illness? Were you the designated caretaker of one or both parents? Describe any physical or sexual abuse, violence, rage, or other inappropriate behaviors in the family. Please take as much time as needed to write about this using your journal for additional space.

_____
_____
_____
_____
_____
_____
_____
_____
_____
_____
_____
_____
_____
_____

Toxic Shame

Toxic shame is a pervasive feeling that we are defective and irrevocably flawed. Toxic shame can be expressed in areas of our life where we are extremely sensitive. Areas of shame could be around competence, adequacy, appearance, weight, worthiness, self-esteem, or sexuality, to name a few. The thousands of negative, critical and unloving verbal and non-verbal messages received from our caregivers have been internalized into believing that we are damaged goods; then we attempt to hide these beliefs and feelings from ourselves and others. In what areas do you feel unhealthy shame?

Example:
I'm ashamed to ask for a raise. Even the thought of asking terrifies me.
I can't ask my boyfriend for a commitment to this relationship. He'll leave me.

_____
_____
_____
_____
_____
_____
_____
_____
_____
_____
_____
_____

When we feel deep shame and humiliation, we feel pain. We are terrified of exposure and vulnerability and, as a defense measure, may develop an outer shell of hardness or defiance. No matter how we adapt to our shame, there is always fear of intimacy with another. We may even hide the truth about our shame from ourselves. We don't want to expose our flaws for fear that others will see that we are intrinsically undeserving and damaged.

Does shame or fear of humiliation keep you from sharing your true story with others?
Yes _____ No _____

How does toxic shame affect your relationship with others? Do you avoid telling them certain things? Do you try and confuse them about yourself? Are you afraid of revealing who you are? Please elaborate:

_____
_____
_____
_____
_____
_____
_____

Messages Received

What did your parents or significant caretakers tell you about yourself? How did they express to you in <u>non-verbal</u> ways what they thought of you? They could have communicated with a *look*, *tone of voice* and/or *facial expression* and *body language*.

Example:
When I would start to talk to my aunt about what was happening in the family, my mom would get this nasty look on her face that meant "you'll be sorry."

_____
_____
_____
_____
_____

_____
_____
_____
_____
_____

Are your beliefs about yourself similar or dissimilar to how you were viewed by your parents? Do you define yourself by their standards, beliefs, and assessments of you? For each example of how your parents responded to you, please find a corresponding belief in your present life.

Example:
Because my dad didn't care about my report card, I've found it very hard to excel. I'm apathetic. Because it was forbidden to talk about family matters, I find it hard to tell others about myself and what's going on with me.

_____
_____
_____
_____
_____

_____
_____
_____
_____
_____

This kind of investigation is a lifelong process. The parental mandate is one of obedience to their will, which usually means settling for way less than we deserve. We resist any evidence to the contrary because our indoctrination is deeply ingrained. Our worldview is distorted – our view of ourselves based only on what others might think. We seemingly rebel against our past, but in fact, we are merely self-destructing. We must walk a different way, rebirth, re-parent and reconsider why we are resistant to new ideas.

CONTINUE USING THE ABOVE TEMPLATES FOR MORE EXAMPLES.

Differentiating Our Feelings

Often, we don't know what we're feeling or we don't want to feel anything. Events from childhood that caused our initial pain: sorrow, grief, and loss are forgotten or little understood. These feelings may confuse us but it is important to know what we're feeling.

This list of feelings should be consulted each day until we become more trusting in our ability to know what we are feeling. Learn to *check in* with your feeling state, giving yourself permission to feel whatever you feel without judgment.

I am feeling _____   I am feeling _____

I am feeling _____   I am feeling _____

I am feeling _____   I am feeling _____

Family Rules About Feelings

As you go through this list of feelings, choose those that apply to you and be aware of certain emotions that seem to occur over and over again. These will become your Predominant Feelings. Also some emotions may have been considered inappropriate to express in your family. For example, anger was fine, but sadness was frowned upon. There may be gender typing in relation to your emotions, such as acceptable feelings for boys as opposed to girls. We are attempting to feel our emotions not judge what we are feeling as good or bad.

My Predominant Feelings are: _____

_____

_____

_____

_____

What emotions seem unacceptable or uncomfortable to feel because of my family history?

_____

_____

_____

_____

_____

_____

_____

PLEASE USE YOUR JOURNAL TO ELABORATE ON ANY OF THESE EXERCISES.

PLEASE XEROX THIS LIST OF FEELINGS TO CHECK IN WITH YOURSELF EACH DAY. WRITE DOWN HOW YOU'RE FEELING IN YOUR JOURNAL DAILY.

Positive Feelings		Painful Feelings	
Affectionate	Grateful	Abandoned	Ignored
Alive	Gratitude	Angry	Impatient
Accepted	Grieving	Anxious	Inadequate
Amused	Happy	Apprehensive	Indignant
Anticipatory	Healthy	Ashamed	Inferior
Beautiful	Hopeful	Awkward	Inhibited
Blissful	Humorous	Betrayed	Insecure
Brave	Independent	Bitter	Irritated
Calm	Joyful	Bored	Isolated
Capable	Lovable	Confused	Jealous
Caring	Loyal	Contemptuous	Lonely
Centered	Optimistic	Defeated	Lustful
Cheerful	Passionate	Dejected	Melancholy
Cherished	Peaceful	Dependent	Miserable
Comfortable	Playful	Depressed	Misunderstood
Compassionate	Pleased	Despairing	Muddled
Competent	Proud	Desperate	Needy
Concerned	Quiet	Devastated	Outraged
Confident	Relaxed	Disappointed	Overwhelmed
Content	Relieved	Discouraged	Panicked
Courageous	Respected	Distrustful	Paranoid
Curious	Safe	Embarrassed	Sad
Delighted	Satisfied	Envious	Sensitive
Eager	Secure	Exasperated	Shocked
Ecstatic	Self-sufficient	Fearful	Stressed-Out
Empathic	Sexy	Foolish	Stubborn
Encouraged	Silly	Frantic	Toxically Shamed
Enlightened	Special	Frustrated	Touchy
Esteemed	Spiritually connected	Furious	Trapped
Exhilarated	Strong	Gloomy	Troubled
Excited	Supportive	Grumpy	Unappreciated
Forgiving	Sympathetic	Guilty	Unattractive
Friendly	Tender	Hateful	Uncertain
Full of Faith	Warm	Helpless	Uncomfortable
Fulfilled	Worthy	Hopeless	Uneasy
Generous		Horrified	Unfulfilled
Glad		Hostile	Unhealthy
Good		Humiliated	Worried
		Hurt	

STEP ONE EXERCISES

This step requires us to acknowledge that we have a problem that is unmanageable. You may be abusing or addicted to drugs or alcohol. It may be that you are abusing or addicted to some other form of negative substance or mood-altering behavior that has brought devastating consequences into your life, or you may be severely co-dependent.

If you experience problems in your relationships with others, on the job, with friends, family, spouses, children or others that are a direct consequence of your abuse of drugs, alcohol, computer games or other computer-related addictions, gambling, food, anorexia, binging/purging cycle, mental illness, personality disorder, shopping/debting, fixing others, sex, or any other kind of compulsive behavior, then you are probably experiencing unmanageability in your life. Addictions get worse, never better. If you have decided you've had enough, then you are ready for more self-examination.

Problem Behaviors

In Chapter One, in the Section entitled ***Some of Our Problems***, I have listed many dysfunctional behaviors that ultimately create crisis in a person's life. Looking back over this list and any other behaviors not on the list that are causing you problems, please describe how a particular behavior or behaviors are causing negativity in your life.

Behavior: _____

Problems this behavior creates:_____
_____
_____
_____
_____
_____
_____
_____

Behavior: _____

Problems this behavior creates: _____

_____
_____
_____
_____
_____
_____
_____

Crisis in Your Life-Past & Present

Addiction is a pathological (diseased or disordered) relationship with any mood or mind altering substance or behavior that comes between you and feelings you don't want to feel that ultimately creates crisis in your life.

Behaviors you described in the previous section may have escalated or increased, reaching uncontrollable levels creating chaos or crisis. In the past year have you experienced crisis in your life? If so, please describe what the crisis was, what impact it had on you and your relationships, and if the crisis was resolved or is ongoing

The crisis I experienced was: _____

_____
_____
_____
_____
_____

What impact did this crisis have on you or your relationships with others? _____

_____
_____
_____
_____
_____
_____

If this crisis was resolved, how did it get resolved? _____

_____
_____
_____

_____
_____
_____

Is there a current, ongoing crisis in your life now? If so, please describe this crisis:

_____
_____
_____
_____
_____
_____

CONTINUE USING THIS TEMPLATE FOR EVERY CRISIS YOU EXPERIENCE.

Defending Our Addictions/Dysfunctions

The ego also uses ineffectual coping strategies in order to maintain an illusion that it is intact and functional. However, an unhealthy ego will dominate us, intimidating us into believing that these coping mechanisms are successful when they are, in fact, an elaborate, defensive psychological construct that keeps us from getting the help we need. What kinds of behavior do you find yourself having to defend on a regular basis either to yourself or to others?

Example:
Playing computer games.
Missing work when I have a hangover.
Spending rent money on gambling.

_____
_____
_____
_____
_____
_____
_____
_____

Defenses

How do you defend your addiction to mind or mood altering substances or behavior to others? Your dysfunctional behaviors? Your co-dependency? How do you defend these behaviors to yourself? For each behavior listed above, choose as many defenses as apply. If you rationalize, explain, minimize and justify, then list all of them as defenses.

Rationalize	Attacking
Blaming others	Joking
Being smug or superior	Debating, arguing
Justifying	Shouting
Deluding ourselves	Theorizing
Switching conversations	Manipulating
Projecting	Playing the Victim
Accusing others	Withdrawing
Evading, dodging	Silence
Defiance	Threatening
Verbalizing, talking	Glaring
Generalizing	Staring
Minimizing	Explaining
Trying to intimidate	Giving excuses
Distorting the truth	Others

We use behaviors to defend behaviors. From the section on behaviors you often have to defend to others, choose from the list above *how you defend* those behaviors. Add any defenses that might not be on the list. For each behavior you have to defend and the defense you use, describe how this works for you and the outcome.

Example:

Behavior: Missing work because of a hangover

Defenses used: **Explaining** to my boss that I was sick. Giving this as an excuse. To myself, I **blame** the pressures of the job for why I have to drink. When someone looks at me as if they're blaming me, I **stare them down**. When someone asks about where I was yesterday, I **change the subject**.

On whom: My boss and co-workers

How does this feel: I feel relieved that the pressure's off.

Outcome: It gets me a reprieve from answering any more questions. It gets the boss off my back for the moment.

Behavior: _____

Defenses used: _____

_____

On whom? _____

How does this feel? _____
_____
_____
_____
_____

Outcome?_____
_____
_____
_____
_____

Behavior: _____

Defenses used: _____
_____

On whom? _____

How does this feel? _____
_____
_____
_____

Outcome? _____
_____
_____
_____
_____

The more you use this exercise the easier it will be for you to become aware of how you use defenses to resist reality and deflect accountability for your behaviors. This is important to any lasting recovery program. We can't change what we don't think needs changing.

CONTINUE USING THIS TEMPLATE AS NEEDED FOR THIS EXERCISE.

Acting Out Leads To Unmanageability

When we act out in addiction or dysfunction our lives become unmanageable. Please describe how that occurs in your life for each of the behaviors identified in this Section.

Example:

My life is unmanageable when my sister doesn't call me and then my feelings get hurt. I get angry and feel like getting even with her for not appreciating me and our relationship. I lose my serenity and peace of mind and get stuck in thinking about her and her problems.

My life is unmanageable: _____

_____

_____

_____

_____

My life is unmanageable: _____

_____

_____

_____

_____

CONTINUE USING TEMPLATE FOR LIFE AREAS THAT ARE UNMANAGEABLE.

Hitting Bottom

What circumstances, emotions or behaviors have you thinking you may have *hit bottom*?

Lost job because of addictions
Lost husband (boyfriend) because of addictions
Lost wife (girlfriend) because of addictions
Lost custody of children because of addictions
In jail because of addictions
In diversion program because of addictions
Feel tremendous shame because of addictions
Feel guilt because I'm avoiding people
Isolating myself because of addictions and other behaviors
Feeling incomprehensible demoralization
Feel lonely and abandoned by everyone
Shame over behavior while under the influence of drugs/alcohol or other substance
Can't think straight anymore
Overwhelmed with guilt or shame
Hate myself
Can't control my drinking and/or dysfunctional behavior

Can't control someone else
Someone in my life is addicted
Someone is my life is abusing me
I am abusing someone else
I need help
I am in emotional pain
I am in mental anguish

For each of the feelings and/or behavior that pertain to you, describe in detail what events, things, people or states of mind cause these feelings or behavior, and how this might trigger your addiction or dysfunction.

Example:

I feel lonely and abandoned by everyone. These feelings overwhelm me and I get depressed and lethargic. To pep myself up, I take a drink; then another, and another, until I feel better and ready to go out on the town. The booze gives me courage to meet people. Yet, then I act stupidly, and get so drunk that I can't control myself. I am ashamed of this.

_____
_____
_____
_____
_____
_____
_____
_____
_____
_____
_____

CONTINUE USING THIS TEMPLATE.

Surrendering

The act of surrender directly opposes the mandate of the ego's need to be in control. It becomes necessary to repeat the process of surrender over and over again throughout our lives. What must you surrender today? Who must you surrender today?

Example:
I surrender the need to know how I'm going to stay sober today and instead go to a meeting.

I surrender: _____

_____

_____

_____

_____

I surrender: _____

_____

_____

_____

_____

CONTINUE USING THIS TEMPLATE FOR FURTHER WORK IN THIS AREA.

STEP TWO EXERCISES

Defining Insanity for Ourselves

As children, we were locked into our family system, powerlessness to act in our defense or to challenge the dysfunction. We learned to accommodate many kinds of insanity and repeated behaviors and actions designed to keep us from any real solution or happiness. We now have to deprogram ourselves from the automated responses of our childhood and examine certain behaviors so that we can transcend the distorted messages of our family. Try to remember some of the insanity of your family dynamics. Your parents or primary caregivers cultivated ideas or acted upon beliefs that seemed absurd to you. Yet you were required to act as if these ideas, beliefs and actions were normal.

Example:
My grandmother would make me wash my clothes in our back porch sink even though we had a washing machine.

_____
_____
_____
_____
_____
_____

_____
_____
_____
_____
_____
_____

What realities were you forced to ignore? What events were *glossed* over and reinvented? How did you respond to these events? With appropriate or inappropriate emotions?

Example:
I ignored that my father was calling Colleen names. My brother and I would start to giggle out of nervousness and fear.

My mother and I ignored that Mike (my stepfather) wouldn't eat dinner with us whenever I visited. I responded by not responding. I felt hurt, but ignored that hurt. Upon returning home to grandma's, I would always have an upset stomach.

_____
_____
_____
_____
_____

_____
_____
_____
_____
_____

What events in your life today are upsetting you yet you find yourself responding in similar ways as when you were a child or teenager?

Example:
I find myself being nice to someone who has hurt me instead of being honest. I laugh when I don't find that person funny. I guess I have a fear of confrontation.

_____
_____
_____
_____

_____
_____
_____
_____

CONTINUE USING THIS TEMPLATE FOR WORK IN THESE AREAS.

More Insanity

Insanity: "Doing the same thing over and over expecting different results." Please make a list of actions that you repeat over and over again with the vague **hope** that somehow your action will change the outcome when the outcome has never changed before.

Example:
Action: I yelled at my boyfriend to stop ogling other women.
Result: He stills ogles women and doesn't stop.

Action: _____
_____
_____
_____

Result: _____
_____
_____
_____

Action: _____
_____
_____
_____

Result: _____
_____
_____
_____

CONTINUE USING THIS TEMPLATE.

Learning to Trust and Be Trusted

Hope is the first step in believing that our circumstances can change instead of clinging to broken strategies and tools. Each time we use unproductive tools and strategies, we fail, become discouraged, go back to our addictions, neuroses and dysfunctions in a vicious cycle.

Do we trust ourselves and others? If we don't, that's okay. Trust must be earned. Can we recognize the characteristics of trustworthiness in ourselves and others? How can we recognize when someone is friend or foe? When are we being our own worst enemy? We must develop trust in ourselves and a faith in a Higher Power. How? By seeing what are positive characteristics in a friend, a spouse, a partner and how we need to view ourselves. Another person is being trustworthy when they:

- Honor your choices
- Consider your viewpoint
- Empathize with your feelings, situation, and/or crisis
- Listen and are receptive to your ideas, plans and goals
- Accommodate your growth
- Nurture your positive changes
- Accept you as you are
- Approve of you
- Offer encouragement
- Support your decisions
- Offer advice and direction when asked
- Praise your efforts at change
- Champion your cause
- Defend against your detractors

Go through this list and imagine how it would feel if you treated yourself in this manner. Can you ask for these things from another? Ask someone to give you something from this list, such as, to accept you as you are or listen and be receptive to your ideas, plans and goals. In this way, in small steps, we can learn to ask for what we need that is reasonable, healthy and appropriate. Be prepared to accept if the answer is "no, I can't give you that."

Today I asked _____ to _____

_____

They responded by: _____

Today I asked _____ to _____

_____

They responded by: _____

How do you treat others? Try taking one item from the list and treat another in this way; such as, considering their viewpoint, or approving of them.

Today, I showed _____ that I could be trusted by: _____

_____

Today, I showed _____ that I could be trusted by: _____

_____

Challenging Belief Systems

There are several types of therapies within the cognitive-behavioral prototype that apply various techniques to change beliefs that are false, destructive or self-limiting. Many of these therapies teach us to challenge our thoughts by asking ourselves whether these thoughts, which form the foundation of our belief system, are actually true.

The following are common mental and cognitive distortions:

1) **Black and white thinking**: A person applies an all or nothing perspective. If someone doesn't say hello, then that person *hates* you. If you make a mistake, then you're a loser.
2) **Overgeneralization**: Seeing a single negative event or behavior as a never-ending occurrence. A fight or argument as "We'll never get along."
3) **Mental filter:** Obsessing on only the negative event or detail and excluding any positives.
4) **Disqualifying the Positive**: Rejecting a positive experience as being a *fluke* and not counting for some non-relevant or vague reason, and thereby, maintaining a negative attitude. "Oh, I got a promotion, but that's because Alice quit last month. She was supposed to get this promotion, not me."
5) **Catastrophizing or minimization**: Exaggerating or minimizing a situation or someone's actions. Seeing things worse than they are or better than they are. Not seeing reality correctly.
6) **Jumping to conclusions:** Thinking that you know what is going on even though you may not have all the facts.
   • **Mind-reading:** Assume that you know what another is thinking.
   • **Fortune-Teller Error**: Anticipating the worse of a situation or person.
7) **"Should" or "must" statements:** Instead of applying a pro-active stance, we beat ourselves up with statements that hold us hostage to a certain kind of pre-ordained behavior or hold others to a standard that we create in our minds. "He should have been more polite." These kinds of statements anger and frustrate us.
8) **Emotional reasoning:** Letting negative emotions determine the truth about something, rather than realizing that emotions are fleeting and can be modified with correct logic and perception about a situation or person. You feel it, therefore it must be true.
9) **Labeling & Mislabeling:** Attaching a negative label on yourself or others. Extreme form of overgeneralization. Highly colored and emotionally charged descriptions of others, yourself or situations.
10) **Personalization:** Perceiving that you are at fault over a situation which is not your responsibility.

Over the years these thought styles become ingrained. We must learn to challenge these erroneous beliefs by countering them with more logical, rational ones. In the following exercise, write out your thought then challenge the thought that fuels the belief.

Example:

<u>My negative thought</u>: If I tell my husband the truth about my addiction, he'll leave me.

<u>My cognition distortion:</u> Jumping to conclusions – mind reading & fortune telling.

<u>Is this thought true?</u> No, I really don't know what will happen. He might get very angry, but I don't know if he'll divorce me.

<u>Where is the evidence that this thought and subsequent belief is true?</u> There is no evidence, because I've told my husband some unpleasant things before and he hasn't left me.

Please write each negative thought you have during the course of the day. Then examine each thought for cognitive distortions of the past. Challenge each negative thought as in the example.

My negative thought: _____

_____

_____

What cognitive distortion could this be? _____

_____

Is this thought true? _____

_____

_____

_____

Where is the evidence that this thought and subsequent belief is true? _____

_____

_____

_____

_____

CONTINUE TO USE THIS TEMPLATE FOR OTHER NEGATIVE THOUGHTS.

<u>*Positive Affirmations*</u>

As you see how your negative beliefs are being repeated in your mind, perhaps it becomes apparent that you can use positive affirmations to counteract these automatic negative thoughts (ANTS) that come from our conscious and subconscious fears and anxieties.

Negative thought: I am a terrible person:

Affirmation: I, _____, am a kind and loving person.

Negative thought: I don't deserve anything good to happen.

Affirmation: I, _____, deserve all good things.

                      (Put your name in the blank) Now you try it.

Negative thought: _____
_____

Affirmation: _____
_____

Negative thought: _____
_____

Affirmation: _____
_____

CONTINUE WITH THIS EXERCISE IN YOUR JOURNAL.

Some other helpful ideas would be:

- Write out your positive affirmations many times.
- Sing your affirmations.
- Record your affirmations and play them back.
- Look into the mirror and tell yourself, "I love you."

These suggestions are only the beginning. Many wonderful books are out there on affirmations. I am giving you an introduction so that you understand how the concept interfaces with your 12 Step program.

Getting in Touch with a Higher Power

Many of our ideas about God originate from our families, schools, churches and communities. Our beliefs may stem from our background or we may have renounced those beliefs. Our families may have not been religious or spiritual. It is important to examine our beliefs about God and how they affect our lives today.

What did your primary caregiver think about God, faith, religion, or spirituality?

_____
_____
_____
_____
_____
_____

How much of what they believed do you still believe?

_____
_____
_____
_____
_____
_____

How are your beliefs different from their beliefs?

_____
_____
_____
_____
_____
_____

From what other sources did you get your beliefs about God, faith, religion, or spirituality?
Example: school, church, neighbor, etc.

_____
_____
_____
_____
_____
_____

How much of what they believed do you still believe?

_____
_____
_____
_____
_____
_____

How are your beliefs different from their beliefs?

_____
_____
_____
_____
_____
_____

Challenging Our Beliefs About God

Old ideas about God or a Higher Power may influence your conscious or subconscious mind. We are at a crossroads in our lives where belief that a Power greater than ourselves can restore us to sanity can mean the difference between life or death.

We can explore and challenge our beliefs about God just as we do any other beliefs by using exercises in the previous Sections. Where are the facts or evidence that makes this true? Makes it false? Who really knows? Does it hurt me to believe in a Power greater than myself? Does it help me to believe in a Power greater than myself?

In the next few days, write down what you feel about God, during the course of the day. Do you find yourself praying or thinking about a more spiritual life for yourself as an answer to your dilemma?

_____
_____
_____
_____
_____
_____
_____
_____
_____
_____
_____

If you believed a Higher Power could restore you to sanity, what would this Higher Power be like for you? Write out your description of your perfect Higher Power. It can be your 12 Step Group, the Sun, the Moon, or the Stars. Anything that helps you feel connected to a Higher Power. What does your Higher Power do for you? How does It respond to you?

_____
_____
_____
_____

_____
_____
_____
_____
_____
_____
_____
_____
_____
_____

If God/Higher Power loves you unconditionally, then what kind of plans would God/Higher Power have for you?

_____
_____
_____
_____
_____
_____
_____
_____
_____
_____
_____
_____
_____

STEP THREE EXERCISES

It may, or may not, become apparent what God's Will is for you. My sponsor once said that when something is God's Will, and not my own misdirected will, events move toward God's purpose for your life *like ball bearings and butter*. However, in early sobriety, we often fight for dominance and control over people, places and things, disrupting any hope for serenity or peace of mind.

You vs. Them

Please list the situations where your will and other people's will clash.

I clash with/over/about: _____

_____

_____

_____

Who usually wins the battle? _____

Does this resolve the issue? _____

If no, what happens after that? _____

_____

_____

_____

If you were to pray and turn it over to your Higher Power, what would this feel like or look like?

_____

_____

_____

_____

_____

I clash with/over/about: _____
_____
_____
_____

Who usually wins the battle? _____

Does this resolve the issue? _____

If no, what happens after that? _____
_____
_____
_____
_____

If you were to pray and turn it over to your Higher Power, what would this feel like or look like?
_____
_____
_____
_____
_____

CONTINUE THIS EXERCISE, AS NEEDED, IN YOUR JOURNAL.

Self-Will Run Riot

When is it our own *best* thinking? List situations, events, persons or beliefs in your life that exemplify *self-will run riot*.

Example:
Continuing to make love with an unfaithful partner – risking contracting a sexually transmitted infection or disease.
_____
_____
_____
_____
_____
_____
_____
_____

_____
_____
_____
_____
_____
_____

Unreasonable Expectations

Your serenity will be directly linked to your expectations. The more expectations you harbor, openly or secretly, the more you will undermine your peace of mind. Yes, I wish for certain conditions. If married, I wish my mate to respect me, but if they don't, how can I expect them to change? Something must change in me. This is the only power I have. I can choose to leave this person or accept that they don't respect me. When I realize my choices do not include changing my partner over whom I have no power, then I can stop all the lying, manipulation, selling out my integrity, threatening and other forms of coercion to get the other person to do it my way.

Please make a list of expectations that you have regarding people, places and things in your life. Examine these and determine whether these are reasonable expectations.

I expect: _____
_____
_____
_____

I expect: _____
_____
_____
_____

I expect: _____
_____
_____
_____

Unreasonable Dependencies Upon Another

Along with unrealistic expectations, we have burdensome dependency needs. People are human and will fail us at some point or another. How do we handle this? With anger? Depression?

Resentment? Self-pity? Please write out examples of your over-dependence upon others for your well-being and serenity and determine how you feel when these dependency needs are not met.

I need: _____
_____
_____
_____
_____

When I don't get what I need, I feel: _____
_____
_____
_____
_____

I need: _____
_____
_____
_____
_____

When I don't get what I need, I feel: _____
_____
_____
_____
_____

I need: _____
_____
_____
_____
_____

When I don't get what I need, I feel: _____
_____
_____
_____
_____

CONTINUE THE ABOVE EXERCISES, AS NEEDED, IN YOUR JOURNAL.

Who or What Did You Make God Today?

To whom, or what, do you normally turn your life and will over to? Such as partner, job, boss, lover, father, mother, friend, husband, drugs, alcohol, pornography, or any other abnormal attachment to a material thing, person or place.

Person, place or thing I turn my life and my will over to: _____
_____
_____

What happens when I turn it over to this person, place or thing?
_____
_____
_____
_____

How do I feel about that? _____
_____
_____
_____

Is there something else I could do? _____
_____
_____
_____
_____

Person, place or thing I turn my life and my will over to: _____
_____
_____

What happens when I turn it over to this person, place or thing?
_____
_____
_____
_____

How do I feel about that? _____
_____
_____
_____

Is there something else I could do? _____
_____
_____
_____
_____

CONTINUE THIS EXERCISE, AS NEEDED, IN YOUR JOURNAL.

Turning Point – How Bad Is It? How Bad Does It Have to Get?

Please name the problem and decide how bad it is. Bad enough to get help? Bad enough to stop engaging in that behavior? This is how we can ***hit bottom*** with ourselves and realize that life can be so much better when we get out of the driver's seat.

Problem: _____
_____
_____
_____
_____

How bad is it? _____
_____
_____
_____
_____

Could it get worse? _____

What would this problem or behavior look like if it got worse? _____
_____
_____
_____
_____

How can you stop this problem or behavior now? _____
_____
_____
_____

Problem: _____
_____

_____

How bad is it? _____

_____

Could it get worse? _____

What would this problem or behavior look like if it got worse? _____

_____

How can you stop this problem or behavior now? _____

_____

Turning It Over

List those people, places or things that you can _**turn over**_ to God today.

I am turning over: _____

_____

I am turning over: _____

_____

I am turning over: _____

_____

Your Higher Power's Will

There might be things that you have left undone that continue to cause unnecessary chaos in your life. Your Higher Power wants you to experience peace, harmony and serenity. What do you need to do to make that happen? Each day make a list (as below) for yourself so you can stay on course, turning over your life and will to the care of your Higher Power.

Example:
God's Will for me today is: Going to my 12 step meetings every day.
God's Will for me today is: Getting a job to be self-supporting through my own contributions.

God's Will for me today is: _____
_____

God's Will for me today is: _____
_____

God's Will for me today is: _____
_____

CONTINUE TO USE THE ABOVE TEMPLATES AS NEEDED.

Sacredness

Take a moment to think about those things that are sacred to you and make you feel as if you are one with the Universe. Choose an activity or make quiet time to get in touch with your HP.

Example:
When I listen to a CD of soothing spiritual music
Bonding with my child
Laughing with my husband

STEP FOUR EXERCISES

Before we begin our 4th Step, we take time to reflect and pray for guidance from our Higher Power having faith that we are being gently shown the error of our ways. We must make a searching and fearless look at ourselves. We then examine the morality and integrity of our past actions and decisions. Many times, our perspectives and decisions were most likely self-serving.

Character Defects & Assets

In our quest for honesty and humility, we are called upon to recognize where our instincts have gone awry and mutated into more grievous character flaws. These defects are moral blind spots that have chipped away at our ability to discern the true nature of our condition. We are working toward a balanced perspective of ourselves and others that will become more apparent as we delve deeper into the Fourth Step. We are never going to achieve perfection

To begin the process, we need a comparison of both positive and negative traits that will either assist in our spiritual growth, or hamper our development. The most glaring character defects will be quite obvious to those who know us best. To become more intimate with ourselves, the good, the bad and the ugly, we need to understand our character – defects and assets.

The list below is fairly comprehensive and will be used for work in the 4th, 5th, 6th and 7th Steps. This list is for reference purposes as we move through the inventory process.

CHARACTER DEFECTS	CHARACTER ASSETS
Fearful	Trustworthy
Resentful	Honest
Over-dependent	Modest
Egoistic	Fair
Self-seeking	Generous
Sell-out of principles and values	Cheerful
Angry	Kind
Irritable	Humble
Easily frustrated	Sincere
Worried	Helpful
Moody/Temperamental	Competent
Sense of entitlement	Open to learning new things
Passive-aggressive	Prudent
Sarcastic	Temperate
Critical	Courteous
Arrogant	Courageous
Lazy	Selfless
Uses profanity	Hopeful
Judgmental	Faithful
Selfish	Industrious
Dishonest	Grateful
Procrastinating	Accountable
Bigoted	Responsible
Jealous	Charitable
Envious	Compassionate
Lustful	Just
Impatient	Patient
Revengeful	Dependable
Grandiose	Mature
Conceited	Forgiving
Remorseless	Persistent in the face of obstacles
Irresponsible	Loyal
Undependable	Punctual
Self-Pitying	Non-Judgmental
Perfectionistic	Speaking good of others
Obsessive	Empathetic
Shameless	Nurturing
Overly sensitive	Comforting
Blind to others rights & boundaries	Respectful of others' boundaries
Disrespectful to others	Receptive listener
Bully	Supportive
Assassinating others' characters	Accepting
Self-Righteous	Perseverant
Fiscally irresponsible	Fiscally responsible
Closed off to others	Willing to be vulnerable

The truth is that these defects and assets, and how they are applied in our daily interactions with others, will not only determine our moral progress, but have a great deal to do with how good we feel about ourselves, how we navigate in our relationships, and determine, to a great degree, how successful our lives will become. Our stumbling blocks, in the form of character defects, are ways that we sabotage our lives.

Fear Inventory

We make a list of our fears. Fear is useful to us as humans, sounding the alarm of danger, giving us the strength and adrenaline to run from threats. Fear is reasonable under these circumstances. However, our fears can also have no basis in fact. From a vague feeling of unease, to an overwhelming sense of impending doom, we must understand our fears in the light of our new criteria. Are these real fears, or are these fears rooted in selfishness, dishonesty, self-absorption, or self-seeking? Have we really sought a solution to the problems that generate fear? The more you are in fear, the less you walk in faith. Bringing the darkness of your fears to the light, examining them under the microscope of your newfound faith, will help you grow in a solid foundation of reliance upon your Higher Power.

Staying sober/recovery	Health
Children	Financial matters
Abandonment	Rejection
What others think	Getting older
Relationship	Losing my spouse
Losing control	Not performing sexually
Not having enough	Others taking advantage
Work	

Listed above are just some of the fears that dominate our lives. Please fill in the blanks with other fears not on the above list as you elaborate upon your greatest fears and how these fears impact your life:

My fear is: _____

_____

This fear impacts my life by: _____

_____

_____

_____

My fear is: _____
_____

This fear impacts my life by: _____
_____
_____
_____
_____

CONTINUE THE ABOVE EXERCISES, AS NEEDED, IN YOUR JOURNAL.

What Can I Do About My Fears and Anxieties?

Begin a pro-active campaign to name the fears and address them with practical solutions, or in the event the fears are not solvable at this time, with acceptance. In the 3rd Step Workbook Section, we recognized cognition distortions and how to challenge fear-producing thoughts. Incorporate those techniques for use with this exercise.

Example:
I am anxious about my boss's behavior. He doesn't seem to like me and I'm afraid I'll lose my job. **My anxiety causes** me to stay up nights worrying. **I can alleviate my anxiety** by turning the problem over to my Higher Power, doing the best I can on the job, and asking for feedback from my boss about my job performance.

I am anxious about:_____
_____
_____
_____
_____

My anxiety causes me to: _____
_____
_____
_____
_____

What can I do to alleviate my anxiety? _____
_____
_____
_____
_____

I am anxious about: _____

_____

_____

_____

_____

My anxiety causes me to: _____

_____

_____

_____

_____

What can I do to alleviate my anxiety? _____

_____

_____

_____

_____

Is there a solution to the problem that generates fear? If not, can I let go and let God? Can I accept my fear and live with it? Challenge my fear with cognitive strategies? Use affirmations to manifest conditions I want in my life? You must identify how your fears mutate into destructive behaviors and pray for guidance to eliminate these negative responses to your fear.

What's Your Motive?

You are now going to get in touch with your self-seeking agendas. You will write out a situation in your life that makes you uncomfortable, where you have conflict with another, or when you are doing something for an ulterior motive.

Example:

Situation: Going to the family function even though I get into a fight with my mom every time.

Hidden
Agenda: My dad's real sick and I don't want him to cut me out of his will like he keeps threatening. If I stay away, my brothers will say bad things about me behind my back and influence my dad.

Motive: I'm not really going to see my dad because I love him even though I do love him. We haven't resolved our issues and I'd like to confront him about how he's treated me badly through the years, but I'm afraid he'll get mad and cut me out of the will. **Self-seeking, dishonest, afraid**.

Situation: Alice puts my sister Cindy down all the time.

Hidden   I don't want to get involved because it puts me in an awkward position because if
Agenda   I stick up for Cindy then Alice gets mad at me.

Motive: I need Alice more than I need Cindy. Alice gives me money for drugs and
lets me crash on her couch sometimes. **<u>Selfish and self-seeking. Dishonest.</u>**

Motives could have been for different reasons – like jealousy of Cindy for accomplishments; or better Cindy than me. Use your 4th step notebook to continue writing about the situations in the past where you had motives directed by fear, self-seeking, selfishness and dishonesty. For each circumstance or situation, please also write out <u>several resolutions</u> for each problem wherein you can regain your integrity, even if it means **<u>getting honest, getting humble and asking forgiveness, taking responsibility for your actions, reviewing your value system, etc</u>**.

Situation: _____
_____
_____
_____

Hidden Agenda: _____
_____
_____
_____

Motive: _____
_____
_____
_____

How can this be resolved? _____
_____
_____
_____
_____

Situation: _____
_____
_____
_____

Hidden Agenda: _____

_____

_____

_____

Motive: _____

_____

_____

_____

How can this be resolved? _____

_____

_____

_____

CONTINUE USING THESE TEMPLATES FOR MOTIVES & HIDDEN AGENDAS.

Resentments

Next, we are going to learn to examine how thoughts, words and/or actions in our past have set up present circumstances that make us angry, resentful and self-pitying. Remember that every action has a reaction, either negative or positive. We can waste enormous amounts of time trying to blame someone else for what could have been prevented if we had taken responsibility for ourselves. We could also make peace with and accept our circumstances.

You have two options as the format for this inventory. The Big Book uses a column system, which is illustrated below, or you can fill in the blanks provided as a template. For each incident resulting in a resentment and anger on your part, write out in detail who/what you resent, the cause of your resentment, and what this resentment/anger has affected.

Each resentment affected the following: **self-esteem (ego), finances, ambitions, personal relationships, security, sexual relationships, or pride. Please also indicate whether these threats are the result of fear and include this for each resentment alongside initial threat.**

Use either format to write out **EACH RESENTMENT/ANGER for EACH PERSON, PLACE, OR INSTITUTION** that you harbor. You may have 20 separate resentments for one person (you might have had a long-term relationship), or an institution that angers you like the government (my personal favorite).

I resent:	Reason for my Resentment	Affects My:
My employer	He fired me for no reason.	Finances: (fear) I can't pay my bills without a job. Self-esteem (ego): I feel like a loser. I'm depressed. Security: (fear) I own a home and need the income. I'm afraid I might not find another job.

Your templates:

I resent:	Reason for my Resentment	Affects My:

Example:
I resent my employer because he fired me for no reason.

This affects my finances (fear) because I can't pay my bills without a job.
This affects my self-esteem because I feel like a loser.
This affects my security (fear) because I own a home and need the income.

I resent _____ because _____
_____
_____
_____
_____
_____

This affected my: _____
_____
_____
_____
_____
_____

I resent _____ because _____
_____
_____
_____
_____
_____

This affected my: _____
_____
_____
_____
_____
_____

I resent _____ because _____
_____
_____
_____
_____
_____

This affected my: _____

_____

_____

_____

_____

_____

Resolving Resentments

As you examine each resentment look deeply for what fuels the resentment, such as fear, selfishness, self-centeredness, and dishonesty.

Look over the Character Defects list and determine if expressing a defect, such as greed or jealousy, resulted in someone else's negative behavior or attitude towards you. Perhaps you were fiscally irresponsible and your roommates kicked you out of the apartment for non-payment of rent. You may resent them for that, however you set these circumstances into motion by not paying your rent. We must get honest with ourselves about any behaviors that contributed to the subsequent resentment we have towards another.

Write down any Character Defects that contributed to your resentment. Be honest.

Example: Getting Fired
This resentment is a result of my FEAR. Fear that I won't be able to get another job and pay my bills. Then, I look for where I contributed to my getting fired. Could I have done something differently? Did I get to my job on time every day? Did I give 100% to my job? Did I do the job to the best of my ability?

My wrongdoing: I was late a lot of the time, I took extra time for lunch and was out sick many times. My character defects: laziness, dishonesty, procrastination and sense of entitlement.

If I did nothing wrong that I can see, then I realize that having a resentment keeps me from my greatest good. I can then go about looking for another job leaving the results in God's hand.

In any event, our resentments keep us angry and fired up. If we truly want peace and serenity, we're going to have to practice letting go of our resentments.

***CONTINUE WRITING OUT RESENTMENTS IN YOUR 4TH STEP NOTEBOOK.
FOLLOW WITH THE SECTION RESOLVING RESENTMENTS.***

Parenting Inventory

As a parent, we have a responsibility to our children. Children don't ask to be brought into the world and have no choice about who will raise them. Children love their parents no matter what, even if they have been abused, abandoned, or neglected. How have you handled your responsibility toward your child(ren)? Answer the questions below, if applicable.

When you were using or drinking did you expose your child(ren) to unnecessary harm or emotionally damaging scenarios?

Did your child(ren) ever see you doing your addiction and/or dysfunctional behavior?

Has this behavior affected your child(ren) and how?

Have you used your child(ren) as an emotional sounding board when going through tough times, thereby robbing them of their childhood?

Did you give your child(ren) too much information, or information that only an adult can handle?

Have you neglected the care of your child(ren)?

Have you taken responsibility for your child(ren) by giving them nutritional food and other care they (s/he) needed?

Have you accused your child(ren) of being like his or her father/mother (the person you dislike)?

Have you guilted your child(ren) into being with you when s/he wanted to be with the other parent?

Have you used your child(ren) to gain sympathy for your plight or situation?

Have you violated the boundaries of your child(ren) when intruding upon them inappropriately, i. e. reading their diary, hugging them when they didn't want to, teasing or embarrassing them, criticizing, or using sarcasm to belittle them?

Have you been inappropriately permissive and letting the child(ren) get out of control because it was too much trouble to discipline and correct your child(ren)?

Have you spent quality time with your child(ren)?

Do you contribute financially to the care of your child(ren)?

Have you left the care of your children to other people?

Do you have contact with your child?

Do you let your child know s/he is loved and not to blame for your problems, dysfunctions and/or addictions?

The above questions give you a starting point in examining your role as a parent, if so indicated.

WRITE YOUR ANSWERS IN YOUR 4ᵀᴴ STEP JOURNAL. CREATE A PICTURE OF HOW YOU HAVE PARENTED YOUR CHILDREN FOR USE IN THE 5ᵀᴴ STEP. DETERMINE WHERE YOU HAVE BEEN DISHONEST, AFRAID, SELFISH OR SELF-SERVING.

Financial Inventory

As in other matters, when addicted or dysfunctional it is common to go astray in financial matters. In some instances, we are going to have to pay money back or make financial amends further down the road. In order to get a clearer picture of what our financial transgressions were, please answer any questions below, as they pertain to you and describe in detail, what happened and how you behaved irresponsibly:

Have I borrowed money that I didn't intend to pay back?
Have I been a spendthrift, spending money I didn't have?
Have I gambled away other people's money and asked for more?
Have I gotten myself into debt?
Have I put another person in debt?
Have I shared appropriately what I have with my spouse and/or children and family?
Have I been miserly, keeping my family in financial insecurity?
Have I kept my job to support my family when necessary?
Have I shirked financial responsibility?
Have I been irresponsible with the family finances?
Do I take care of financial business, such as paying bills on time, or other bills and financial obligations, such as child support?

ELABORATE EACH ANSWER IN YOUR JOURNAL.

Sexual Inventory

We are all sexual beings. We are defined by our gender, and children often start acting according to gender roles as early as 3 years old. Society has many different ways of perceiving the genders, some of it negative, and some of it positive. Our goal in taking our sexual inventory is to find where we have used our sexuality, our sexual desires, needs and wants in a negative or hurtful way to others, and sometimes to ourselves. If applicable to you, please answer the following questions and describe what happened as it pertains to your sexual behavior.

Have I taken the necessary precautions to protect myself from pregnancy and/or STIs and HIV?
Did I ever infect someone with STI or HIV?
Did I get someone pregnant and refuse to take responsibility?
In my pursuit of sexual release, have I violated the boundaries of another by coercion?
Have I ever used violence to get sexual release?
Have I ignored the rights of others?
Have I ever used force to get another to submit to having sex with me?
Have I ever molested a child or adolescent?
Have I been unfaithful to my partner?

Have I used sex to procure other non-sexual favors, such as money, power, a better job, promotions, or other material gain?

Have I exploited someone's vulnerability to gain sexual favors?

Have I had sex when I wanted love?

Have I used sex manipulatively to get someone to care for me?

Do I look at pornography obsessively?

Do I masturbate excessively?

Do I go to strip clubs and get lap dances?

Am I honest with sexual partners about my intentions?

Have I flirted inappropriately?

Have I been sexually provocative to make someone jealous?

Have I been sexually provocative to get undue attention?

Did I use sex to get love? attention? make someone jealous? get revenge?

These are very important and serious issues. If you have a sexual addiction, you might look at pornography obsessively, keeping this from your loved ones, in effect, being dishonest. You are then taking your partner's choice by withholding vital information (lying) to them.

Please go over your sexual history and answer the questions posed to you above. If there are more serious charges against you, i.e. forcing someone to have sex with you or rape, then you will have to write out these occasions and be willing to make amends in some way. Obviously, if you are a criminal, in order to change you will have to tell your sponsor, ask for guidance from your Higher Power, and not engage in this behavior again. If you feel you can't stop yourself, then you will have to turn yourself in to the authorities.

The behavior: _____
_____
_____
_____

Who was hurt? _____
_____
_____

Where were you wrong? _____
_____
_____
_____
_____
_____
_____
_____

Again, we describe how we were *fearful, selfish, dishonest and/or self-serving*.

CONTINUE USING THE TEMPLATE FOR FURTHER ELABORATION.

Deep, Dark Secrets

We have a saying in AA, that "we are only as sick as our secrets." This is now the time to write out what those secrets might be. This is important to relieve us from the burden of carrying around this darkness.

_____
_____
_____
_____
_____
_____
_____
_____
_____
_____
_____
_____
_____
_____
_____
_____
_____

Positive Inventory

We are both darkness and light. We have done terrible things to ourselves and sometimes to others. We may have hurt ourselves and others, but we have also done good things. There are positive things in our inventory of ourselves, and we are going to enumerate them for ourselves and for our sponsor when we share our 5th Step.

List 5 good things you have done for others:

1) _____
_____
_____
_____
_____
_____
_____

2) _____

3) _____

4) _____

5) _____

List 20 good things about yourself:

1) _____

2) _____

3) _____

4) _____

5) _____

6) _____

7) _____

8) _____

9) _____

10) _____

11) _____

12) _____

13) _____

14) _____

15) _____

16) _____

17) _____

18) _____

19) _____

20) _____

STEP FIVE EXERCISES

Preparation for 5th Step:

It is now essential for you to examine any reservations you have in revealing your innermost self, flaws, problems, secrets, fears, hatreds, bigotries, bad acts, selfishness, or resentments to another person.

Please list any fears or reservations you have about making your 5th Step:

_____
_____
_____
_____
_____
_____
_____
_____
_____
_____
_____
_____
_____
_____
_____

What qualities are most important in the person with whom you share your 5th Step?

_____
_____
_____
_____
_____
_____
_____

_____

_____

_____

Do you have a particular person in mind with whom to share your 5th Step?

Yes _____   No _____

STEP SIX EXERCISES

Though we might not be ready to have **all** our character defects removed, we must cultivate our willingness to look at those areas of our life that are self-limiting and irresponsible. Willingness is the key concept of Six Step. Recognizing when we are expressing negative character traits requires deeper insight into the mechanics of our behaviors and how they affect others. It seems that once we surrender certain moral shortcomings, we are presented with available options for spiritual and emotional growth.

Character Defects & Character Assets

For this next exercise, refer to the list of Character Defects & Assets in Workbook Section in Step Four. Please list some of your Character Defects:

Defect: _____

How do you feel about this defect? _____

_____

_____

_____

Do you have objections to letting this go? _____

If yes, why? _____

_____

_____

_____

How has this defect helped you? Or hurt you? _____

_____

_____

_____

_____

_____

Has this defect hurt others? _____
_____
_____
_____
_____

What Character Asset could you use to replace this? _____

How would you go about using this new Asset? _____
_____
_____
_____

In what situations? _____
_____
_____

With whom? _____
_____
_____
_____

How do you feel about this? Awkward? Empowered? _____
_____
_____
_____

CONTINUE TO USE THIS TEMPLATE FOR EACH CHARACTER DEFECT THAT CAN BE TRANSFORMED INTO A CHARACTER ASSET.

Self-Sabotage

> *Character defects are persistent self-defeating patterns that,*
> *once admitted and accepted, can be alleviated by*
> *the work of the recovery process and God's intervention.*

What conditions in your life are a direct result of self-sabotage because you continue to practice certain character defects?

Example:

I procrastinated and missed a job opportunity because I didn't call in time to get an interview for the job.

Character Defect: Procrastination
Result: Didn't try to get interview
Why did I Self-Sabotage: I don't feel worthy of getting a job that I might enjoy

Parenting presents its own set of problems and characteristics, such as disciplinary actions, spending quality time with children, giving them a sense of belonging and self-respect, among many other things that parents impart to their children.

Character Defect: Letting my children get away with bad behavior
Result: Children are out of control
Why did I self-sabotage: Overwhelmed and compensating for divorce

Character Defect: _____

Result: _____
_____
_____
_____

Why did I self-sabotage: _____
_____
_____
_____
_____
_____
_____
_____

Character Defect: _____

Result: _____
_____
_____
_____

Why did I self-sabotage: _____

_____

_____

_____

_____

_____

_____

_____

_____

CONTINUE TO USE THIS TEMPLATE FOR EACH CHARACTER DEFECT THAT CONTRIBUTES TO SELF-SABOTAGE.

Hitting a Bottom In Sobriety

Sometimes, our self-defeating patterns are so destructive to our lives that we hit a bottom in sobriety. Some of our behaviors result from past, unresolved issues that surface time and time again and are resistant to change. It is important to examine these problem behaviors to determine if they jeopardize your sobriety and if they signal that you are hitting a bottom in sobriety. These issues need to be acknowledged and processed.

Have I hit a bottom in sobriety? Yes _____   No _____

If you've hit a bottom in sobriety, please describe the self-defeating characteristic?

_____

_____

_____

_____

_____

_____

_____

How does this self-defeating characteristic harm me?

_____

_____

_____

_____

_____

_____

_____

_____

_____

_____

_____

_____

How does this self-defeating characteristic harm others?

_____

_____

_____

_____

_____

_____

_____

_____

_____

_____

_____

Remember, you may revisit this step time and time again as you have other *ah-ha* moments in your recovery. As a newcomer, you may not see that a character defect applies to you or that it sabotages your life.

STEP SEVEN EXERCISES

Humility is the main characteristic needed for successful recovery and we are trying to achieve this attribute by practicing Step Seven. In humbly asking our Higher Power to remove our shortcomings, we need to carefully delineate our character defects, understand how they operate in our life and how they contribute to self-sabotage in our life. However, we may still be resistant to having these negative characteristics removed from fear of the unknown or because of pride We may have deemed that certain characteristics, even though negative, are necessary for living life.

Old Ideas – Pride & Grandiosity

Pride very often keeps you from listening to others. Grandiosity prevents others from getting to know the real you. Old ideas die hard and are resistant to change. You need to examine those times and circumstances when you are exhibiting pride rather than humility "teachability" or when you are being grandiose.

Example:
My pride surfaces when I am being questioned about my decisions.
I can become more teachable by listening to other people's input about my choices.

My pride surfaces when: _____
_____
_____
_____

I can become more teachable by: _____
_____
_____
_____

My pride surfaces when: _____
_____

_____

_____

I can become more teachable by: _____

_____

_____

_____

Grandiosity is exhibited in resistance to letting others in or overreaching our true capabilities by our insistence that we know what's best for us without receiving input from others or our Higher Power. This is a coping skill used by the ego as it protects itself from perceived threats from outside sources. In the course of your recovery, though we might have felt we know better, when has our Higher Power revealed a different course of action?

I felt I knew what was best for me when: _____

_____

_____

_____

More was revealed when: _____

_____

_____

_____

I felt I knew what was best for me when: _____

_____

_____

_____

More was revealed when: _____

_____

_____

_____

Humility

How have you become more humble in your life today?

I have become more humble by: _____

_____

_____

I have become more humble by: _____
_____
_____

I have become more humble by: _____
_____
_____

Removal of Addiction

We are a work in progress, surrendering to God's will at times and then backsliding into our own ideas. However, the most important character defect that must be removed is our addiction/ dysfunctional behavior/destructive neuroses.

Did you ask God to remove your addiction/dysfunctional behavior/destructive neuroses?
_____

How do you feel your Higher Power responded to that plea? _____
_____
_____
_____
_____

Removal of Character Defects

How have you assisted your Higher Power in removing certain obstinate character defects from your life?

Example: Going to meetings every day. Avoiding those with whom I used drugs and/or alcohol. Getting a sponsor. Praying. Doing positive affirmations.

I helped my Higher Power remove my character defects by: _____
_____
_____

I helped my Higher Power remove my character defects by: _____
_____
_____

I helped my Higher Power remove my character defects by:_____

_____

_____

_____

7ᵗʰ Step Prayer

*My Creator, I am now willing that you should have all of me
good and bad. I pray that you now remove from me
every single defect of character that stands in the way
of my usefulness to you and other people.
Grant me strength, as I go out from here,
to do your bidding. Amen.*

STEP EIGHT EXERCISES

Our defense mechanisms can keep us from making amends to those we have harmed. As we familiarize ourselves with Step Eight, we must explore those areas of denial about our resentments, anger and lack of accountability. This resistance perpetuates destructive cycles. We begin with an examination of our feelings.

Step Eight reveals our conscience in dealing with others, tests our ability to make an honest assessment, listing those we have harmed and our willingness to make amends. Step Nine actually has us making these amends.

Feelings About Amends Process

Please refer to your ***FEELINGS LIST*** on Page 155 and make a list of the painful feelings, or other reasons, that prevents your willingness to make amends:

Example:

I feel angry about making amends. My other reasons for being reluctant are: It doesn't seem fair that I didn't do hardly anything, but it got so complicated and I don't know how to do it. It seems so unfamiliar to me. It'll all blow over like it always does. They don't remember that I even did that. . . etc., etc., etc.

I feel _____ about making amends. My other reasons for being reluctant are: _____

_____

_____

_____

I feel _____ about making amends. My other reasons for being reluctant are: _____

_____

_____

_____

CONTINUE USING THIS TEMPLATE AS IT APPLIES TO YOUR RESISTANCE

<u>*Why You Need to Become Willing to Make Amends*</u>

Example:
I need to continue to clear up the wreckage of my past.
I need to feel clean again.
I need to resolve these issues before I can move on.

_____
_____
_____
_____
_____
_____
_____
_____
_____
_____
_____
_____
_____
_____
_____
_____
_____
_____

<u>*Reviewing the 4ᵗʰ Step*</u>

If we have done our inventory thoroughly, we have recognized that those who have harmed us were emotionally, mentally, and spiritually disturbed and that we also suffered from similar afflictions. However, we must go farther than mere acknowledgement. Some steps are contemplative and some steps are action steps. The 8ᵗʰ Step helps us to discover ourselves as fallible beings capable of harming others even when there is no intention to do so. Please list those peoples, places and institutions to whom we caused harm by our selfishness, self-seeking, manipulation, fear, dishonesty, prejudice, intolerance, impatience, bigotry, pride anger/rage and resentments:

Example:
My <u>prejudice</u> caused pain to <u>my co-worker, Lorraine,</u> by <u>gossiping behind her back about her son that got arrested for drug possession</u>. This happened <u>approximately 4 years ago,</u> and <u>since I don't work at this place anymore we don't speak</u>, but I feel <u>bad</u> that I did that. I want to <u>correct this wrong I did</u>. I plan on doing that by <u>writing her a note and apologizing for my behavior</u>. I expect <u>nothing in return</u>.

My _____ caused pain to _____ by _____
_____
_____.

This happened _____
_____.

I speak/don't speak <u>(why)</u> _____ to _____
_____.

I feel _____. I want to _____.
_____

I plan on _____
_____
_____. I expect _____
_____

My _____ caused pain to _____ by _____
_____
_____.

This happened _____
_____.

I speak/don't speak <u>(why)</u> _____ to _____
_____.

I feel _____. I want to _____.
_____

I plan on _____
_____
_____. I expect _____
_____

CONTINUE TO USE TEMPLATE TO EXAMINE PAIN YOU CAUSED OTHERS.

<u>Resistance</u>

In some instances, we may have reservations and conditions about who does or doesn't deserve amends. Our ego defenses kick in and mount credible arguments in our favor. Please explore your resistance to making certain amends.

The incident: _____
_____
_____
_____

Why it wasn't my fault: _____
_____
_____
_____

Why it was my fault: _____
_____
_____
_____

I am _____ to approach the parties involved and make amends
for my part because _____
_____
_____
_____
_____
_____

The incident: _____
_____
_____
_____

Why it wasn't my fault: _____
_____
_____
_____

Why it was my fault: _____
_____
_____
_____

I am _____ to approach the parties involved and make amends
for my part because _____
_____
_____
_____
_____
_____

CONTINUE TO USE THIS TEMPLATE TO EXPLORE RESISTANCE.

Fixing Others

When have you tried to _**play God**_ and fix others? This can lead to boundary violations, co-dependence, enabling, blaming others for not following your rules and wishes, intolerance of the recovery process in others, and self-serving agendas. If we seek someone else's recovery so our lives can be better, or we want someone to get _**fixed**_ so that they can love us the way we weren't loved by our parents, then we're doing it for the wrong reasons.

Who did I try to _fix_? _____

What were the circumstances? _____
_____
_____
_____

Am I violating his/her boundary? _____

How? _____
_____
_____
_____
_____

What is my _real_ agenda in this matter? _____
_____
_____
_____

How does this help me? _____
_____
_____
_____
_____

How does this help the other person? _____
_____
_____
_____

Is this right course of action? Yes _____   No _____

Do I need to make amends for violating their boundary? Yes _____ No _____

Who did I try to *fix*? _____

What were the circumstances? _____
_____
_____
_____

Am I violating his/her boundary? _____

How? _____
_____
_____
_____
_____

What is my *real* agenda in this matter? _____
_____
_____
_____

How does this help me? _____
_____
_____
_____
_____

How does this help the other person? _____
_____
_____
_____

Is this right course of action? Yes _____ No _____

Do I need to make amends for violating their boundary? Yes _____ No _____

CONTINUE USING THIS TEMPLATE TO EXAMINE OTHER BOUNDARY VIOLATIONS THAT REQUIRE AMENDS.

Examining the Harm Done

We must continue to examine the harm we have done to others, our feelings about what we have done, mixed or otherwise, and how we intend to go about making amends for wrongdoings committed. As you do this exercise, use visualization to imagine the person you need to make amends to.

Please make a list of those persons you have harmed, how they were harmed by you, what you feel about the wrongs done, and what you could do to make amends.

The person I have wronged is: _____

I harmed them by: _____

_____
_____
_____
_____
_____
_____

My feelings about this are: _____

_____
_____
_____
_____
_____
_____

I could make amends by: _____

_____
_____
_____
_____
_____
_____

The person I have wronged is: _____

I harmed them by: _____
_____
_____
_____
_____
_____
_____

My feelings about this are: _____
_____
_____
_____
_____
_____
_____

I could make amends by: _____
_____
_____
_____
_____
_____
_____

CONTINUE TO USE THIS TEMPLATE AS NEEDED.

Harm To Myself

In harming others, you have harmed yourself, eroding your good feelings about who you are and your values. Our standards or values make up the content of our character and when we act in accordance with those values, we build our self-esteem and self-respect. By using drugs, alcohol and engaging in other mind or mood altering behaviors, we have done great harm to ourselves. By remaining co-dependent and tolerating unacceptable relationships, we have harmed ourselves. And there are other ways we have done harm. Please examine some of this harm.

I harmed myself by: _____
_____
_____
_____
_____
_____

How can I make it up to myself? _____
_____
_____
_____
_____
_____

I harmed myself by: _____
_____
_____
_____
_____
_____

How can I make it up to myself? _____
_____
_____
_____
_____
_____

CONTINUE TO USE THIS TEMPLATE AS NEEDED.

Those Affected By My Harming Myself

There were people in your life, or institutions that were affected by your addictions, neuroses, and dysfunctional behaviors. Either those people were frustrated in their attempts to help you, or you pushed them away, or any other number of scenarios occurred as a result of the dysfunction in our life. Please list those who have been affected, how they were affected, what has changed since your recovery, and how you can make amends to those who have been distressed by your behaviors.

The person affected by my dysfunctional behaviors: _____

If they tried to help me, how did I respond? _____
_____
_____
_____

How were they affected by my attitude and behaviors? _____
_____

_____

_____

Have I exploited their good will, exhausted their patience? Describe the nature of your behavior and how it affected your relationship with this person: _____

_____

_____

_____

_____

How am I willing to adjust my attitude toward this person? _____

_____

_____

_____

_____

_____

The person affected by my dysfunctional behaviors: _____

If they tried to help me, how did I respond? _____

_____

_____

_____

How were they affected by my attitude and behaviors? _____

_____

_____

_____

Have I exploited their good will, exhausted their patience? Describe the nature of your behavior and how it affected your relationship with this person: _____

_____

_____

_____

_____

How am I willing to adjust my attitude toward this person? _____

_____

_____

_____

_____

_____

CONTINUE TO USE THIS TEMPLATE AS NEEDED.

Forgiveness

There are those who have harmed us, either unknowingly, or out of their own spiritual and emotional sickness. Holding onto the hurts and resentments toward these people only harms us in the end. Please describe the harm done to you, bearing in mind that you may have harmed them also, and that it is your responsibility to make amends to those people you have harmed.

I felt harmed by: _____

This person harmed me by: _____
_____
_____
_____
_____
_____

If I did forgive this person it would feel: _____
_____
_____
_____
_____
_____

I can forgive this person by: _____
_____
_____
_____
_____
_____

I can forgive this person but I don't want them in my life anymore because: _____
_____
_____
_____
_____
_____

I felt harmed by: _____

This person: _____

_____

_____

_____

_____

_____

If I did forgive this person it would feel: _____

_____

_____

_____

_____

_____

I can forgive this person by: _____

_____

_____

_____

_____

_____

I can forgive this person but I don't want them in my life anymore because: _____

_____

_____

_____

_____

_____

CONTINUE TO USE THIS TEMPLATE AS NEEDED EXPLORING FORGIVENESS.

STEP NINE EXERCISES

Opening ourselves to vulnerability and risking our false pride and ego defenses, we find that we are becoming more available for intimacy with others. However, important relationships may have suffered during our insanity and addiction/dysfunction, and it's time to find out how we are being perceived and repair the damage from past mistakes. To get a realistic perspective of how you affect others, go to those closest to you, even if you sense there are no problems, such as your wife, partner, relatives, children, employer, or others. Please do the following exercise.

Getting Closer to Others

I went to: _____

Their feelings toward me are: _____
_____
_____

Their perception of me is: _____
_____
_____
_____

They said I did/did not harm them: _____
_____
_____
_____
_____

The plans for improving the relationships are: _____
_____
_____
_____
_____
_____

We have resolved our differences by: _____
_____
_____
_____
_____
_____
_____

I went to: _____

Their feelings toward me are: _____
_____
_____

Their perception of me is: _____
_____
_____
_____

They said I did/did not harm them: _____
_____
_____
_____
_____

The plans for improving the relationships are: _____
_____
_____
_____
_____
_____

We have resolved our differences by: _____
_____
_____
_____
_____
_____
_____

CONTINUE TO USE THIS TEMPLATE AS NEEDED.

Investigation

From your 8th Step, you have determined who you have harmed. In some cases you may have harmed one person in several ways. Please list those you have injured or harmed below:

- **<u>Those you have harmed who have not harmed you</u>**

To further elaborate upon those you have harmed, describe this incident and how you will make amends.

Who was harmed? _____

How were they harmed? _____

_____
_____
_____
_____
_____
_____

How do you feel about what you did? _____

_____
_____
_____
_____
_____

How do you intend to make amends? (unless to do so would injure them or others)

_____
_____
_____

What will you say? _____

_____
_____
_____
_____
_____
_____

What will you do? _____

_____

_____

_____

_____

_____

_____

If your amends would injure them, in what other ways can you make amends?
> *Example:*
>> Make restitution anonymously.
>> Donate to a charity in their honor.
>> Pray for this person for 30 days.

_____

_____

_____

_____

Who was harmed? _____

How were they harmed? _____

_____

_____

_____

_____

_____

_____

How do you feel about what you did? _____

_____

_____

_____

_____

_____

How do you intend to make amends? (unless to do so would injure them or others)

_____

_____

_____

What will you say? _____
_____
_____
_____
_____
_____
_____

What will you do? _____
_____
_____
_____
_____
_____
_____

If your amends would injure them or others, in what other ways can you make amends?
> *Example:*
>> Make restitution anonymously.
>> Donate to a charity in their honor.
>> Pray for this person for 30 days.

_____
_____
_____
_____

CONTINUE TO USE THIS TEMPLATE AS NEEDED.

- **<u>Those we have harmed and have also harmed us</u>**

Who was harmed? _____

How were they harmed? _____
_____
_____
_____
_____
_____

How were you harmed? _____

_____

_____

_____

_____

How do you feel about what you did? _____

_____

_____

_____

_____

_____

How do you feel about what they did to you? _____

_____

_____

_____

_____

Will making amends jeopardize our safety? Yes _____ No _____

If yes, in what other ways can you make amends?
> *Example:*
>> Make restitution anonymously.
>> Donate to a charity in their honor.
>> Pray for this person for 30 days.

_____

_____

_____

_____

If no, how do you intend to make amends? (unless to do so would injure them or others)

_____

_____

_____

What will you say? _____

_____

_____

_____

_____

_____

_____

What will you do? _____

_____

_____

_____

_____

_____

_____

CONTINUE TO USE THIS TEMPLATE AS NEEDED.

- **Those who have harmed us and whom we resent**

Resentments are a useless activity that drain our spiritual reserves and eventually cause greater harm to our recovery, perhaps even leading to relapse.

If we've been harmed, how can we overcome our resentment? _____

_____

_____

_____

_____

CONTINUE USING THIS TEMPLATE FOR EACH PERSON YOU RESENT.

- **Those who have done nothing to us and whom we resent**

How can we overcome our resentment? _____

_____

_____

_____

_____

_____

CONTINUE USING THIS TEMPLATE FOR EACH PERSON YOU RESENT.

- **Those who hold a resentment toward me that I have not harmed.**

Who resents me? _____

Could I have provoked this person by my self-righteousness, grandiosity, criticism, selfishness, dishonesty, fear, or other character defect that I was unaware of at the time that triggered their resentment? If yes, please describe what happened:

_____
_____
_____
_____
_____
_____

If no, indicate how you will approach this person in the future: _____

_____
_____
_____
_____

CONTINUE USING THIS TEMPLATE FOR EACH PERSON WHO RESENTS YOU.

- **Those we have harmed but to make amends would injure them**

Use template for ***those we have harmed but have not harmed you***, in particular the section that lists other ways you can make amends without direct contact.

- **Those we have harmed but to make amends would injure others**

Please use the applicable template, indicating how you will make amends without direct contact, releasing damaging information, or making the other person uncomfortable.

How could this amends cause harm to others? _____

_____
_____
_____
_____
_____

- **Those we have harmed, but to make amends would injure ourselves**

How could this amends cause harm to ourselves? _____

_____
_____

_____

_____

_____

_____

Did we consult with our sponsor or spiritual advisor about the nature of the harm done and possible injury to ourselves? Yes _____ No _____

What did our sponsor/spiritual advisor suggest? _____

_____

_____

_____

_____

_____

_____

What do we feel should be done? _____

_____

_____

_____

_____

_____

_____

CONTINUE USING THIS TEMPLATE FOR EACH PERSON HARMED.

- **Those we have harmed but now live far away**

If direct contact is not possible, is it wise to write a letter? Yes _____ No _____

Please outline the major points your letter will address:

_____

_____

_____

_____

_____

_____

_____

_____

_____

_____

CONTINUE USING THIS TEMPLATE FOR EACH PERSON HARMED.

- **Those we have harmed who are now dead but not because of us**

Again, we can write this person a letter and read it aloud.

Please outline the major points your letter will address:

_____
_____
_____
_____
_____
_____
_____
_____
_____
_____

- **Those we have harmed who are now dead because of us**

First, if causing further injury is indicated, we make no direct approach to those affected by the death of their loved one.

Who died because of us? _____
_____
_____

What happened? _____
_____
_____
_____
_____
_____
_____
_____

How do we feel about this? _____
_____
_____
_____
_____
_____

_____
_____
_____

Are there other ways to make amends to the memory or spirit of this person? Please indicate below:

_____
_____
_____
_____
_____
_____
_____
_____
_____
_____

Before and After

To eliminate procrastination, please indicate to whom, when and what you will say for each person you will make direct amends to listed in the prior categories:

I will make amends to: _____
I will make amends on (date): _____
I will tell them: _____
_____
_____
_____
_____
_____
_____
_____

CONTINUE TO USE THIS TEMPLATE AS NEEDED.

After Your Amends

I made amends to: _____

I feel now: _____
_____
_____

_____
_____
_____

They responded: _____
_____
_____
_____
_____
_____

They want me to: _____
_____
_____
_____
_____
_____

I plan to carry out their wishes by: _____
_____
_____
_____
_____
_____
_____
_____

I made amends to: _____

I feel now: _____
_____
_____
_____
_____
_____

They responded: _____
_____
_____
_____

_____

They want me to: _____
_____
_____
_____
_____
_____

I plan to carry out their wishes by: _____
_____
_____
_____
_____
_____
_____
_____

CONTINUE TO USE THIS TEMPLATE AS NEEDED.

Consequences of Making Amends

The possible consequences of my amends are: _____
_____
_____
_____
_____

Who should be told of these consequences? _____
_____
_____

How do I intend to handle these consequences? _____
_____
_____
_____
_____

CONTINUE TO USE THIS TEMPLATE AS NEEDED.

Realizing the Promises

If we have been diligent in our recovery to this point, the Big Book has made some bold statements. Though our lives may not be perfect the work we have accomplished is rewarded with these promises:

THE PROMISES

**We are going to know a new freedom and
a new happiness.**

**We will not regret the past
nor wish to shut the door on it.**

We will comprehend the word serenity.

We will know peace.

**No matter how far down the scale we have gone,
we will see how our experience can benefit others.**

The feelings of uselessness and self-pity will disappear.

**We will lose interest in selfish things and
gain interest in our fellows.**

Self-seeking will slip away.

Our whole attitude and outlook upon life will change.

Fear of people and of economic insecurity will leave us.

We will intuitively know how to handle situations which used to baffle us.

**We will suddenly realize that God is doing for us
what we could not do for ourselves.**

If you feel you have realized some of the promises, write down what they are:

Example: I have realized the promise of knowing intuitively how to handle certain situations. I was confused about how to approach my boss when it dawned on me that he is wondering whether or not I'm planning on leaving. Once I assured him I staying with the job, he seems more relaxed and easier to talk to.

I have realized the promise of: _____

_____

How? _____

_____

_____

_____

_____

_____

_____

I have realized the promise of: _____

_____

How? _____

_____

_____

_____

_____

_____

_____

STEP TEN EXERCISES

You can use any part of these exercises to help you more deeply analyze your motives, intentions, agendas and problem areas. It is suggested that you prepare a Nightly Inventory. A Spot Check Inventory is also available or you can use your own template. It helps to prepare this template beforehand so that it can be available in a timely manner-when your back is up against the wall!

Unfinished Business

Please list those in your family who are resistant to your recovery:

_____
_____
_____
_____
_____

Do some of your present difficulties seem to correspond with how you previously interacted with your family of origin? If so, please explain.

_____
_____
_____
_____
_____
_____
_____
_____
_____

List the recurring patterns: _____
_____
_____
_____

_____
_____
_____
_____

What can you do differently? *Example:* Instead of arguing – I can leave.

_____
_____
_____
_____
_____
_____

Devise a plan to handle difficult family members:

_____
_____
_____
_____
_____
_____
_____
_____

Adaptability

Our ability to adapt is what makes us successful as a human species. Survival equals adaptation. Consider the butterfly or moth that changes its color to match the tree or bush that it lands on to camouflage itself from predators. What does adaptability means to the recovering person? In order to thrive, we must have tools. Some tools are listed below:

Compromise
Listening
Clarification
Support
Removing yourself
Setting new boundaries
Advise of new boundaries
Redefining old boundaries
Acceptable limits of behavior on the part of others
Acceptable limits of behavior on your part
Acceptance of conditions as they are
Forgiveness

Process of Acceptance

What person, place or thing is not acceptable to me right now?

_____
_____
_____

I can't accept this because:_____
_____
_____
_____
_____

My serenity is compromised because: _____
_____
_____
_____

Practice serenity: Sit quietly and imagine accepting these conditions for five minutes.

Can I change myself or these circumstances?   Yes _____   No _____

If yes, outline a plan for change:

_____
_____
_____
_____
_____
_____
_____

Practice manifestation : Sit quietly and imagine yourself changing and in your new circumstances or conditions for five minutes.

Spot Check Inventory

I'M FEELING OK _____   NOT OK _____

WHAT CAN I DO RIGHT NOW TO FEEL BETTER?

<u>Say the Serenity Prayer</u>
God grant me the serenity to accept the things I cannot change
The courage to change the things I can
And the wisdom to know the difference

<u>Other Ideas</u>
Get to a meeting
Call sponsor/spiritual advisor
Take 10 deep breaths
Walk away and say the serenity prayer again
Write out where you veered-off course
Can you make amends or an apology?
Detach yourself from the moment
Imagine that you're at your favorite place
Challenge your prevailing perception
Examine where you might be wrong
Are you being selfish, dishonest or afraid?
Give someone a time-out
Shout "STOP" in your head
Practice acceptance
Listen to soothing music

Since you know your circumstances best, please list other things you might do now that would be appropriate:

_____
_____
_____
_____
_____

IN YOUR EARLY RECOVERY, YOU MIGHT XEROX SEVERAL COPIES OF THIS SEC-
TION AND TAKE ONE WITH YOU EACH DAY.

The Personal Inventory

The personal inventory is directed toward our behavior with others that is predatory, ma-nipulative, selfish, dishonest and fearful. Our relationships cannot flourish nor can we achieve intimacy if we continue practicing old behaviors acknowledged in our 4th Step, but that persist despite our awareness of them. In this exercise, we investigate hidden agendas, motives and reasons behind our seemingly *nice* behavior, *bullying* behavior, or *indifferent* behavior, or any other behavior that is calculated to get us what we want from another person. In turn, our behavior can create conflict or dishonesty on the part of another who is just *people-pleasing* you. Our relationships will never be perfect but to continue in recovery we must recognize our own manipulations.

Hidden Agendas and Motives

The reasons behind the reasons we are doing or saying something. Can you spot your hidden agendas? Are you <u>pulling your own covers</u>? For each situation, please elaborate:

Who was involved? _____
_____
_____

What was said or done? _____
_____
_____
_____
_____
_____

Why did you say or do what you did? _____
_____
_____
_____
_____

Was this an entirely truthful statement or action? _____
_____
_____
_____
_____

What were you not really saying or doing? _____
_____
_____
_____
_____

What were you really trying to get out of this situation? _____

_____

_____

_____

_____

_____

_____

If I'm trying to get something, have I stated my intentions clearly, giving the person a choice to say yes or no? _____

_____

_____

Were you selfish? _____

_____

_____

_____

_____

Self-seeking: _____

_____

_____

_____

_____

Dishonest:_____

_____

_____

_____

_____

Afraid: _____

_____

_____

_____

_____

How will you *promptly* admit you are wrong?

_____

_____

_____

_____

_____

Who was involved? _____

_____

_____

What was said or done? _____

_____

_____

_____

_____

_____

Why did you say or do what you did? _____

_____

_____

_____

_____

_____

Was this an entirely truthful statement or action? _____

_____

_____

_____

_____

_____

What were you not really saying or doing? _____

_____

_____

_____

_____

_____

What were you really trying to get out of this situation? _____

_____

_____

_____

_____

_____
_____

If I'm trying to get something, have I stated my intentions clearly, giving the person a choice to say yes or no? _____
_____
_____

Were you selfish? _____
_____
_____
_____
_____

Self-seeking: _____
_____
_____
_____
_____

Dishonest: _____
_____
_____
_____
_____

Afraid: _____
_____
_____
_____
_____

How will you *promptly* admit you are wrong?
_____
_____
_____
_____
_____

CONTINUE TO USE THIS TEMPLATE FOR INVENTORY.

Conflict Resolution

Please describe the conflicts you that are now occurring with others.

Who did you have the conflict with? _____

What caused it? _____
_____
_____
_____
_____
_____

Did this get resolved? _____
_____
_____
_____
_____
_____

Why not? _____
_____
_____
_____

Did the other person make an attempt to resolve this conflict? _____

How? _____
_____
_____

Did you make an attempt to resolve this conflict? _____

How? _____
_____
_____

Who did you have the conflict with? _____

What caused it? _____
_____
_____
_____
_____
_____

Did this get resolved? _____
_____
_____
_____
_____
_____

Why not? _____
_____
_____
_____

Did the other person make an attempt to resolve this conflict? _____

How? _____
_____
_____

Did you make an attempt to resolve this conflict? _____

How? _____
_____
_____

CONTINUE TO USE THIS TEMPLATE FOR INVENTORY.

Nightly Inventory

Review your day for those times you were at peace and serene. Describe below.
_____
_____
_____

_____
_____
_____
_____
_____
_____
_____
_____
_____
_____

How was your behavior different today than before your recovery?

Example:

Before my recovery, I would have stormed out of the meeting. Today, I sat in my anger, took several deep breaths, and just stayed quiet while others took over. After I felt calm, I then began participating.

Before my recovery, I would have gone out looking for a *fix*, now I sat in my emotional pain, then called my sponsor to help me through it.

Before my recovery, I would have: _____
_____
_____
_____
_____
_____

Now, I: _____
_____
_____
_____
_____
_____

Before my recovery, I would have: _____
_____
_____
_____
_____
_____

Now, I: _____

_____
_____
_____
_____
_____

Review your day for times when you were emotionally upset or physically in pain. Describe below:

_____
_____
_____
_____
_____
_____
_____
_____
_____
_____
_____
_____
_____

Review any conflicts you had within yourself. Describe your internal conflicts:

Example:
I'm afraid to set my boundaries with my partner for fear he'll leave me.

_____
_____
_____
_____
_____

Review any conflicts you had with others:

_____
_____
_____
_____
_____
_____

Can you see where you have gone off-course? Describe:

_____
_____
_____
_____
_____
_____
_____
_____

What spiritual principles can you apply to this conflict?

Example:
Acceptance, Humility, Forgiveness, Brotherly Love, Integrity, Tolerance

_____
_____
_____
_____
_____

Boundaries

Many times, boundary issues cause conflict, either because we intrude on another's boundary or they breach our boundaries. We have a right to our emotional and physical space, and we get to determine the amount of space we need. We have no right to try and coerce another to do it our way, even if we feel it's for their good. This is called ***enabling***. Just as problematic is our inability to set our boundaries. Be clear about boundaries.

Examples:

Physical boundaries:	Inappropriate touching from others and how we touch others.
Verbal boundaries:	Abusive or sexual language.
Emotional boundaries:	Not allowing others to manipulative us or not manipulating others. Being honest and expecting honesty from others.

Did you set your boundaries today? If yes, please describe:

_____
_____
_____
_____
_____
_____

If no, please describe:

_____
_____
_____
_____
_____
_____

Did any problem arise because of weak boundaries, either from you or another? If, yes, describe:

_____
_____
_____
_____
_____
_____

Did anyone ignore or breach your boundary after you informed them of what they are? If yes, describe:

_____
_____
_____
_____
_____
_____

What did you do? _____
_____
_____
_____
_____
_____

Will this resolve the boundary issue? If so, why? _____
_____
_____
_____
_____
_____

If not, what will you do in the future?

Example:
My employer continues to make sexual innuendos. I'm afraid to tell him that it's unacceptable for fear of losing my job. FEAR: We must tell someone regardless of our fear. We accept our fear, but let go and let God in telling our boss to stop the language when he is around us. Tell him that his behavior is not appropriate, then leave quietly. We need to have faith that God will provide for our needs, including another job if so indicated. If necessary, consider reporting your employer to the State Labor Board. We do what's in front of us to do.

_____
_____
_____
_____
_____
_____
_____
_____
_____
_____

CONTINUE USING THE TEMPLATE TO EXPLORE BOUNDARY ISSUES.

Plan for Tomorrow - What's in Front of You

In our recovery program, we take action on those matters that are immediately in front of us, such as securing gainful employment, paying off our debts, getting a place to live, sharing custody of our children and any other responsibilities that we have delayed or postponed. Procrastination only makes those things loom larger and more insurmountable – so plan in small increments to accomplish what you can each day.

What's in front of me to do? _____
_____
_____
_____
_____

What's one step I can take to accomplish the ultimate goal?

Example
Goal: Get a job
Step taken: Sent out 3 resumes online

Goal: _____

Step(s) Taken: _____

_____
_____

Attitude of Gratitude

No nightly inventory is complete without encouraging our new-found attitude of gratitude. What do I have to be grateful for today?

Example:
That I got through the day without using my addictive drug/behavior of choice.

_____
_____
_____
_____
_____
_____
_____

Transformation and Transcendence

Each day that we seek to live by spiritual principles and metaphysical fundamentals, we are being reborn and redeemed into another reality. Reality is unpleasant only when we have neglected our spiritual growth. Each day is a revelation of our Higher Purpose. We may not know why something is happening to us, but as we say in AA, <u>more will be revealed</u>. I have always found it so.

RELAPSE PREVENTION

The addiction field has broadened the interpretation and scope of 12 Step programs to include a wide variety of issues that face a newly recovering person. There are many areas of life that have been neglected as we pursued our substance and behaviors of choice with a vengeance. One thing is clear: if we put the same energy into our recovery, we will make great strides in a short amount of time. Relapse prevention strategies, such as, knowing when we are in trouble, recognizing the symptoms of imminent relapse, and learning how to intervene before irreparable harm is done, are critical to continuing recovery and feeling safe inside our own skin.

Relapse Triggers

Negative emotional states are primarily responsible for relapses. Feeling good, surprisingly, can also trigger relapse. Can you identify your primary emotional state(s) most of the time to determine if you are setting yourself up for a relapse?

Isolation	Depression
Self-pity	Loneliness
Anger	Family Pressure
Frustration	Resentment
Stress	Elation
Indecision	Social Pressure
Complacency	Denial

Using the above, or from your own emotions, describe the emotional state: _____

_____

_____

_____

_____

Does it make you think about using your drug/dysfunction of choice?_____

_____

_____

_____

_____

Please list some ways you plan to cope with these feelings:

_____
_____
_____
_____
_____
_____
_____
_____
_____
_____

Who? Where? What? Why? When?

With whom do you associate that might lead into a relapse?

_____
_____
_____

Do you have plans to change this association? Yes _____ No _____

How can you limit your contact with this person?

Example:
Make new friends
Be busy with other, more productive activities

_____
_____
_____
_____
_____
_____

Where are the places most associated with your addictions/dysfunction and neuroses?

_____
_____
_____
_____
_____

Do you plan on avoiding these places? Yes _____ No _____

How can you avoid these places?

Example:

Take another route to work or when you do errands.

Take someone with me when I have to go to this place.

_____

_____

_____

_____

_____

_____

What could be the most compelling reasons for your relapsing?

Example:

I am in too much emotional pain.

I still have cravings.

_____

_____

_____

_____

_____

_____

For each of the reasons you have listed above, please use your decision-making abilities and coping skills to argue against relapsing.

_____

_____

_____

_____

_____

_____

_____

_____

Example:

I can start going to a therapist for this terrible emotional pain. It's so hard to understand what's going on with me.

My cravings pass pretty quickly. I can go outside for a walk when I get a craving or call my sponsor.

_____

_____

_____

_____
_____

Why would you relapse?

Example:
I don't think I can't make it.
My family is against me.
I don't know how to cope.

_____
_____
_____
_____
_____
_____
_____

For each of the reasons you have listed above, please use your powers of discernment to balance these reasons with other compelling reasons to continue your recovery, which is making your life so much better.

Example:
I have some self-respect today.
I looked in the mirror yesterday, and I actually liked myself a little.

_____
_____
_____
_____
_____
_____
_____
_____
_____
_____

When is the time of day that you are most vulnerable to going back to old behaviors, addictions, and/or dysfunction?

For me that was around 5:00 p.m., after work, or when I was relatively free of my hangover. My drinking would start for the day and continue, of course, throughout the evening, night, and sometimes into the next day.

_____
_____
_____

_____
_____
_____
_____

Substituting Activities

For each of the times of day listed above, please substitute another activity that would help you get through that time of day more easily.

_____
_____
_____
_____
_____
_____
_____
_____

Example:
Going to a meeting.
Taking my child to the park.
Going to the library and doing internet research.
Working on one of my goals.

_____
_____
_____
_____
_____
_____
_____
_____

Money Issues:

Having money to spend may lead to a false sense of security. Those with gambling, drug and other addictions that require money to engage in are particularly vulnerable. You may want to plan ahead how you will handle money matters. Some strategies are:

- Don't get an ATM card
- Carry only small amounts of cash
- Have a trusted family member or friend handle your money
- Don't go alone to the bank

- Share any financial information about potential windfalls with your sponsor, trusted family member or friend, counselor or therapist
- Write out checks for your immediate needs; i.e. grocery shopping, haircut, drugstore items, dry cleaning, rent, phone bills
- Have your check deposited directly into your checking account

If you feel the money matters could lead to a relapse, please outline your plan for handling money matters below:

I intend to handle my money: _____

_____
_____
_____
_____
_____
_____
_____

Relationship Issues

Dating and starting new relationships with those who are not recovering can be problematic since you are on an emotional roller coaster with intense highs and lows which must be discharged in meetings, sober groups (going out to coffee), with our sponsor and/or therapist. It might be wise to abstain from dating, but if not, be prepared for navigating unfamiliar territory – being with people without your drug of choice. Some strategies for meeting people in or not in recovery programs are:

- Go to 12 Step dances and conventions.
- Go to 12 Step retreats.
- Take a class at a community college.
- Go to movies with recovering friends.
- First date: Don't go to a bar or other kind of place where you have used or engaged in your addiction.
- Tell the other person that you are a recovering _____.
- Have your sponsor's number on speed dial.

If you decide to remain solo for a while, remember it's wise to discharge some of your feelings by talking about issues of loneliness with your recovery group and sponsor. It's important to stay in touch with your feelings. You don't have to act on your feelings of loneliness by hooking up with someone out of desperation. But if you do, be prepared to manage the fallout – go to more meetings and discuss your feelings with other recovering friends.

Please describe what kind of relationship you would like to have with recovering or non-recovering persons and what impact this might have on your continued recovery:

_____
_____
_____
_____
_____
_____
_____
_____
_____
_____

If Partner Still Uses or is Dysfunctional

If your partner still drinks, uses drugs, gambles or engages in other addictive behavior, it may tempt you to indulge in your drug or dysfunctional behavior of choice at certain times. Having a plan how to deal with your partner's addictive behavior is crucial for your continuing sobriety.

- Leave the house when the person is using or engaging in their addiction of choice.
- Get to a meeting.
- Join Al-Anon or CODA for help with your co-dependent behavior.
- Detach emotionally from the *drama* that his/her addictive behavior provokes.
- Plan an intervention with your partner or spouse's closest friends and family to get him or her the help they need.
- Stop enabling that person to indulge in their addiction of choice.
- Keep boundaries firmly in place.
- Don't say "yes" when you mean "no."
- Work your program – not theirs.
- Take care of your needs first.

You must ask yourself if you can continue to remain in recovery and also be in this relationship. If the other person isn't ready to get help and stop their addiction and/or dysfunctional behavior, you need to detach in order to stay sane. You need to evaluate the reasons why you are in this relationship and, if recovery means leaving, how you can communicate your love to your partner or spouse while taking care of yourself. Without your recovery you have nothing. If you can remain detached and stay in the relationship, that's great. Don't ever let someone jeopardize all you've worked for – it isn't worth it.

Please list below some new strategies you plan to use in your relationship to maintain recovery:

_____

_____

_____

_____

_____

_____

_____

_____

Intimacy with Ourselves & Others

Intimacy with yourself. Terry Kellogg says that the catalyst for co-dependency is a lack of intimacy with ourselves. Check off any of those qualities listed below that indicate how you feel when you are with yourself.

You
Love	_____	Acceptance	_____
Trust	_____	Surrender	_____
Understanding	_____	Empowerment	_____
Connectedness	_____	Joy	_____
Clarity	_____	Vulnerability	_____
Spontaneity	_____		

For those qualities you did not check off, how can you incorporate them into your life to feel more intimate with yourself and to help you feel better about yourself?

Example:
Listen to my feelings.
Go out with myself and enjoy just being with me
Tell someone how you really feel.
When I begin to doubt myself, go with it anyway

_____

_____

_____

_____

_____

_____

<u>Others</u>

Love	_____	Acceptance	_____
Trust	_____	Surrender	_____
Understanding	_____	Empowerment	_____
Connectedness	_____	Joy	_____
Clarity	_____	Vulnerability	_____
Spontaneity	_____		

What qualities above would you like to develop in your relationship? What action can you take to bring you closer to intimacy with another?

Example:
Talk honestly to my partner about my past.
Acknowledge my feelings of shame and in what areas of life I have these feelings.
Introduce your partner to this list and get their reaction to it.
Develop these qualities in my relationship with myself.

_____
_____
_____
_____
_____
_____
_____
_____

Negative Qualities That Destroy Intimacy

The relationships we choose will indicate the level of intimacy we are capable of. Sustaining intimacy is difficult for recovering people. We are afraid of intimacy, feeling that if we let someone see all our darkness and damage they won't continue to love us. We have been shamed to our core and letting someone in is very risky. We fulfill this prophecy by either pushing people away or finding others unable to sustain intimacy. This creates that wonderful roller coaster relationship where emotional highs and lows are a daily occurrence. If we continue with these kinds of relationships with ourselves and others, our recovery will be seriously jeopardized. It is helpful to know what destroys intimacy and to evaluate how these negative behaviors impact you and your relationships. This is a step toward deeper understanding of what really motivates us. We're good at saying we want intimacy, then picking someone who isn't ready to engage us at an intimate level. Below, please describe the behaviors that have kept you from intimacy, directed toward yourself or another.

Rage

With whom: _____

Describe the incident:

_____
_____
_____

How did this impact the relationship?

_____
_____
_____
_____
_____

Criticism

With whom: _____

Describe the incident:

_____
_____
_____

How did this impact the relationship?

_____
_____
_____
_____
_____

Sarcasm

With whom: _____

Describe the incident:

_____
_____
_____

How did this impact the relationship?

_____
_____
_____
_____
_____

Withdrawal

With whom: _____

Describe the incident:

_____
_____
_____

How did this impact the relationship?

_____
_____
_____
_____
_____

CONTINUE USING THIS TEMPLATE OR MODIFY IT TO SUIT YOUR SITUATION WITH EACH PERSON WITH WHOM YOU HAVE A RELATIONSHIP.

Family and Friends

I related to you the story of my first New Years' Eve. Listed below are some ways to prevent getting into problems with family and friends who are still addicted to their mood and mind-altering behavior and substances:

- Take a recovering friend with you to all family functions.
- Make sure everyone understands you're leaving at the first sign of trouble.
- Leave when you no longer feel safe – no matter what.
- Say "no."
- Maintain your boundaries.
- If someone violates your boundaries – let them know about it.
- If someone tries to offer you your drug of choice – leave immediately.

In many cases, we must retrain people how to treat us. If we're newcomers, we can't expect that our families are going to **get** it right away. They will continue trying to sabotage us because they want to maintain the dysfunctional **status quo**. But that is destructive to you and your newfound recovery, so you'll have to make some difficult choices. If they can't respect you, then you can't be around them until they do. You don't have to explain this to them. Believe me, they already understand – they're just choosing not to. It's called denial. Remember our old friend. Give them time – love them, and try and forgive them. But above all, take care of yourself first. You owe it to yourself.

Please describe below some possible problems you might have with family members because you're now in recovery:

_____
_____
_____
_____
_____
_____
_____
_____
_____
_____

Please describe below some possible problems you might have with close friends because you're now in recovery:

_____
_____
_____
_____
_____
_____
_____
_____
_____
_____

List some strategies you might use to manage the problems with families and friends:

1) _____
_____

2) _____
_____

3) _____
_____

4) _____
_____

Relapse Prevention and Skill Building

Social Skills

Developing ways to interact with others is very important to our continuing recovery. List some ways that you are improving your social skills:

_____
_____
_____
_____
_____
_____
_____

If you've taken a risk in a social situation, describe it:

_____
_____
_____
_____
_____
_____

CONTINUE TO USE THIS TEMPLATE FOR FURTHER WORK.

<u>Each time you use one of your strategies, reward yourself by doing something you want to do:</u> Some examples might be:

- Going to a movie.
- Inviting a friend out to coffee and telling them what you did.
- Buying yourself a little something to commemorate your success.
- Taking a nice long bath.
- Taking a scenic walk.

Please list other rewards that are specific to you:

1) _____

2) _____

3) _____

4) _____

5) _____

6) _____

7) _____

8) _____

Anger Management

Anger can be related to many other emotional states and can be used as a ***catchall*** emotion for many, in particular, men. It is socially unacceptable for men to display many emotions such as sorrow, hurt feelings, worry, and, heaven forbid, a man should cry. This is all nonsense. Our emotions are guideposts to areas that need processing and release. Using anger can become a bad habit. Usually anger signals stress levels have gone up and someone else (not you) is to blame. Therefore, in order to cope, we must limit our stress levels and remove ourselves from stressful situations. Blaming others is also not likely to restrain our anger in the long run.

You have made an examination of anger issues in 4th Step Exercises. If this has remained a problem, you may need anger management therapy and in-depth counseling for this resistant issue.

Job Skills

Without the ability to support ourselves, we are left at the mercy of people, places and things and our lives will become unmanageable. Even if we do get a job, the newly recovering person may experience difficulties, however we can be assured of the protection of our Higher Power, if we are doing everything within our human power to take care of ourselves, those we are responsible for and the needs of those concerned.

Please list any job skills that might translate into a job:

1) _____

_____

2) _____

_____

3)_____

_____

4) _____
_____

5) _____
_____

6) _____
_____

7) _____
_____

It is helpful to see that character traits can also translate into the job market, such as an outgoing personality, the ability to positively negotiate with others for win/win outcomes, even being a housewife or mother can be a skill that supports a career in organizing materials or information.

Take personality tests, assess your interests and investigate careers that correspond to your personality and temperament.

There are many websites on job skills and job finding searches. Two that I found particularly enjoyable were www.jobsearch.about.com and www.deed.state.mn.us (click other, then C in the alphabet, then Creative Job Search).

There are short-term and long-term options. In others words, you might have to do a job that you don't like to move you forward into a job that you might love. Paying our dues is a common term, but, in most cases, an apt description of a process that might take you a couple of years to complete. You might need more skills training, education, experience or any number of components. You might have to evaluate your appearance and change certain things to make yourself more marketable to prospective employers.

Parenting Skills

If we are parents, there will be a certain amount of guilt towards our children as they've been exposed to our addictions/dysfunctions and neuroses. Now that recovery is achievable, we must begin to repair our relationships with our children. In the book, I have made several suggestions, such as parenting classes and books. Also available are community resources such as Easter Seals and others who specialize in assisting parents or primary caregivers to transition out of addiction and other disorders, and help them gain control over the family system. The family unit can be any size and include many different numbers of persons and several generations. There are others who have combined families when two people marry that each have children. Even close friends or aunts and uncles can be considered part of the extended and blended family system. Please list below those whom you consider to be a member of your family system.

_____
_____
_____
_____
_____
_____
_____
_____
_____

Are you currently having any conflict with any of these individuals? Yes _____ No _____

If you currently have conflict will this affect your children? Yes _____ No _____

Do you feel safe having your children around those people? Yes _____ No _____

List ways you can keep your children safe below:

Example:
I can leave them with a family member with whom my children are safe.
I can stop letting my children spend time at the homes of unsafe family or friends.
I can go to court and get an order of protection for my children.

_____
_____
_____
_____
_____
_____
_____
_____

Parenting classes are a helpful resource for those of us who learned ineffectual parenting from our own parents. Compensating for our addiction, divorce, or other factors in our lives, can derail the parenting process by over-permissiveness and others parenting mistakes.

Suggestion: Depending upon the age of your child or children, you can invite them into the process with family meetings, using the first one to explain that you are on a new and better road to recovery and that you love them and things will change for the better, although sometimes it won't seem that way to them.

Romanticizing the "Good Old Days"

Recovery is a lot of hard work, changing core beliefs and destructive behavior. Sometimes we might feel that "it wasn't sooooo bad." This is romanticizing the drug, addiction, behavior or neuroses that we used and seeing a rosy cloud around it. We have artfully removed the chaos, pain, degradation, humiliation, and incomprehensible demoralization that our drug of choice put us through. This is A BIG LIE.

Play the real movie in your head

One of the ways that I kept sane and sober was to play the movie of my drunken life in my head, going over those particularly painful and humiliating episodes. You can get some of these from your 4th Step – your deepest, darkest secrets – or from just remembering. Play the movie and clearly put yourself in it exhibiting all the disgusting and self-annihilating behavior which you took part in. Give yourself a big close-up and then imagine someone that you love watching this movie; your children, your new boyfriend or your mother. Because no one really knows every little, demeaning detail of your former life, do they? So put yourself back there, and then run the pictures of your new life, new friends, new ideas, new plans, goals, jobs, behaviors and feelings about yourself. Which do you prefer?

New Hobbies and Interests

It is very important to develop other interests and hobbies to replace the dysfunctional behaviors of the past and that can utilize our free time in positive ways.

List some interests and/or hobbies that you'd like to investigate or get involved yourself with, that you either thought about before or that have recently interested you:

1)_____
_____
2)_____
_____
3)_____
_____
4)_____
_____

STEP ELEVEN EXERCISES

Starting the Day

How can we start the day with a positive attitude? Please choose for yourself an affirmation that you can think or speak aloud first thing upon awakening.

Example:
My Higher Power directs and guides my course today.
I am Divinely inspired.
I am in the service of my Higher Power today.

_____
_____
_____
_____
_____
_____
_____

Getting Connected

Is there a simple way you can get connected to your Higher Power? Here are some examples:

Reading from an inspirational book
Reading from the Big Book or Twelve and Twelve
Reading from Twenty-Four Hours a Day
Meditating for five minutes
Praying for someone who's going through a tough time
Calling your sponsor or spiritual advisor
Going to a meeting
Reaching out to someone newer than you on the program
Working on a Step
Saying a prayer
Affirming a positive

Short Affirmations for Emergency Use

In the beginning of my sobriety, I got a part-time job as a legal secretary with a rather conservative lawyer. I made a few mistakes and became convinced he was going to fire me. I was paralyzed with panic. I would run into the bathroom and start saying out loud "God Is My Source." I would repeat this over and over again until I knew that jobs might come or go – my ultimate support is God – not people, places or things. I would immediately feel calmer. Can you think of a short affirmation that you can use in emergency situations that would help you? Please write them down.

_____
_____
_____
_____
_____
_____

The Law of Non- Resistance

It says in the Big Book that "we cease fighting anything or anybody" and, while this may be the ideal, it doesn't become our mantra until we've gone a few rounds with ourselves, our old ideas, and/or fighting with everyone over everything. We finally get plain tuckered out from the fight.

Who are you fighting today? _____
_____
_____
_____

What does your Higher Wisdom reveal about this situation? _____
_____
_____
_____

Is there someone you need to forgive? _____ Yes _____ No

If you need to forgive someone, how can this be done?

You can hold them in the light. Release any burden you have placed on this person to satisfy your ego, your needs, wants or desires It is not up to this person, place of thing to be responsible for these things. You can say the words:

"I release you to the light. I forgive you and whatever has happened between us that was distressful or that I felt was wrong is now forgotten. I am free of the burden of needing you to be anything at all. I am freeing myself of the burden to be anything you might want me to be."

In this way you can release the person, place or thing and move forward in your journey and in the light.

Distinguishing Between Our Will & God's Will

This may be difficult at first because our wills so dominate our lives in the beginning. Denial has a strong foothold on our consciousness and going against it, is going against the grain of our disease. But that is the point. Our disease leads us into chaos and pain. There are two kinds of pain: constructive pain that guides you to the next level of your recovery, and unnecessary pain that you bring on yourself by trying to fit a square peg into a round hole. Pain could be God's will, but you can be sure that when you feel pain that is a result of a wrong decision, it is not God's will. You've got to feel your way through it to know whether or not it's right.

The incident causing you pain: _____
_____
_____
_____
_____

Have I experienced this pain before? _____ Yes _____ No

If yes, and the situation you find yourself in, or decision you have made is repetitive behavior, describe prior incidents or decisions:
_____
_____
_____
_____
_____
_____
_____
_____

Do you think it's God/Higher Power's Will for you to repeat this pattern? Yes _____ No _____

If this is not God's Will, then what do you need to do to be in alignment with God's Will?

_____

_____

_____

_____

_____

_____

_____

_____

STEP TWELVE EXERCISES

Spiritual Values & Principles

We have come quite a far way from our first faltering steps. We have gained confidence and clarity in our newly created life. We have developed spiritually. We have experienced both psychological and spiritual epiphanies and awakenings and discovered inner strength and, alternatively, the vulnerability that contributes to our ability to become intimate with ourselves, with God, and with others.

What new values have you added to your life?

My new values are: _____
_____
_____
_____
_____

These values contribute to my life by: _____
_____
_____
_____
_____

My new values are: _____
_____
_____
_____

These values contribute to my life by: _____
_____

_____
_____
_____
_____

Referring to the text, what spiritual principle would you like to work on in the next month?

I would like to work on the spiritual principle of _____

Why? _____
_____
_____
_____

How will this strengthen your recovery? _____
_____
_____
_____

Being of Service

In what ways can I be of service?

In my 12 Step meetings: _____
_____
_____
_____

On my job: _____
_____
_____
_____

To my family: _____
_____
_____
_____

To my friends: _____
_____
_____
_____

To those who don't know me: _____

_____

_____

_____

To my community: _____

_____

_____

_____

Carrying the Message

In what ways do I carry the message to other addicts? _____

_____

_____

_____

_____

_____

_____

_____

_____

_____

_____

Prayer of. St. Francis

God, let me be an instrument of your peace
Where there is hatred, let me sow love
Where there is injury, pardon
Where there is doubt, faith
Where there is despair, hope
Where there is darkness, light
And where there is sadness, joy
O, Divine Consciousness, grant that I may not so much
Seek to be consoled as to console
To be understood as to understand
To be loved as to love
For it is in giving that we receive
It is in pardoning that we are pardoned
And it is in dying that we are born to eternal life. . .

Glossary of Recovery Terms
and 12 Step Sayings

13th Step: When a person with a considerable amount of sobriety, or recovery, initiates or engages in a sexual liaison or relationship with a person new to the program.

Accommodating the insanity: Allowing another person to manipulate, use, hold you hostage in shame or guilt, or otherwise engage in inappropriate behavior around you or direct this behavior towards you.

Act as if: Acting as if helps us to make the transition from resistance to acceptance of any idea presented in recovery that we find unacceptable. If we pretend that we are patient, then we may attain patience. If we pretend we are willing, we may be surprised to feel that we become willing over time.

Addict: Anyone who is severely co-dependent on mood or mind-altering substances or behavior.

Addiction: A pathological (diseased or disordered) relationship with any mood or mind altering substance or behavior that comes between you and feelings you don't want to feel that ultimately creates crisis in your life.

Attitude Adjustment: The internal/mental repositioning of expectations gained by adjusting ourselves to circumstances and not demanding that circumstances adjust to our will.

Attitude of gratitude: Making a mental (or physical) list each day of those things in our life that we are grateful for to reinforce how fortunate we are to be in recovery. When we do this, we find that we begin to internalize a more positive attitude and gratitude for what we are receiving, and do not live in disappointment for what isn't there.

Behavior will dictate the quality of your life: Despite good intentions to change certain behaviors or insight into our psyches, actual outward behavior directed toward the world, will impact our relationships, careers, and feelings about ourselves, either positively or negatively.

Big Book: Officially the title of this book is Alcoholics Anonymous, but over the years it has been nicknamed the "Big Book" because people must have thought it was both big in size and in ideas about alcoholism. This book contains the 12 Steps of Alcoholics Anonymous.

Boundary: Psychological or physical walls or barriers that encourage integrity of the self and the family system.

Boundary violation: A trespass by someone who crosses our perimeters of self; physically, mentally, emotionally or psychologically. We have a right to think, feel and act for ourselves and in our best interests.

Bring the body the mind will follow: If we get ourselves to meetings, one of the first steps in changing behavior, the mind will soon hear the message if we are open, honest and willing.

Carrying the message: By our continued sobriety and recovery from debilitating addictions and behaviors, we are an example to those who seek their salvation in recovery and to the world at large. We can speak of our recovery and help others to incorporate the principles of the program and strength they need to continue on their recovery journey.

Change is the antidote to crisis: When crisis becomes a pattern of life, then only through changing our thinking, behavior, and actions will we find relief.

Cognitive distortions: Habitual and persistent thought processes that distort reality. Negative automatic thoughts based on faulty and irrational logic.

Conscious contact: A connection to a Power greater than ourselves. No matter how small, this connection can grow through prayer, meditation and growing faith.

Course correction: The course we're on must be wrong if our behaviors produce negative responses from others and chaos in our lives. It is necessary to assess our situation honestly and change our actions.

Definition of insanity: Doing the same thing over and over expecting different results. Accommodating the inappropriate behavior of yourself and others.

Denial: The mental blind spot that allows a person or group of people to deny the truth of a situation. It is condition peculiar to those who are the most in need of intervention.

Don't quit five minutes before the miracle happens: Often we become impatient when anticipated results are not forthcoming in our timeframe. But are we really able to gauge the time it should take for God to give us the results we want? Our limited viewpoint of the universe versus God's unlimited and infinite perspective makes it impossible for us to understand what is for our greatest good, and therefore we need to let God do Its work instead of giving up prematurely before we receive the miracle of Divine intervention.

Dry drunk: When we are feeling restless, irritable and discontented with an accompanying lack of gratitude, emotional immaturity, selfishness, self-obsession and irrational fears.

Easy Does It: Slowing down the pace and taking stock of feelings, surroundings, attitudes and mental states so that we don't overdo as we did when we were submerged in our disease.

EGO (Edging God Out): The sneaky ego tricks us into taking back our lives and our wills because we think we know better than our Higher Power.

Enmeshment: Not knowing where you and another person begin or end. Unidentified. Over-identified with another. Fused with another.

Faith is a lighted doorway, but trust is a dark hall: Faith can lead us through the darkness as we learn to trust that each new step brings us closer to the light. Trust is putting one foot in front of the other even in the dark of the unknown.

False Evidence Appearing Real (FEAR): Assuming the worst about the circumstances presented to you. Jumping to conclusions and being afraid, rather than gathering more data and making an evaluation based on facts.

Fear is the absence of faith: The more faith you have in your Higher Power and It's will for you, the less you will fear present circumstances.

Fellowship: The people in the rooms of 12 Step groups who become like family. Our sponsors and others in our support network. Attending fun activities in 12 Step, such as sober dances, seminars, meetings, both stag and mixed.

First things first: Do what's in front of you to do that is indicated to be a priority.

Flooding: Overwhelming feelings that are triggered by remembering past traumatic life events. These feelings are intense and sometimes frightening. We might feel hysterical or that we're going to go out of control.

Footwork: Any action necessary for continued involvement in our recovery program. This could include answering ads for jobs, doing necessary paperwork for various purposes, cleaning our house, making amends, praying for direction and guidance.

Giving unsolicited advice: Giving advice to someone who did not request it.

H.A.L.T.: Never get too hungry, angry, lonely or tired as these conditions could lead to faulty thinking and relapse.

Half measures avail us nothing: We must fully commit ourselves to the program and do what we are being led and asked to do, rather than trying it our way one more time.

Higher-powered: Our lives are powered by something other than our fear, selfishness and dishonesty. We have turned our lives over to the care of something greater than ourselves with absolute assurance that we will be fine.

Hit a relationship bottom: Unable to choose relationships with individuals that are loving, support-ive, kind or nurturing, we continue to practice old, self-defeating patterns by having relationships with those who are incapable of vulnerability or intimacy. This is also "broken picker" syndrome. When we become demoralized about our choices, and have hit a bottom of pain and anguish, we are ready to surrender the relationship matter to our Higher Power for Its intervention in our lives.

Hitting Bottom: Reaching a point of incomprehensible demoralization. Ahead lies death by suicide, accident or unfortunate incident or insanity.

If it's meant to be...I can't stop it. If it isn't God's will...I can't make it happen: Illustrates that circumstances meant to happen will manifest regardless of our meddling and interference in God's plan for us. Conversely, with all the willfulness and ego-driven ambition at our disposal, we just can't bend circumstances, people or things to our plan.

If it works. . . don't fix it: Don't repair things that already are working in your life just because somebody else might disapprove or thinks it should be done differently.

If you think you're different, you've come to the right place: Many of us have come to feel alienated in our own lives, different, shame-based, weird, crazy and mainly out of control. There is a place where others like us can identify with our pain and dysfunction and can also help us to see ourselves as "survivors" not "victims."

It's an inside job: There are no external methods of attaining serenity, peace, freedom, joy or happiness. New cars, clothes, material goods may make us momentarily happy, but that happi-ness fades and another "new" thing takes its place. What makes us truly serene, content, and comfortable in our own skins is the continuing journey to understand ourselves and our motives, the process of self-examination in the face of a world that offers only a superficial rendering of the truth. To love ourselves unconditionally as we love others unconditionally.

It takes what it takes: If the experiences in our lives culminate into surrender and a new way of thinking and behaving, then all our experiences were necessary to motivate us into recovery

<u>It works if you work it</u>: We must apply the principles of the program to our lives, work the Steps, carry the message, and remain sober from our mind and/or mood altering substances and behaviors.

<u>Let go and let God</u>: When we have tried it our way again and again, and end up in horrible pain and destruction of our spirit, then we may be able to surrender and let God handle our lives.

<u>Life on life's terms</u>: We do not get to dictate the terms of our own path because we have shortsighted vision and can't see that far down the road. We must be willing to accept what is in front of us, work within those perimeters and, perhaps, if we can handle that, we will be given an even larger assignment.

<u>Life's in session</u>: Recovery demands that we pay attention to life and do what is in front of us to do because, more than likely, that is what our Higher Power is directing us toward. Don't spend all day in 12 Step meetings, get out in the mainstream of life and work the program, practice your coping skills and new belief system.

<u>Live and let live</u>: If someone doesn't agree with us we don't argue unnecessarily with that person. It is not the time for them to see what you see. That is their choice and we have no right to interfere in God's will for that person.

<u>More will be revealed</u>: Our Higher Power will reveal the way to us the more we are healed. Many times what we heard at the beginning of our recovery didn't make much sense, but as we continue on the path of recovery, more and more becomes clear, and more and more of what we learn and feel can be applied to our lives in a positive way.

<u>Neurosis</u>: A benign mental disorder characterized by (a) incomplete insight into the nature of the difficulty (denial); (b) conflicts; (c) anxiety reactions; (d) partial impairment of personality; (e) often, but not necessarily, the presence of phobias, digestive disturbances, and obsessive-compulsive behavior.

<u>No human power</u>: It has been observed that human intervention, without the support of a Higher Power, is not enough to support long-term sobriety and recovery from our addictions, dysfunctions or neuroses. By working in partnership with our Higher Power, we can learn new strategies, skills and gain spiritual strength sufficient to keep us in recovery.

<u>One day at a time</u>: We can only breathe in one breath at a time. We cannot force ourselves to take giants steps when chards of glass from our former path have cut our feet bloody and raw. It is necessary to take small, tentative steps as our feet and our souls heal. Live each breath. You are in only one moment – this one.

People pleasers: Afraid of rejection and/or abandonment, we agree and please people out of fear. We are "nice," unassuming and agreeable even in the face of obvious boundary violations and abusive interactions.

Process feelings: Letting feelings come in, rather than fighting or fixing them, while investigating their origin. We let ourselves feel the truth of our emotions as they guide us toward understanding what occurred, such as traumatic and disturbing events. We are better able to function without the distortion of our dysfunctional family of origin interfering with the discovery process.

Practice these principles in all our affairs: Using the primary principles of 12 Step ideology to inform our actions and life decisions.

Principle before personalities: In any given situation, personalities will complicate the issues with personal agendas, motives, selfish desires, and self-aggrandizement. If there is to be any sanity in our lives, we must utilize the principles of the 12 Steps as we make decisions or judgments in our lives. Personalities cloud the issues while principles enlighten us to the course we must pursue.

Pulling our own covers: Admitting the truth regardless of how hard we try to hide it from ourselves. Having the courage to face ourselves in the harsh light of reality, still love ourselves, and try to improve to the best of our ability.

Recovery phenomenon: The unexplainable reason behind the recovery of so many through the 12 Steps of Alcoholics Anonymous.

Reliance Not Defiance: The ability to discard stubbornness and pride and allow ourselves to take another approach. We lay down our arsenal of defenses and rely upon a Power greater than ourselves for guidance.

Restless, irritable and discontented: A sign of impending relapse that begins with uncomfortable emotional states and continues until we are angry, stressed out, blaming others for our conditions and questioning our recovery.

Self-supporting through our own contributions: Pulling our own weight by contributing to life in whatever way we can afford. This could be financially, in work, or in service to others.

Self-will run riot: The times when ego is running the show and creating havoc in our lives and personal relationships.

Sick and tired of being sick and tired: Your addictions/dysfunctions/neuroses are bringing chaos, crisis and confusion in a never-ending series of disasters, which leave you feeling drained, exhausted, powerless, and in despair.

Slippery slope: People, places or things that bring us dangerously close to acting out in negative and addictive old behaviors.

Sponsor: A recovering individual with a significant length of sober time, who has worked all of the Steps and can take a newcomer through the program of recovery via the 12 Steps by spending time, energy, and patience for a sustained period of time.

Stinking thinking: Plummeting into a downward spiral of unproductive feelings about yourself and others. Reverting to old thinking that leads to resentment, anger, discontent and a possible relapse.

Suit and show up: The character building skill of getting up in the morning, putting on one's clothes and showing up for whatever God has put in front of us to do that day. We stop overanalyzing those actions that are seemingly ours to accomplish.

Switching addictions: Achieving sobriety from one substance only to revert to another addictive behavior or develop a new addiction. This usually occurs when recovery is incomplete – all of the 12 Steps were not done with full dedication, willingness and commitment.

Taking a hostage: One person uses guilt or feelings of responsibility, insecurity and indecisiveness against another. This person then intimidates and challenges the "victim" with hostility, abuse, anger, and other violent emotional and physical strategies, to keep the victim from leaving them. This is about one person controlling another person, leaving the hostage feeling uncomfortable but powerless to assert themselves against the hostage taker.

Take another person's inventory: Looking at another person's faults and character defects as an excuse for our own behavior. Judging another person's actions in a negative way.

The road to disappointment is paved with expectations: Once we begin the vicious cycle of expecting others to think, believe, or act as we would like them to, we set ourselves up for pain, hurt and anguish when they don't comply with our designs and plans.

The will of God will not take you where the grace of God will not protect you: If some action is indicated to be God's will, God will take care of the results and make sure you are protected.

Them that matter don't mind and them that mind, don't matter: True friends and partners accept us for who we are at the moment, even though we have flaws and defects. We are in the process of growing and getting better. So to hell with those who are bothered by our growth, our surrender, our program, or our changes in beliefs. If we are continually seeking the approval of others, then we have stopped asking God's approval for our plans or actions. Others are as short-sighted as us and we don't rely upon their interpretation of our actions.

This too shall pass: No matter what circumstance in which you find yourself that may be problematic or difficult, nothing stays the same for long. This problem or difficulty will either get resolved or accepted or time will give us greater perspective or it may simply disappear. One thing is for sure, it will pass.

Toxic shame: The kind of shame that is undeserved based on shaming communications, both verbal and non-verbal, that are received in childhood and adolescence and internalized as beliefs that we are defective, flawed or damaged goods.

Triggers: People, places and things, smells, odors, thoughts, feelings, colors, and sense memories that we became habituated to during our destructive use of drugs, alcohol and other dysfunctional behaviors and that can set off an extreme urge or craving to engage in these behaviors or addictions again.

Turn it over: Again, another great saying in 12 Step that simply means to give the matter to God and stop obsessing, thinking or raging about it.

Two sickies don't make a wellie: Two dysfunctional people in recovery or not in recovery do not make one well person. Two sickies are unable to help each other unless they can accept each other unconditionally. Two sick people are unable to help each other because of their self-centeredness and tendency to blame each other for the shortcomings in the relationship. It is best to seek our own recovery first and then, when our hearts and heads are on a healing path, to find someone who accepts and loves us as we are and that we are able to feel the same in return.

Walking the talk: Refers to those in the program who put the principles of recovery into their daily lives not just when they speaking at a meeting or to other 12 Steppers.

Willpower: Bending or forcing circumstances to our will without considering the greater good for ourselves and others.

Willingness: A conscious adjustment of our will as we set aside preconceived beliefs and ideas to accommodate new information and solutions to our problems.

<u>Willing to be willing</u>: Finding some small measure of voluntary action on our behalf to change.

<u>Works if you work it</u>: Working the 12 Steps, going to meetings, writing on our feelings and inventories and any other thought or action that is indicated for us to do that encourages our growth in recovery.

<u>You can't save your face and your ass at the same time</u>: A reluctance to expose our vulnerabilities to others. Not asking for help when life gets tough and instead, pretending things aren't that bad. This is particularly true of high bottom addicts and co-dependents who may not have lost everything to their drug of choice.

<u>You're exactly where you're supposed to be</u>: We can never be or feel or act differently than we are supposed to because that would be impossible. We are in the moment, in the NOW, with our feelings, thoughts and behavior. We don't know why, but many times the purpose behind circumstances are revealed to us later.

<u>You're only as sick as your secrets</u>: Secrets in dysfunctional family systems become a way of life and fester in the darkness of our shame. Bringing the secrets out into the light strips them of power to harm us. We are unburdened and free of the sickness that keeps us from loving ourselves and letting others love us. We are not perfect and that's okay.

<u>Your best thinking ain't in your best interest</u>: When your pain and dysfunction blinds you to the paths of enlightenment that await you, your thinking can only destroy you and that is not in your best interest. Therefore, it's "best" to put your thinking aside for the moment and listen to the counsel of others who have your best interests at heart.

<u>You've got to give it away to keep it:</u> In paradoxical fashion, in order to hold onto our continuing recovery, we've got to help others attain recovery. In this way, we pass the gift onto others that are willing to accept the gift. We are not in charge of the results of our efforts – if someone is not ready for recovery – we allow them to fall until they, hopefully, hit bottom. But we are there when they need us.

Bibliography

Addiction

Carnes, Patrick. *Out of The Shadows: Understanding Sexual Addiction.* Center City, MN: Hazelden. 1994

Daley, Dennis C., Moss, Howard B. and Campbell, Frances. *Dual Disorders: Counseling Client with Chemical Dependency & Mental Illness.* Center City, MN: Hazelden. 1987

Fellowship of Alcoholics Anonymous. *Alcoholics Anonymous: The Story of How Many Thousands of Men and Women Have Recovered from Alcoholism.* New York, NY: Alcoholics Anonymous World Services Organization. 1939, 1955, 1976

Fellowship of Alcoholics Anonymous. *The Little Red Book.* Center City, MN: Hazelden. 1986

Fellowship of Alcoholics Anonymous. *Twelve Steps and Twelve Traditions.* New York, NY: Alcoholics Anonymous World Services Organization. 1955

Grateful Members. *The Twelve Steps for Everyone . . . who really wants them.* Center City, MN: Hazelden. 1975

Johnson, Vernon E. *I'll Quit Tomorrow: A Practical Guide to Alcoholism Treatment.* New York, NY: Harper & Row. 1980

Larsen, Earnie. *Stage II Recovery: Life Beyond Addiction.* New York, NY: HarperCollins Publishers. 1985.

Lawson, Gary W., Lawson, Ann W. and Rivers, P. Clayton. *Essentials of Chemical Dependency Counseling.* Gaithersburg, Maryland: Aspen Publications. 2001

Miller, Merlene, Gorski, Terence T. and Miller, David K. *Learning to Live Again: A Guide for Recovery from Chemical Dependency.* Independence, MO: Herald House/Independence Press. 1982, 1992

Unknown. *Twenty-Four Hours A Day.* Center City, MN: Hazelden. 1975

Affirmations/Visualization

Addington, Jack and Addington, Cornelia. *Your Needs Met.* Marina Del Rey, Calif.: DeVorss & Company, 1966

Barker, Raymond Charles. *Treat Yourself To Life.* New York, NY: Dodd, Mead & Company. 1954, 1988

Fox, Emmet. *The Sermon on the Mount: The Key to Success in Life.* New York, NY:: Harper-Collins Publishers. 1934, 1989

Gawain, Shakti. *Creative Visualization.* Mill Valley, Calif: Whatever Publishing. 1979

Hay, Louise L. *You Can Heal Your Life.* Santa Monica, Calif.: Hay House, Inc. 1984

Lerner, Rokelle. *Daily Affirmation For Adult Children of Alcoholics.* Deerfield Beach, Fla.: Health Communications. 1985

Ponder, Catherine. *Open Your Mind To Receive.* Marina del Rey, Calif.: DeVorss & Company, 1983

Shinn, Florence Scovel. *The Game of Life and How To Play It.* New York, NY: Florence Scovel Shinn. 1925

Wilde, Stuart. *Affirmations.* Taos, New Mexico: White Dove International, Inc. 1987

Roman, Sanaya and Packer Duane. *Creating Money: Keys to Abundance.* Tiburon, Calif: HJ Kramer, Inc. 1988

Co-Dependency

Beattie, Melody. *Codependent No More.* San Francisco, Calif.: Harper & Row. 1987

Beattie, Melody. *Codependent's Guide to the Twelve Steps.* New York, NY: Fireside. 1998

Kellogg, Terry. *Broken Toys, Broken Dreams: Understanding & Healing Codependency, Compulsive Behavior & Family.* Amherst, MA: BRAT Publishing. 1990

Wegscheider-Cruse, Sharon and Cruse, Joseph R. *Understanding Co-Dependency.* Deerfield Beach, Fla.: Health Communications. 1988

Family of Origin Issues/Self-Parenting/Inner Child

Bradshaw, John. *Healing the Shame That Binds You.* Deerfield Beach, Fla.: Health Communications. 1988

Bradshaw, John. *The Family: A Revolutionary Way of Self-Discovery.* Deerfield Beach, Fla.: Health Communications. 1988

Capacchione, Lucia. *Recovery of Your Inner Child.* New York, NY: Simon & Schuster. 1991

Engel, Beverly. *Healing your Emotional Self.* Hoboken, New Jersey: John Wiley & Sons, Inc. 2006

Fossum, Merle A. and Mason, Marilyn J. *Facing Shame: Families in Recovery*. New York, NY: W.W. Norton & Company. 1986

Friends in Recovery. *The 12 Steps for Adult Children.* San Diego, Calif.: Recovery Publications. 1987

Middleton-Moz, Jane and Dwinell, Lorie. *After the Tears: Reclaiming the Personal Losses of Childhood.* Deerfield Beach, Fla.: Health Communications. 1986

Miller, Alice. *Drama of the Gifted Child.* New York, NY: Basic Books. 1981

Oliver-Diaz, Philip and O'Gorman, Patricia A. *12 Steps to Self-Parenting for Adult Children of Alcoholics.* Deerfield Beach, Fla.: Health Communications. 1988

Whitfield, Charles L. *Healing the Child Within.* Deerfield Beach, Fla.: Health Communications. 1987

Trauma/Incest/Abuse

Bass, Ellen and Davis, Laura. *The Courage to Heal: A Guide for Women Survivors of Child Sexual Abuse.* 3rd Ed. New York, NY: HarperCollins Publishers, Inc. 1994

Evans, Katie and Sullivan, J. Michael. *Treating Addicted Survivors of Trauma.* New York, NY: The Guilford Press. 1995

Herman, Judith. *Trauma and Recovery.* New York, NY: Basis Books. 1992

Middelton-Moz, Jane. *Children of Trauma: Rediscovering The Discarded Self.* Deerfield Beach, Fla.: Health Communications. 1989

Psychology

Bourne, Edmund J. *The Anxiety & Phobia Workbook.* Oakland, CA: New Harbinger Publications, Inc. 2000

Flores, Philip J. *Group Psychotherapy with Addicted Populations: An Integration of Twelve Steps and Psychodynamic Theory.* Binghamton, NY: The Haworth Press, Inc. 1997

Kaufman, Gershen. *The Psychology of Shame: Theory and Treatment of Shame-Based Syndromes.* New York, NY: Springer Publishing Company. 1989

Keirsey, David and Bates, Marilyn. *Please Understand Me: Character and Temperament Types.* Del Mar, Calif: Prometheus Nemesis Book Company. 1978

Tieger, Paul D. and Tierger, Barbara Barron. *Do What You Are.* Boston, MA: Little, Brown and Company, 1992

Young, Jeffrey E. and Klosko, Janet S. *Reinventing Your Life.* New York, NY: Dutton. 1993

Spirituality & Meditation

Bloch, Douglas. *Listening to Your Inner Voice.* Minneapolis, MN: CompCare Publishers. 1991

Briggs, Dorothy Corkille. *Celebrate Your Self: Enhancing Your Own Self-Esteem.* New York, NY: Doubleday. 1977

Gawain, Shakti. *Creating True Prosperity.* Novato, Calif.: New World Library. 1997

Jampolsky, Gerald G. *Forgiveness: The Greatest Healer of All.* Hillsboro, Oregon: Beyond Words Publishing. 1999

Miller, Carolyn. *Creating Miracles: Understanding the Experience of Divine Intervention.* Tiburon, Calif.: HJ Kramer, Inc. 1995

Peck, M. Scott. *The Road Less Traveled: A New Psychology of Love, Traditional Values and Spiritual Growth.* New York, NY: Simon & Schuster. 1978

Stratton, Elizabeth K. *Seeds of Light: Healing Meditations for Body and Soul.* New York, NY: Simon & Schuster. 1997

Wilde, Stuart. *Infinite Self: 33 Steps To Reclaiming Your Inner Power.* Carlsbad, Calif: Hay House, Inc. 1996

Made in the USA
Lexington, KY
27 June 2014